Economic Development, Poverty, and Income Distribution

Other Titles in This Series

Westview Special Studies in Social, Political, and Economic Development

Economic Development, Poverty, and Income Distribution
edited by William Loehr and John P. Powelson

The increasing inequality and poverty that seem inevitably to accompany economic growth in developing countries have become more and more evident in recent years. The search for development paths that lead to growth with equality—all too difficult to find—is now an area of central concern for development economists. One result of their concern is this volume, in which internationally known representatives of a range of disciplines address themselves to ways in which growth with equity might be successfully achieved. The book begins with both empirical and theoretical background to the development issues involved, and with an overview of the experience of the international development assistance community. Part 2 focuses on operational definitions of the poor that will permit analytical, policy-oriented research to lead to useful conclusions. Specific concern is expressed for small-business owners, women, peasants, and recent migrants from rural to urban areas.

The basic question, of course, is what can be done about poverty and inequality. Part 3 includes suggestions for specific measures and provides a comprehensive comparison across a wide range of policy options. The book does not solve the problem, but it does point to directions that promise a reasonably high probability of success. And throughout, suggestions are made for the kind of interdisciplinary research required to raise that probability even further.

William Loehr is associate dean and associate professor of economics in the Graduate School of International Studies, University of Denver. John P. Powelson is project director of the Institute of Behavioral Science and professor of economics at the University of Colorado.

Economic Development, Poverty, and Income Distribution

edited by William Loehr
and John P. Powelson

Westview Press
Boulder, Colorado

*Westview Special Studies in Social, Political,
and Economic Development*

Copyright © 1977 by Westview Press

Published 1977 in the United States of America by
  Westview Press, Inc.
  1898 Flatiron Court
  Boulder, Colorado 80301
  Frederick A. Praeger, Publisher and Editorial Director

Library of Congress Cataloging in Publication Data
Main entry under title:

Income distribution, poverty, and economic development.

(Westview special studies on social, political and economic development)
1. Underdeveloped areas—Addresses, essays, lectures.
2. Underdeveloped areas—Income distribution—Addresses, essays, lectures.
I. Loehr, William. II. Powelson, John P.
HC59.7.I47   330.9'172'4   77-23270
ISBN 0-89158-248-7

Printed and bound in the United States of America

Contents

Preface

The papers in this volume were originally presented in the spring of 1976 at a conference on economic development and income distribution sponsored by the Institute of Behavioral Science, University of Colorado, at Estes Park, Colorado. The conference was attended by more than seventy people representing many academic institutions and public agencies as well as a wide range of interests in the social sciences. Most were motivated by concern about trends toward greater income inequality and poverty in a large number of developing countries.

Many countries and international agencies have recently begun attempting to devise policies aimed at narrowing the income gap between rich and poor. These efforts have been hampered, however, by lack of understanding of the causes of inequitable income distribution. One purpose of the Estes Park conference, therefore, was to explore the propositions that (1) the income gap is growing in developing countries and (2) the poor are becoming relatively poorer, and perhaps even poorer in an absolute sense.

The first part of this book is designed to shed some light on the study of income distribution from both theoretical and empirical perspectives. A summary of recent data and findings (Loehr) and a report of the experience of the international development assistance community (Chenery) provide a starting point. The most important theoretical question—whether the related objectives of growth and equity are compatible—is tackled by Ranis, and the specific tasks facing one developing country, Tanzania, are explained by Guruli.

Distinguishing that category of people whom we might label "the poor" in developing countries is not as easy as it might at first appear. Problems immediately arise in trying to define the poor in such a way that the group is amenable to analysis. In Part 2, Hackenberg presents some of the prob-

Preface

lems as they were encountered in the Philippines, but also demonstrates the payoffs, in terms of insights into urban poverty, that can be gained through trying to solve those problems. Powelson concerns himself with a definition of poverty, but even more with a behavioral approach to determining what makes poor people behave the way they do. A specific mode of behavior, conditioned by the concept of the "limited good," is examined by Irene Stoller, while Elise Boulding demonstrates how the exclusion of women as objects of study has distorted our perceptions about inequality and about our options for achieving greater equity and growth.

The main topic of discussion in any such conference usually centers around what can be done about the problems that have been uncovered. This conference was no exception. In Part 3, a wide range of policies is formally surveyed by Adelman, Morris, and Robinson, and structural change along Marxist lines is suggested by Martha Gimenez et al. Specific factors affecting poverty and inequality—such as water in acceptable quantity and quality and appropriate technology—are examined by White and Wehr respectively.

The papers presented in this book are, of course, only a start; conference participants subsequently spent the better part of a day (and night) discussing alternative policies that might be considered, theories that had gone untested, and data that had gone uncollected. In the end, there was considerable agreement that, if we are to make much progress in our understanding of poverty and equity, high priority must be assigned to several factors:

1. Poverty groups must be carefully defined, so that homogeneous behavioral characteristics can be identified. We must be able to distinguish between those who can be productive and those who cannot. Only in this way can we design realistic poverty-oriented policies that will help those poor who are in a position to help themselves and provide transfers to those who cannot. The poor, as we currently view them, comprise such a heterogeneous group that few generalizations are valid; thus considerable interdisciplinary

work is needed in order to provide a clearer view of the behavioral characteristics of specific poverty groups.

2. The rural-to-urban migration that is taking place very rapidly in developing countries is associated with increasing inequity and poverty. The reasons for such migration are not fully understood, and even the measurement and comparison of rural and urban incomes are hampered by imprecise ways of comparing equivalency in incomes across sectors. Whether the urban poor are better off or worse off than the rural poor is still in question, but there seems to be general agreement that inequality is greater in urban areas and that rapid urbanization increases overall inequality.

3. Many questions related to rural development become relevant once we begin seeking solutions to problems created by rural-to-urban migration. At least in part, such migration is due to perceptions of greater income opportunities in urban areas. Thus, stemming migration will require creating additional opportunities in rural areas. Land reform and rural industrialization come to mind as potential policy variables; however, especially in regard to the latter, much remains to be done before we can fully understand the overall impact of these factors on income inequality and growth.

4. Technology has often been blamed for excessive unemployment in developing countries. Although we are quick to recommend that more "appropriate" technology be used, we do not always understand how that technology is to be located and selected.

5. Rapid population growth is associated with increasing inequality. Countries that have slowed their population expansion usually have simultaneously improved income equity. Here we have a "chicken-and-egg" problem, in that we do not know which is the dependent variable. Clearly, reducing population growth can reduce absolute poverty and probably stimulate growth. Whether or not increased income equity will follow is a question yet to be answered.

6. Foreign economic assistance may have caused increasing income inequality in the past by stimulating capital-intensive growth in urban centers. Aid must be, and is being,

channeled into projects and programs which stimulate both growth and favorable changes in income distribution. Monitoring systems must be established to ensure that progress is made on these fronts.

The one conclusion that received unanimous endorsement at the Estes Park conference was that the quality of data about all these factors is poor, and that until the data are improved only limited progress can be made. Much more effort must be exerted toward performing the difficult (and often unglamorous) microstudies that will provide well-developed data on the behavior of specific groups which interact in the eventual determination of growth, poverty, and income equity.

Many people helped make the conference and this volume possible. The solid support of Gilbert White and the Institute of Behavioral Science at the University of Colorado was indispensible. The authors of each chapter worked hard both before and after the conference to put their ideas—some of them controversial—on record. Kenneth Boulding, in a way that we have come to expect and yet still find delightfully surprising, composed the poetry preceding each section while participating in the panel discussions. Other participants on the panels helped clarify our ideas: Charles Howe, Dwight Brothers, Donald Castillo, James Dugan, Gottfried Lang, Noel Osborn, Paul Shankman, Juan Wicht, Charles Wood, Beverly Hackenberg, Ragaei el Mallakh, Wyn Owen, James Mudge, and Richard Goode earned our gratitude for their help. The participation and support of these people, and of the other sixty or so conference participants, have helped move us a bit closer to policies which are accurately aimed at achieving growth with equity.

William Loehr
John P. Powelson
Boulder, Colorado
December 1976

Contributors

Irma Adelman, Professor of Economics, University of Maryland

Elise Boulding, Professor of Sociology and Project Director, Institute of Behavioral Science, University of Colorado

Hollis Chenery, Vice-President, World Bank

Martha E. Gimenez, Assistant Professor of Sociology, University of Colorado

Edward Greenberg, Associate Professor of Political Science, University of Colorado

Kassim Guruli, Professor and Chairman, Department of Economics, University of Dar es Salaam (Tanzania)

Robert A. Hackenberg, Professor of Sociology and Program Director, Institute of Behavioral Science, University of Colorado

William Loehr, Assistant Professor of Economics, Graduate School of International Studies, University of Denver; Research Associate, Institute of Behavioral Science, University of Colorado

Thomas Mayer, Associate Professor of Sociology and Program Director, Institute of Behavioral Science, University of Colorado

Ann Markusen, Assistant Professor of Economics, University of Colorado

Cynthia Taft Morris, Professor of Economics, American University

John Newton, Graduate Student in Economics, University of Colorado

John P. Powelson, Professor of Economics and Project Director, Institute of Behavioral Science, University of Colorado

Gustav Ranis, Professor of Economics and Director, Economic Growth Center, Yale University

Sherman Robinson, Assistant Professor of Economics, Princeton University

Irene Philip Stoller, Teaching Assistant in Anthropology, University of Colorado

Paul Wehr, Associate Professor of Sociology and Project Director, Institute of Behavioral Science, University of Colorado

Anne U. White, Research Associate, Institute of Behavioral Science, University of Colorado

Part 1: The Problem

Whether the poor are getting poorer
Is a question that creates a furor,
For Prejudices all grow greater
On absent, or invalid data.

Of Poverty, the Measurement
Is little more than good intent,
For all the various orthodoxies
Produce a bunch of feeble proxies.

We can't avoid the imputations
That *Measures* mean *Evaluations,*
And *Indicators* spark debates
On who will set the value weights.

Kenneth Boulding

1. Economic Underdevelopment and Income Distribution: A Survey of the Literature

William Loehr

International comparisons of income distributions in developing countries (LDCs) began in earnest only in the early 1960s. By then some of the first data on income structure were beginning to appear, reporting mainly on developed countries (DCs) around 1950. Kravis (1960) made an early attempt to compare income inequality crossnationally and to search for reasons why income inequality generally appeared greater in less-developed countries than in developed countries. He compared before-tax income among consumer units in ten countries with that of the United States, and found that in three countries there was less inequality (Denmark, the Netherlands, and Israel), in three other countries there was about the same degree of inequality (Great Britain, Japan, and Canada), and in four countries inequality was considerably greater (Italy, Puerto Rico, El Salvador, and Ceylon (now Sri Lanka). Greater equality generally appears where industrialization and the socioeconomic changes necessary to support it have proceeded furthest. Also, statistically, there is a tendency for low incomes and inequality to go hand in hand. While the data are very poor for this purpose, Kravis (p. 410) found that the primary area of differences in inequality lies in the upper income brackets. There appears to be somewhat less dispersion in the lower income levels in developing countries than in developed ones, but much greater concentration at the top in the former.

Comparisons such as these can be very misleading because of biases in measurement which may creep into the data. The following biases have a tendency to understate the inequality existing in LDCs in comparison with DCs, a fact of which Kravis was aware (p. 408):

1. Nonmonetary income plays a much larger role in total income in LDCs than in DCs, and usually is not reported as part of income.
2. A long-run view (longer than one year) would probably show a relative reduction in inequality in DCs because of their generally greater socioeconomic mobility.
3. Old-age pensions are generally prevalent in DCs but not in LDCs.
4. There apparently is a greater tendency for high incomes to escape the reporting system in LDCs than in DCs.

Other biases tend to understate the degree of inequality in the DCs:

1. Income data usually exclude income from capital gains, expense accounts, etc. These usually accrue only to persons in higher income groups.
2. Differences in price structures in various countries may tend to create a relative overstatement of inequality in LDCs. In the DCs, markets are likely to function more perfectly than they function in LDCs, so that all persons in DCs face more or less the same set of consumer prices. In LDCs, price distortions are likely, causing urban dwellers (higher income groups) to face a set of consumer prices which are high compared to prices in rural areas (lower income groups).

Unfortunately, Kravis' conclusions about what causes international differences in income distribution are not very helpful in any analytical sense. He attributed these differences to (a) human characteristics of the populations concerned, (b) such barriers to economic mobility as racial discrimination and rigid class structure maintained by tradition or legal systems, (c) an economic structure which does not permit highly differentiated forms of work but which nevertheless permits high income differentials, and (d) social and political organization. These "reasons" for inequality probably could have been discussed without any empirical evidence whatsoever, since they are in no way derived from Kravis' empirical exercise. In criticizing these points, Oshima (1962) indicated that the major determinant of income dispersion, at least among Asian countries, appears to be the weight of the farm or rural sector in the total economy. "Other factors appear to be trivial" (p. 442).

Oshima's argument was based upon an examination of the assumptions behind the measures of inequality used by Kravis.[1] He demonstrated that in fact these measures yield conflicting readings of the relative distributions being examined. An examination of income distributions in several Asian countries—breaking each into two sectors, agricultural and nonagricultural—proved instructive. In most cases (Japan was the exception), the income distributions within the sectors were different, in that income frequency distributions peaked at different income levels, the agricultural sector normally peaking below that of the nonagricultural sector. Depending upon the preponderance of agriculture, the shape of the combined distribution (for a country as a whole) could assume almost any form. Oshima (1962; p. 441) showed that by using an alternative measure, the standard deviation of quintile shares, the overall distributions in all countries in his sample (five countries) came out with approximately the same shape.[2] Thus, international comparisons were easier to make and yield less ambiguous results than was the case with the measures used by Kravis and others.

Perhaps the main contribution of the Oshima article was that it laid the blame for income inequality on the shoulders of dualism. In his words (p. 442), "the major determinant of the dispersion of quintile shares between countries is the weight of the farm or rural sector in the total economy," as well as the extent to which the agricultural and urban areas are economically integrated. Secondarily, he found that within the rural and urban sectors the standard deviation of quintile shares was largely influenced by the dispersion of land holdings within the rural sector and the dispersion of capital per worker in the urban sector. This explanation— that sharp dualism creates sharp income inequality—

appears time and again in economics literature, some of which will be examined in detail in this chapter (Adelman and Morris, 1973).

One of the first fairly comprehensive studies of income distribution and levels of economic development and growth was that of Kuznets (1963). His analysis was based upon data which are inadequate for very precise descriptions of the distributions in question. As he pointed out (p. 12), evidence about the distribution of income is more along the lines of "synthetic estimates" than of precise readings; the ingenuity of the research adjusts for the deficiencies in the data in order to make the latter usable. Nevertheless, our early insights into the relationship between economic development and income distribution were provided by Kuznets.

For comparing income distributions crossnationally, Kuznets was able to generate usable data on sixteen countries, nine of them developing. In classifying before-tax family income in these countries by quintiles, he was able to make the following observations:

1. The income shares of the highest income groups in developing countries are significantly larger than the shares of the same groups in the developed countries. The top decile of families in the developing countries received about 40–45 percent of all income (average 43 percent), while the same group in the developed countries received about 30–35 percent (average 32 percent). Any bias in measurement is likely to be along lines which would understate the incomes of the upper decile in developing countries because of poor reporting systems, as well as the reluctance of upper-income persons to accurately report their incomes for fear of incurring extra tax burdens. Thus, if anything, the extent to which upper income groups in developing countries have larger income shares than the same groups in developed countries is likely to be increased by adjustments which eliminate the biases involved.

2. The income share of the lowest quintiles is about the same in developed and developing countries. The poorest 60 percent of families in developed countries received about 29–33 percent of income, while in LDCs they received 25–32 percent.

3. It follows from items 1 and 2 above that there must be greater equality among middle income groups in LDCs than

in such groups in DCs. If there is greater inequality in LDCs at the top of the income structure, and the same degree of inequality at the bottom, there there must be greater equality in the middle groups. This is not, of course, to say that the middle income groups are vastly better off than the lower ones. What seems to be the case is that there simply isn't much difference between the lower and middle income groups, and that the entire scale is characterized by a fairly even income distribution up to, but not including, the upper 5 to 10 percent of families. In the developed countries, the inequality starts much lower down in the income structure, and, therefore, never becomes quite so extreme as that in the developing countries.

In an attempt to explain his findings, Kuznets relied primarily upon the distribution of property income and what he called "participation" income. Property income (i.e., income from dividends, interest, rent, etc.) constitutes about the same share of total income in DCs as in LDCs, but there is reason to believe that it is more concentrated in the upper income groups in LDCs than in DCs. First of all, savings are much more highly concentrated in the former, and only a relatively small portion of the population has a consistent ability to accumulate earning assets. Second, the equalizing effects of tax legislation and economic mobility are greater in the developed countries. This is true despite the fact that Kuznets was able to show that racism may tend to widen income disparities within the U.S. States with the highest proportions of nonwhite population were shown both to be among the poorest and to display the greatest degrees of income inequality. Third, any monopoly power of high income groups in LDCs is likely to be more easily maintained than in DCs, because of the fragmented markets in the former. Participation income has to do with the distribution of products and income among industries. Kuznets observed the widest differences in participation income by sector within the LDCs. This is particularly true when comparing the agricultural and nonagricultural sectors, partly because of technology and partly because of institutional forces. As earlier studies indicated, it appears that dualism is a major cause of uneven income distribution.

Kuznets' data were on the whole rather crude; they were based on a wide variety of sources and they referred primarily

to years around 1950. Since his article appeared, new estimates on income distribution have been made. As a check on
the Kuznets data, we have collected more recent estimates for
the same countries which were used in his analysis.[3] Most of
these estimates, appearing in Table 1, were compiled by Jain
(1974) as part of ongoing work at the World Bank. While
again some of these new data come from a variety of sources,
much was generated by the activities of the World Bank and
thus could be expected to be more accurate and consistent
than the Kuznets data.

One immediately notes that our mid- to late-1960s data
show higher Gini coefficients from the LDCs than do the
Kuznets data. The overall arithmetic average Gini for the
LDC group rose from .45 to .48. Only two countries in this
group, Sri Lanka and Barbados, appear to have experienced
increased equality on the basis of the Gini coefficient.
Excluding them from the LDC group, the average ratio for
the group rises from .45 to .52. On the other hand, the group
of developed countries does not seem to have experienced
much change. The Kuznets Gini averaged .39 and still does.
West Germany and the Netherlands are the exceptions
among the DCs for which we have data. They are the only
countries to show a rise in the Gini coefficient—a particularly sharp rise in Germany (from .37 to .46). Excluding West
Germany, the DC group shows a drop in the Gini coefficient
from .39 to .37. We would normally say that not much can be
made of these comparisons, since the data bases are different.
However, the consistency with which income in the LDCs
appears more unequal and that of the DCs appears less
unequal gives us the strong impression, at least, that inequality differences between the DCs and LDCs are widening.

Let us also compare the conclusions about income groups
that can now be made with those of Kuznets:

1. The relatively greater inequality of income distribution among upper income groups in the developing countries is still evident, but on the average appears to have
declined slightly. The average share of the top decile has
declined from 43 percent to 39 percent. This finding, however, hides the fact that there seems to have developed a much
wider variability in upper-decile income shares because of
movements toward greater equality in some countries

TABLE I
SHARES OF ORDINAL GROUPS

	0-20	21-40	41-60	0-60	61-80	81-90	91-95	Top 5%	GINI
INDIA									
K (1950)	7.8	9.2	11.4	28.5	16.0	12.4	9.6	33.4	.45
J (1967-68)	4.8	8.3	12.9	26.0	20.8	16.7	11.5	25.0	.47
SRI LANKA									
K (1952-53)	5.1	9.6	13.3	27.7	18.4	13.3	9.6	31.0	.46
J (1969-70)	7.2	10.8	16.1	34.1	21.0	15.6	10.3	19.0	.37
KENYA									
K (1949)	N/A	N/A	N/A	N/A	N/A	N/A	N/A	50.9	.46
J (1969)	3.8	6.2	8.5	18.5	13.5	11.7	12.0	44.3	.61
MEXICO									
K (1950)	6.1	8.2	10.3	24.6	15.6	10.8	9.0	40.0	.51
J (1969)	4.0	6.5	9.5	20.0	16.0	13.0	15.0	36.0	.57
COLOMBIA									
K (1953)	N/A	N/A	N/A	31.4	12.2	8.0	6.8	41.6	.43
J (1964)	3.6	6.9	11.4	21.9	13.2	11.0	9.5	46.0	.58
EL SALVADOR									
K (1946)	N/A	N/A	N/A	32.2	15.7	8.5	8.1	35.5	.40
J (1969)	3.6	9.1	13.8	26.5	21.5	18.5	13.5	20.0	.46
GUATEMALA									
K (1947-48)	N/A	N/A	13.2	28.8	15.8	11.6	9.3	34.5	.46
BARBADOS									
K (1951-52)	3.6	9.3	14.2	27.1	21.3	17.4	11.9	22.3	.45
J (1969-70)	6.9	11.7	16.3	34.9	21.4	14.7	8.7	20.3	.36
PUERTO RICO									
K (1953)	5.6	9.8	14.9	30.3	19.9	16.6	9.5	23.4	.42
W (1963)	4.5	9.2	14.2	27.9	21.5	17.0	11.6	22.0	.45

TABLE 1 (Con't)
SHARES OF ORDINAL GROUPS

	0-20	21-40	41-60	0-60	61-80	81-90	91-95	Top 5%	GINI
ITALY									
K (1948)	6.1	10.5	14.6	31.2	20.4	14.4	10.0	24.1	.40
R (1969)	5.4	11.0	15.9	32.3	22.2	15.7	29.8*		.38
GREAT BRITAIN									
K (1951-52)	5.4	11.3	16.6	33.3	22.2	14.3	9.3	20.9	.38
J (1968)	6.0	12.8	18.2	37.0	23.8	15.2	9.0	15.0	.33
WEST GERMANY									
K (1950)	4.0	8.5	16.5	29.0	23.0	14.0	10.4	23.6	.37
J (1964)	5.3	10.1	13.7	29.1	19.0	11.5	7.7	33.7	.46
NETHERLANDS									
K (1950)	4.2	9.6	15.7	29.5	21.5	14.0	10.4	24.6	.33
R (1967)	4.3	11.1	16.6	32.0	22.6	15.9	29.6*		.39
DENMARK									
K (1952)	3.4	10.3	15.8	29.5	23.5	16.3	10.6	20.1	.42
D (1966)	5.4	11.3	17.2	33.9	24.3	16.0	25.8*		.35
SWEDEN									
K (1948)	3.2	9.6	16.3	29.1	24.3	16.3	10.2	20.1	.43
J (1963)	4.4	9.6	16.4	31.4	24.6	16.1	10.3	17.6	.40
U.S.									
K (1950)	4.8	11.0	16.2	32.0	22.3	15.4	9.9	20.4	.40
J (1966)	4.0	11.0	17.0	32.0	24.0	15.0	10.0	19.0	.40

*Top 10%

SOURCES: Data labeled K are from Kuznets (1963); J are from Jain (1974); D are from Dich (1970); R are from Roberti (1974); W are from Weisskoff (1970).

(especially Sri Lanka and Barbados) and increasing inequality in others. The share of the top decile fell in five cases and rose in three, causing the range of top decile shares to widen from 35-50 percent to 29-55 percent over approximately 20 years. Meanwhile, in the DCs (excluding West Germany), the average top-decile share dropped from 32 percent to 28 percent. Again with the exclusion of West Germany (which now has an income distribution similar to that of India), the range dropped from 30-35 percent to 24-30 percent. Overall, the only convincing indication is that the income share of the upper decile in DCs has dropped, while in the LDCs the results are mixed.

2. At the very lowest levels, average income shares have remained about the same for all countries: on the average, about 5 percent of income is received by the lowest quintiles in both DCs and LDCs. However, Kuznets' observation that the lowest three quintiles received about the same share of income everywhere can no longer be sustained. Where he found the share of that group in LDCs averaging about 29 percent, it has dropped recently to 26 percent. With the exception of Sri Lanka and Barbados, the only two LDCs to distribute a larger share to the poorest 60 percent, that share is now only 23 percent. All the developed countries except the U.S. (where the share was constant) showed a rising share going to the poorest 60 percent. This was true even in Germany and the Netherlands, where overall inequality has increased. Overall, the average share for the lowest three quintiles rose from about 30 percent to 33 percent. Again we observe a trend similar to that observed in (1) above: there appears to be a movement toward greater inequality at the low end of the income spectrum in LDCs, while the opposite is occurring in the DCs.

3. The Kuznets conclusion that there is greater equality in the middle income groups in developing countries than in the DCs can no longer be sustained. Our new data show that families in the eighth decile of income earners received about the same average proportion in both classifications of countries (15 percent). This concept of "middle" income groups is a rather ambiguous one; but even if we could define the term precisely, there is now no evidence leading us to expect that group to experience greater income equality in LDCs than DCs.

We are, of course, aware of the limitations of these still-deficient data. We do not yet have standardized, comparable data on income distributions across countries. Yet methods are improving, and we think it significant that some of the relative differences between DCs and LDCs observed by Kuznets now appear to have become greater. It is likely that we are observing, not just a change in the quality of data available, but trends toward greater inequality in developing countries.

Scholars concerned with income distribution during the early 1960s generally found greater income inequality in developing countries than in developed ones. As explanations of this, several factors have been mentioned which continue to appear in economic literature. We briefly summarize them here:

1. The uneven distribution of *human resources* causes wide disparities in productivity and thus in income.
2. *Barriers to economic mobility* are greater in developing countries than in developed ones. These barriers may take the form of open racism, restrictive legislation, unrealistic job qualifications, ignorance, or tradition.
3. The *economic structure* of a country may tend to concentrate income in a few hands. This structure may determine the ownership of property and location of specific resources such as minerals.
4. The *social and political organization* of a country may not be conducive to a widespread sharing of income.
5. *Dualism*, an element of economic structure, may create a situation in which there is an "automatic" tendency for income to become concentrated despite rapid economic growth.

Not all of these factors can be expected to be operative at any one time in all countries. In general, however, they are found in most of the literature dealing with income distribution which has appeared in the past fifteen years.

Growth and Income Distribution

Considerable attention has been directed toward the

idea that as countries move from very low levels of development toward higher levels, income at first becomes more inequitably distributed. After a "middle" development level is reached, further growth is associated with increasingly equal distribution of income. Paukert (1973) examined data on income distribution in fifty-six countries ranked in order of GDP per capita, lowest to highest. He found a sharp increase in inequality (on the basis of Gini indices) as one moved from the lowest per-capita GDP countries up to those in the $300–$500 per-capita range. (The $300–$500 range represents those countries with the most extreme inequality.) As higher per-capita income levels were approached, inequality became progressively less. He pointed out that one should not generalize from the simple fact that the share of the poorest 20 percent of families in countries below $500 per capita falls as income increases. Subsistence certainly sets a floor to family income; and, in each of these countries, if the poorest 20 percent are at subsistence level, their share of total income must fall as income increases.

It has also been observed that countries experiencing the most rapid rates of economic growth suffer from increasing inequality. Adelman and Morris (1973), Fishlow (1972), and Wells (1974) point to the increasing inequality accompanying rapid growth in Brazil in the late 1960s, and Arndt (1975) finds similar trends in Indonesia. Trends toward greater inequality along with economic growth have been witnessed by Chenery et al. (1974) in many countries; in Argentina, Mexico, and Puerto Rico by Weisskoff (1970); and in India by Swamy (1967), though the latter case is not so clear-cut (Kumar, 1974). Our survey here is by no means conclusive, since it represents a rather long list of investigators, using various methods, who have found a correlation between inequality and growth in LDCs.

Adelman and Morris (1967, 1973, 1974) have devoted considerable attention to both generating accurate sets of data on variables important in explaining economic development and discovering the statistical relationships among them. Their 1974 paper and recent book (1973) examine data on forty-three developing countries, searching for relationships between patterns of income distribution and thirty-one indices of economic, political, and social forces which could be expected to influence it. Their method of hierarchical

interactions is an analysis of variance technique which scans
a set of data on a sample (in this case a sample of countries)
and chooses the one variable which best splits the sample
into two subgroups. The split is performed on the basis of
the smallest possible combined dependent variable variance
within the subgroups.[4] The method admits nonlinear interactions and is openly empirical rather than theoretical, since
the "theories" of income distribution are not yet specified to
the point where parametric tests are appropriate.

The findings of Adelman and Morris (1974) confirm the
hypothesis that, at the lowest levels of development, growth
tends to increase inequality. Broadly speaking, in the poorest countries, growth works against the poorer segments of
the population. The allocation of income to the poorest 60
percent of the population is best "explained" by the extent of
socioeconomic modernization and the expansion of educational services.[5] Throughout the entire sample, the poorest
60 percent of the population received 26 percent of total
income, but in two subgroups the share of the poorest 60
percent was relatively high (30–34 percent). One of these
subgroups was characterized by a relatively low level of
development accompanied by a predominance of small-scale
or communal subsistence agriculture. The other was a
subgroup of relatively well developed countries where major
efforts to improve human resources had been made. Small
income shares of the poorest 60 percent were most significantly related to sharply dualistic development processes.
On the other hand, the upper 5 percent of income recipients
received about 30 percent of income, on the average. The
largest part of the variation in income of upper income
groups is explained by the endowment of natural resources
and the extent of government involvement in the economy.
Countries in which the share of upper income groups was
relatively small tended to exhibit relatively intensive government participation in the economic environment, as well as
a relatively scarce supply of natural resources. Apparently
the latter variable assumes importance because when resources are abundant they are, more often than not, concentrated
in the hands of a small class of businessmen, landlords, or
expatriates.

Of the variables found important in the Adelman and
Morris study, improvement of human resources and direct

governmental economic involvement seem to offer the most promise for greater equity in income distribution. While dualism was found to be an important explanatory variable, it, in itself, is not a policy variable. But policies can be devised (p. 82) for widening the base for economic growth; e.g., credit can be made available to small entrepreneurs and technical services can be extended.

Recent work by the World Bank (Chenery et al., 1974), summarized in part by Ahluwalia (1974), gives some weak evidence that increasing inequality does not necessarily accompany economic growth. Ahluwalia's work (p. 14) compares the growth in income of the poorest 40 percent of income recipients with the GDP growth rate in eighteen developing countries and finds no clear pattern. In addition, cross-section regression analyses were run on data representing sixty-five countries where income recipients were divided into three groups—top 20 percent, middle 40 percent, and lower 40 percent—and their respective income shares were used as dependent variables. The finding that the growth rate of GDP was *positively* related to the share of the lower 40 percent of income recipients suggests that the dual objectives of growth and equity may not be in conflict.[6] However, when regressions were run again, this time separating countries by income level, it was found (p. 17) that the share of the poorest 40 percent did decline with growth, up to the point where a per-capita income level of about $400 was reached. After that, the share of this group continually increased. Concurrently, the share of the top 20 percent moved in an exactly opposite way, and that of the middle income group remained unaffected.

It is of interest that the World Bank study turned up two variables related to the quantity and quality of human resources as being most closely related to relative income shares. The level and availability of education was positively related to the income shares of the poorest 80 percent. Primary-school enrollment rates most significantly explained the share of the poorest 40 percent, and rates of enrollment in secondary schools played a similar role for the middle 40 percent of income recipients. Population growth, on the other hand, was negatively correlated with the share of the poorest 40 percent of income recipients. In Ahluwalia's words, this effect seems "quantitatively substantial" (p. 17).

All of the foregoing analyses rely upon cross-sectional studies for their conclusions. The paucity of available data usually forces us to work with only one or two points in time for which data on income distribution have been collected. Few developing countries have reliable one-year estimates, let alone time series on income distribution. Time series do exist, however, on some developed countries, and at least one such study (Roberti, 1974) has been made. In his study of Finland, the Netherlands, Norway, Sweden, the U.S., and the U.K. during the postwar period, Roberti found that: (a) deciles below the mean income generally had a higher probability of losing income than those above the mean, (b) except for the top decile, all deciles above the mean gained, or at least maintained their income shares, and (c) the main loser was the top decile. This erosion of the top deciles' share, however, caused an accrual of income, not to the lowest deciles, but rather to middle income groups.

In an attempt to check upon the generality of his findings, Roberti examined the relationship between deciles' income shares and the level of GDP per capita in a sample of twenty-four (developing and developed) countries for which cross-sectional data were available. In general, he found, GDP per capita was negatively related to the top and bottom deciles' shares, positively related to the shares of the fourth through eighth deciles, and not related at all to the shares of the second and ninth deciles.

The data in Table 1 lend support to the idea that, over an extended period of time, the share of the upper income group tends to decline. All but two countries eventually experienced a reduced share for the top 5 percent of income recipients. The evidence for the lowest income recipients is mixed, however, and, because of our limited data, not much can be said about them at all. The general conclusion that gan be drawn is that the hypothesis *as growth occurs, distribution becomes less unequal* is not necessarily true. Furthermore, such aggregate measures as the Gini index might be misleading, since income gains by middle income groups seem to come at the expense of *both* upper and lower groups.[7] Thus, one must examine all income groups and their interaction to understand the distributional changes which are occurring (Webb, 1972). What is called for then are additional indices which allow us to make statements about (1) all income groups and (2) income groups of special interest.[8]

Roberti's findings are consistent with those of Berry's study of Colombia (1974). Since time series of income distribution data do not exist, it was necessary to infer distributional changes from data on wages for groups of workers together with information on occupational structure over time. Overall, between 1934 and 1964 both the top decile and the lowest deciles experienced a slight reduction in their income shares. Meanwhile, gains accrued to the two deciles just below the top. Overall income distribution in Colombia became increasingly unequal from the mid-1930s until the mid-1950s, when it improved somewhat as a result of the increasing share of income accruing to nonagricultural workers. The idea presented by Adelman and Morris (1973, 1974)—that poorer groups suffer an absolute deterioration in real income as growth proceeds—receives some support from Berry's data, in that real agricultural wages were observed to be below their 1935 level for almost the entire 1935–1964 period.

International Comparisons—Nonfamily Units

Almost all empirical studies of income distribution, including those cited previously, rely upon income data related to families. Most censuses collect data in this way, and thus the largest samples for cross-sectional work can be obtained by dealing with family data. This approach has serious shortcomings, however. First, definitions of "family" differ. Some censuses may not include groups of unrelated adults in this category; others do. Some include income information for people who normally live within the family unit but who are temporarily absent at the time of census; others include only those persons in residence at the time. Perhaps more intractable are the differences in the concept of "family" which exist among nations. For income purposes, it is important to know whether we are dealing with a society in which the traditional extended family predominates or whether the nuclear family is the norm. The former, of course, is of much greater relevance in LDCs, while in DCs the (more-easily dealt with) nuclear family is most often observed. In the extended family system, it may be completely irrelevant that individuals are not members of the same household, in the sense that they do not dwell together. For income purposes, such individuals may be just as interdependent as if they lived together. The fact that persons living and working in urban areas support parents living in rural areas complicates any real measurement of "household" income. (For a theoretical analysis in which these factors play an important role, see Sen, 1975.) Further complications arise when we attempt to compare household incomes in societies which are monogamous with incomes in those which are not. Moreover, the limits of the extended family differ; in some societies only parents and siblings are included, while others include uncles, cousins, etc.

Distributions of income based upon the individual may, therefore, be of greater relevance than those relying on the household concept. Unfortunately, such data are difficult to come by, and few censuses collect them.[9] In general, income distributions by individuals are likely to show greater inequality than those compiled on a family basis. To the extent that poorer families in LDCs tend to be larger and more "extended" than richer families, there is likely to be greater inequality in those countries. The nuclear family is the norm in the DCs, and a nuclear family tends to include a smaller number of individuals than the extended family that prevails in LDCs. The larger household incomes of DC families support relatively few individuals, while the smaller household incomes in LDCs must be shared by more people. Thus, the income gap between LDCs and DCs is even wider when distributions are based on individual income.

Sectoral Income Distribution

If different sectors in an economy have different intrasectoral income distributions, and if a major shift in population takes place from a sector with low inequality to one with greater inequality, overall inequality will be seen to rise. This is true even if inequality within each sector is constant. Increasing inequality in LDCs, accompanied by economic growth, can be at least partially explained by this arithmetic truism. We can generally observe in LDCs that inequality tends to be greater in the urban (industrial) sector than in the rural (agricultural) sector (Weisskoff, 1970; Swamy, 1967). Rapid growth usually proceeds in a dualistic fashion, so that growth in the industrial sector is more rapid than growth in the agricultural sector (Adelman and Morris, 1973). In addition, rapid population growth and rural-to-urban migration occur. These factors alone are enough to ensure that, *ceteris paribus*, income distribution will become more unequal overall during the early stages of development and then more equal later on (Robinson, 1976).

Oshima (1970), in a study of inequality in Asian countries, found that changes in income distribution are not a result of economic growth per se. Using his quantile deviation measure, he was able to calculate the share of inequality attributable to each economic sector. He noted that changes in economic structure—i.e., shifts from a rural to an urban focus of economic activity as growth proceeds—were more important than growth per se in explaining changing income distribution. His main conclusion (p. 34) was that undue policy emphasis on industrialization can lead to unemployment, excessive urbanization, regional imbalance, and widening inequality. Thus, he laid the blame for inequality squarely in the lap of dualistic development.

Weisskoff (1970) examined the shift from agriculture to nonagricultural economic activities and also found a resulting overall increase in inequality. Swamy (1967), in a study of inequality in India, was able to separate the increase in inequality into two parts: one attributable to intersectoral inequality, the other to intrasectoral inequality. He found that changes in intrasectoral equality between 1951 and 1960 were small. No observable change took place in the agricultural sector, while the income distribution in the nonagricultural sector became slightly more unequal. Only 15 percent of the overall increase in Indian income inequality could be attributed to changes in the intrasectoral income distribution; the remaining 85 percent was the result of increased intersectoral inequality—i.e., shifts in population from the low-inequality (agricultural) to the higher-inequality (nonagricultural) sector.

Variables which relate the overall personal distribution of

income to sectoral distributions are (a) the relative size
distribution of income within each sector, (b) the weight of
each sector in terms of the number of people it represents,
and (3) the intersectoral differences in income per person
(Kuznets, 1963, p. 22). Kuznets found it useful to array sectors
by increasing product per worker—just as one would array
families by ascending income levels—and then calculate
concentration ratios, where the relevant Lorenz curve has as
many segments as there are sectors.[10] His data clearly show
much wider sectoral inequality in LDCs than in DCs.
Furthermore, although in countries at all levels of development the agricultural sector's product per capita is lower
than the countrywide average, it is close to the average in
DCs and far below the average in LDCs. In general, relative
differences in the sectoral levels of product per worker are
inversely related to levels of economic development
(Kuznets, 1957, p. 45). Over the long-run development of a
country, the relative product per person in the agricultural
sector rises toward the countrywide average, while the same
relative product gradually declines toward the average in
other sectors.

Berry's work (1974), alluded to previously, was based on an
analysis of the sectoral distribution of income in Colombia.
By examining wage information across sectors, he could
imply changes in the incomes of workers across sectors. His
conclusions were somewhat at odds with Kuznets', however,
in that he found continually increasing inequality between
the agricultural sector and the rest of the Colombian economy since the 1930s, despite growth in overall product per
capita.

Regional Income Distribution within Countries

Clearly, to the extent that such sectors as industrial
production and agriculture are location specific, one should
expect differences in income levels between regions of any
given country. But one would also expect differing degrees of
income inequality within regions, since the preponderance
of region-specific types of production implies the generation
of income in a region-specific manner as well. Geographic
limitations as well as occupational immobility would tend

to accentuate whatever tendencies there are for income inequality to develop within some regions. In a very limited sample of countries where data were available (Italy, the U.S., and Brazil), Kuznets (1963) found that income tended to be much more unequally distributed in poorer regions of the countries examined. In Italy, the shares of income in the lower brackets were distinctly lower than the shares for those groups nationwide, and the shares of upper groups were distinctly higher. Data by states in the United States showed a similar pattern. There appeared a negative association between the share of the top income group and the per-capita income of a state *despite* lower property income in poorer states. In 1957, the Gini concentration ratios were .22 for the poorest states and .12 for the richest. Allowing for the effect of the progressive income tax, we see a greater equalizing effect in rich states than in poor, since the rich groups in rich states have higher absolute incomes than the same groups in poor states, and are thus subject to a higher marginal tax rate.[11]

Policy Analyses

Studies of income distribution become purely academic exercises if attention is not paid to the impact of public policy upon income distribution and to the policy recommendations which may be made to change that distribution in one way or another. Studies of public policy and income distribution fall into two very general categories. The first, and by far the most-often studied, is the effect of the fiscal system on distribution. Analyses of this type are very common for almost all developed countries, and methods for delving into tax/expenditure incidence are fairly well formulated (Meiszkowski, 1969; Blinder et al., 1976). The second category deals with the distributional impact of such specific public programs as educational services, agricultural development, and construction projects.

Although studies of fiscal systems in developing countries are few, generally they can be used to exert favorable redistributive pressures within the economy. Snodgrass (1974), for example, indicates that progressiveness within the Malaysian fiscal system has increased noticeably since 1958.

McLure (1975) indicates that, overall, the fiscal system of Colombia exhibits mild progressiveness. On the whole, surveys of general tax/expenditure incidence in LDCs (De Wulf, 1974) indicate that benefits from government expenditures received by upper income groups represent a smaller portion of their incomes than do the benefits received by low income groups. Both conceptual and methodological problems, however, cast serious doubt on the adequacy of these studies in determining whether or not public policy is "pro poor." Usually what is measured is the amount of public expenditure for such items as teachers and irrigation projects, rather than the value of education to those being taught or the marginal value of agricultural products to producers. Since the recipients of public benefits at the low end of the income scale rarely have any say about the quantity or quality of the services they receive, we cannot be sure that their evaluation of such services would correspond to that of public officials.

Many public expenditures provide public goods and services which add particular difficulties to the evaluation of benefit incidence.[12] Because there are no generally accepted ways of allocating these benefits, assumptions about their value must be used only as rules of thumb. One assumption is that all persons benefit equally (since all consume equally); others are that benefits are received in proportion to income or wealth or that benefits are received and valued in some impressionistic way. Unfortunately, the proportion of public goods in most government budgets is large, and assumptions about how benefits are to be assigned largely determine the outcome of studies concerned with overall incidence of public expenditures (De Wulf, 1974, p. 22).

Students of tax/expenditure incidence are further thwarted by poor-quality data. The excellent study by Krzyzaniak and Ozmucur (1972) offers a good illustration. Their analysis of the incidence of taxes in Turkey resulted in estimates of tax burdens for thirty-five income categories and demonstrated that, under varying assumptions, Turkish taxes, overall, probably are proportional. However, the many adjustments needed to make the data comparable (and to force them into a format which allowed a study of this type) introduce the potential for a wide range of errors, thus weakening the validity of their results.

Studies of specific public policies generally show that lower-income segments of the population receive benefits which represent a larger portion of their incomes than richer segments. Studies cited by De Wulf (1974, p. 23) indicate, however, that, because of the extreme inequality of income existing in the first place, the absolute benefits received by upper income groups are far in excess of those accruing to the poor. Colombian data on the distribution of educational benefits, for example, show that the lowest income classes receive benefits (measured by expenditure) equivalent to 13.1 percent of their incomes and that the highest income group receives as little as 0.8 percent. In absolute terms, however, the latter group receives more than six times the educational benefits of the poor. Fields' (1975) study of higher education in Kenya indicates that there is a "systematic process operating against the poor," tending to perpetuate inequities existing there.

Employment programs have captured the attention of many economists of late, and proposals for attacking the problems of unemployment and inequitable income distribution decorate almost any development plan. While most of these efforts can probably be recommended to improve the employment situation, they cannot be seen as panaceas for solving distribution problems. Too many other factors, in addition to employment, affect distribution. Webb (1972), for example, points to the effect of nonlabor income, which appears much more inequitably distributed in Peru than labor income. Jarvis (1974) points to this factor as well as to the distribution of capital ownership and the effect of dualism before concluding that employment programs, as a means of achieving income redistribution, are likely to be of only marginal benefit. Like many other critics of employment policy, Jarvis advocates a more direct government role in income redistribution.

Stabilization policies seem to have been associated with sharply increased inequality. Arndt (1975) analyzed post-Sukarno Indonesia and the stabilization and growth policies pursued there after 1966. With per-capita income growing at a rapid 4 percent per year, ever-larger shares were accruing only to the upper income groups. While the poorest income groups lost part of their relative share, it was Arndt's judgment that they were at least holding their own in absolute terms. The severe stabilization program in Brazil, begun in 1964, also resulted in rapid economic growth and a deterioration in economic equity (Wells, 1974). The data presented by Wells, however (Table 8), show that the poorest decile of the working population could not possibly have been holding its own on an absolute scale, since its relative share dropped by more than 40 percent. Informal reports from Chile indicate that current trends there are mostly along Brazilian lines. Unfortunately, the cases cited present such a mixture of economic and political confusion that few clear economic forces can be observed.

Often, where data permit, simulation exercises can help determine the impact of specific programs upon income distribution. Weisskoff's 1973 study of growth in Puerto Rico, plotting the path of employment and income distribution, probably could not have been done in many developing countries because of data limitations. Via simulation, Thirsk (1972) examined the Colombian policy of subsidizing the mechanization of agriculture. He showed explicitly the changes in income distribution which resulted from the relative changes in prices of productive factors and the changes in GDP which resulted from improvements in efficiency. He was able to show that withdrawing the subsidy both improved income distribution (by increasing labor intensiveness and decreasing the income share of capital owners) and increased GDP (through more optimal allocation of resources).

Occasionally, reference is made in economics literature to policies for improving income distribution as part of an overall development strategy. Development plans are replete with statements about combining distributional objectives with other goals, such as growth and export expansion.[13] Often, however, no analytical framework exists which links distribution with other considerations. Thus, one cannot easily determine whether multiple objectives are consistent with one another or, if there are trade-offs among them, define those trade-offs. In the Chilean case, for example, Foxley and Munoz (1974) indicate that the objectives of the Allende government for 1970–1976—to increase economic growth and employment and reduce foreign indebtedness— were not consistent, given internal savings propensities. Their evaluation of the Chilean situation could generally be applied in other cases: "The way to promote a sustained redistribution effort must . . . make direct redistributive efforts compatible with the savings and investment efforts, and also [compatible] with an increase in efficiency . . ." (Foxley and Munoz, 1974, p. 29).

Overall studies of specific policies or sets of policies usually are deficient in that they do not single out the specific groups which are to benefit or pay the cost. It is insufficient to merely indicate which income classes will feel some impact, since each income class usually consists of a variety of people with different behavioral patterns. What is needed is more information about such specific functional groups as small farmers, shopkeepers, skilled labor, and entrepreneurs. These groups often span several income categories, but all are nevertheless tied together in a set of economic activities which eventually determine what the overall income distribution will be. Since each of these groups operates in a slightly different economic area, their motivations and needs will differ. Studies must, therefore, be designed to analyze the specific needs of each group so that policies can be derived to effectively meet those needs.

Notes

1. These measures were quintile shares, the Gini concentration ratio, coefficient of variation, and the standard deviation of the logs of income.

2. Since perfect equality means that each quintile will receive 20 percent of total income, the standard deviation of quintile shares is taken from 20. Similarly, decile shares, or whatever, could be calculated.

3. Data were available on all countries examined by Kuznets except for Guatemala.

4. The technique is more fully described in Sonquist and Morgan (1964).

5. Though the 1974 paper does not carefully define all the independent variables, these can be found in Adelman and Morris (1973 and 1967).

6. Adelman and Morris (1974, p. 82) noted the same thing. The variables most strongly related to income distribution are not the ones which were found useful in explaining

growth in their 1967 study. The policy implication is that instruments for improving income distribution are not the same as those used to stimulate growth.

7. One well-known defect of the Gini index is that it is not sensitive in comparisons of two Lorenz curves that cross. Also, only the overall inequality, not its location, is indicated.

8. Roberti (1974, p. 633) differentiates between (1) unanimous changes in inequality (i.e., where the population becomes more or less equal throughout, with no groups moving in contrary directions—in this case aggregate measures will suffice) and (2) nonunanimous changes in inequality (i.e., where some groups in society move toward equality while others move away; some individuals would thus regard the final distribution as more equal, and others as less equal—in this case measures comparing groups are clearly called for, in addition to aggregate indices).

9. Household data are easier to collect, since once a definition of "household" is determined the census is faced with a population which is much smaller and much more fixed in location than is the population of individuals.

10. Kuznets' (1957) measure of weighted relative inequality among sectors is calculated as follows: If agriculture produces .3 of total national product and employs .4 of the labor force, the difference (i.e., .1) is really the difference between the relative per-worker product (i.e., .3/.4=.75) and the countrywide average (i.e., 1.00). That difference (.75 - 1.00 = -.25) is then weighted by the share of that sector in the total labor force (i.e., .4). The sum of these differences is a measure of relative inequality among sectoral products per worker, weighted by the share of each sector in the labor force. The index ranges from 0 (complete equality) and approaches infinity as production becomes entirely concentrated in one sector which employs fewer and fewer people.

11. It is interesting to note that Kuznets (p. 41) found that when the 12 highest nonwhite population states were separated from the others, income inequality was shown to be clearly greater in the nonwhite states and greatest in the poorest 6 nonwhite states.

12. Public goods are those which (1) once provided, no one can be excluded from consuming and (2) the consumption of them by one person does not reduce the supply

available to others. The classic example of a "pure" public good is defense. However, rarely are public goods "pure" in the sense of meeting the definition precisely.
   13. For an example, see Republic of Kenya (1974).

References

Adelman, I. (1975). "Development Economics—A Reassessment of Goals." *American Economic Review* 65, no. 2 (May 1975): 302–309.

Adelman, I., and C. T. Morris (1973). *Economic Growth and Social Equity in Developing Countries.* Stanford, Calif.: Stanford University Press.

Adelman, I., and C. T. Morris (1967). *Society, Politics and Economic Development.* Baltimore: Johns Hopkins Press.

Adelman, I., and C. T. Morris (1974). "Who Benefits from Economic Development," in OECD, *Planning, Income, Distribution, Private Foreign Investment.* Paris: OECD, 1974.

Ahluwalia, M. S. (1974). "Income Inequality: Some Dimensions of the Problem," in Chenery et al.

Arndt, H. W. (1975). "Development and Equality: The Indonesian Case." *World Development* 3, nos. 2 and 3 (February/March 1975).

Berry, A. (1974). "Changing Income Distribution under Development: Colombia." *Review of Income and Wealth* 20, no. 3 (September 1974).

Blinder, A., et al. (1974). *The Economics of Public Finance.* Washington: The Brookings Institution.

Chenery, H., et al. (1974). *Redistribution with Growth.* London: Oxford University Press.

De Wulf, L. (1974). "Do Public Expenditures Reduce Inequality?" *Finance and Development*, September 1974.

Fields, G. (1975). "Higher Education and Income Distribution in A Less Developed Country." *Oxford Economic Papers* 27, no. 2 (July 1975).

Fishlow, A. (1972). "Brazilian Size Distribution of Income." *American Economic Review* 62, no. 2 (May 1972).

Foxley, A., and O. Munoz (1974). "Income Redistribution, Economic Growth and Social Structure: The Case of

Chile." *Oxford Bulletin of Economics and Statistics* 36, no. 1.

Jain, S. (1974). "Size Distribution of Income: Compilation of Data." IBRD, Bank Staff Working Paper no. 190 (November 1974).

Jarvis, L. S. (1974). "The Limited Value of Employment Policies for Income Inequality," in Edwards, ed. *Employment in Developing Nations.* New York: Columbia University Press.

Kravis, I. (1960). "International Differences in the Distribution of Income." *Review of Economics and Statistics* 42, no. 4 (November 1960).

Kumar, D. (1974). "Changes in Income Distribution and Poverty in India: A Review of the Literature." *World Development* 2.

Krzyzaniak, M., and S. Ozmucur (1972). "The Distribution of Income and the Short Run Burden of Taxes in Turkey, 1968." Program of Development Studies, Rice University, Houston, Paper no. 28.

Kuznets, S. (1963). "Quantitative Aspects of the Economic Growth of Nations: Distribution of Income by Size." *Economic Development and Cultural Change* 11, no. 2 (January 1963).

Kuznets, S. (1957). "Quantitative Aspects of the Economic Growth of Nations: Industrial Distribution of National Product and Labor Force." *Economic Development and Cultural Change,* no. 4 (July 1957).

McLure, Jr., C. E. (1975). "The Incidence of Colombia Taxes: 1970." *Economic Development and Cultural Change* 24, no. 1 (October 1970).

Meiszkowski, P. (1969). "Tax Incidence Theory: The Effects of Taxes on the Distribution of Income." *Journal of Economic Literature* 7, no. 4 (December 1969), 1: 103-124.

Oshima, H. T. (1970). "Income Inequality and Economic Growth: The Postwar Experience of Asian Countries." *Malayan Economic Review* 15, no. 2 (October 1970).

Oshima, H. T. (1962). "The International Comparison of Size Distribution of Family Incomes with Special Reference to Asia." *Review of Economics and Statistics* 44, no. 4 (November 1962): 439-445.

Paukert, F. (1973). "Income Distribution at Different Levels of Development: A Survey of Evidence." *International Labor Review* 108, nos. 2 and 3 (August/September 1973).

Roberti, P. (1974). "Income Distribution: A Time-Series and A Cross-Section Study." *Economic Journal* 84, no. 335 (September 1974).

Robinson, S. (1976). "A Note on the U Hypothesis Relating Income Inequality and Economic Development." *American Economic Review* 66, no. 3 (June 1976).

Sen, A. (1975). *Employment, Technology and Development.* Oxford: Clarendon Press.

Snodgrass, D. R. (1974). "The Fiscal System as an Income Redistributor in West Malaysia." *Public Finance* 29, no. 1.

Sonquist, J. A., and J. N. Morgan (1964). *The Detection of Interaction Effects.* Ann Arbor: Institute of Social Research, University of Michigan.

Swamy, S. (1967). "Structural Change in the Distribution of Income by Size: The Case of India." *Review of Income and Wealth* 13, no. 2 (June 1967).

Thirsk, W. R. (1972). "Income Distribution, Efficiency and the Experience of Colombian Farm Mechanization." Program of Development Studies, Rice University, Houston, Paper no. 33.

Tokman, V. E. (1974). "Redistribution of Income, Technology and Employment: An Analysis of the Industrial Sectors of Ecuador, Peru and Venezuela." *World Development* 2.

Webb, R. C. (1972). "The Distribution of Income in Peru." Research Program in Economic Development, Woodrow Wilson School, Princeton University, Princeton, N. J., Discussion Paper no. 26.

Weisskoff, R. (1970). "Income Distribution and Economic Growth in Puerto Rico, Argentina, and Mexico." *Review of Income and Wealth* 16, no. 4 (December 1970).

Wells, J. (1974). "Distribution of Earnings, Growth, and the Structure of Demand in Brazil during the 1960s." *World Development* 2, no. 1 (January 1974).

2. The World Bank and World Poverty

Hollis Chenery

The World Bank has taken a circuitous route from financing rich countries to financing poor countries. Established after World War II as the International Bank for Reconstruction and Development, its first main function was to lend funds for reconstruction in European countries. It supplemented the capital subscriptions of its members by borrowing on the world capital market, added a half-percent or so to the interest rate, and reloaned the money. Gradually its clients shifted to the developing countries, but its borrowers were not subsidized except through the bank's acceptance of the risk of default. Only in 1960 did the bank begin lending in any volume to poor countries with the formation of its soft-loan affiliate, the International Development Association, which lends at very low (almost zero) interest rates and with long maturities.

The philosophy of the World Bank in the 1960s remained rather conservative: development was largely synonymous with growth—growth that would be achieved by investing in sound projects. Until recently the bulk of the bank's lending was for infrastructural projects, such as roads and electric power, selected on the basis of their contribution to growth.

As development economists began to question this philosophy, seeing that growth was having little effect on large numbers of people who were left behind in poverty, the bank began to alter its approach. After Robert S. McNamara became its president in the late 1960s, the bank's operations were broadened so as to give more prominence to other sectors, particularly education and agriculture.

At that time, those who doubted that growth was a sufficient goal of development policy were pointing to the evidence of growing unemployment in developing countries. In the early 1970s the International Labour Office began its studies of the "employment problem," but it soon became clear that this was not the most useful focus for research. Since many of the unemployed were not among the poorest people, and since the great bulk of the poorest people did have employment—but at very low levels of productivity—it was clearly necessary to look at other causes of poverty.

The World Bank began doing research on poverty and the distribution of income in the early 1970s. This was not because we were seeking a theory for its own sake, but because we needed to know enough to determine whether what we were doing was wrong—and, if it was wrong, to identify the changes in policy that were needed. At that time the available data on income distribution were so poor that almost any generalization could be supported. The bank set out to remedy this situation by collecting and analyzing new data and by compiling existing studies. Though there are still many serious deficiencies, I think we have become the world's main source of income-distribution data.

In 1973, we sponsored jointly with the Institute of Development Studies in Sussex a meeting at which a group of planners and policymakers pooled their ideas about income distribution. We have yet to find definitive answers to many of the questions which were being raised then: Does income distribution normally get worse before it gets better? Is there necessarily a trade-off between distribution and growth? The scarcity of data, and in particular the lack of time-series data for individual countries, means that we cannot yet make very strong statements about these issues.

But, having persuaded ourselves that poverty problems were not, indeed, being solved by the mechanisms of growth, we have not waited for new theories to be perfected before beginning to reshape our operations. Investments in rural and urban development are monitored so that we can learn from what are now rather large-scale experiments. For example, in conjunction with the $1 billion we are lending this year for rural development, we will spend some $10 million on monitoring programs that will help show us how to design such projects more effectively in the future. Nonetheless, from the outset there have been fundamental questions that could not be answered from looking at individual projects:

First, who are the poor? Any antipoverty strategy must be able to identify poor people and some of the reasons for their poverty. Research on the existing distribution of income in developing countries, by the World Bank as well as the development community generally, has identified certain groups containing the majority of poor people. These groups have characteristics that make it harder for them to benefit from the workings of the market and, particularly, to get into the advanced sector of the economy, where incomes are higher. Not all of these target groups, however, can be reached through existing mechanisms.

Second, if one is interested in the welfare of individuals and not merely in the growth of GNP, what measure does one use to evaluate human-oriented projects, or social programs, or the performance of the economy as a whole? Though GNP is a simple and convenient index, it has obvious deficiencies as a welfare measure. Since the upper 20 percent typically receives more than 50 percent of total income, GNP weights the income of the rich much more heavily than that of the poor. If the objective is to alleviate poverty, one must allow for the fact that an additional dollar of income would make far more difference to the welfare of a poor family than to that of a rich family. This approach yields different answers as to what is a profitable, sound, or efficient project. For example, if the objective is to maximize GNP, I would have to prefer a cattle-raising project with a rate of return of 25 percent, whose main beneficiaries were large landowners, to a small farm development project which benefited many low-income families but whose overall rate of return was only 20 percent. How the incomes of different groups should be weighted is still a matter of experiment in bank work; but research is continuing in this area, and those evaluating projects have taken some important steps in getting away from the simple GNP criterion.

Third, how far can governments redistribute income by

means of fiscal policy, using tax and welfare systems? Studies
we undertook in several developing countries, tracing who
paid taxes and who benefited from the revenues that were
generated, showed that, in general, whatever redistribution
takes place through the fiscal system is perverse. In most
poor countries, the effect of the fiscal system is regressive; the
rich get far more than their share of education, roads,
housing, and most other public services. To a large extent,
this reflects the fact that some three-quarters of the poor live
in rural areas, while most of the well-to-do are urban. People
with power living in urban areas can perceive their own
needs far more clearly than they perceive rural needs.
Outside of China, Tanzania, and a few other firmly rural-
oriented economies, the urban areas receive more than their
fair share of public spending. This perception leads to an
obvious sólution: we need to distribute public investment
more fairly. Since public investment is a large share of the
total, and since this is an area in which the World Bank has
traditionally been involved, controlling its distribution has
been one of the main ways in which the bank has sought to
combat poverty. We may not yet know how to ensure that
small farmers benefit from cooperative credit schemes, but
we do know how to design rural roads. This is one of the few
cases in which diagnosis and cure come quite close together.

This recognition—that distributional effects follow
directly from the type of production, and that, therefore,
distributional aspects of growth have to be considered in
project selection—is what I would call the "minimum
diagnosis" that has led not only the bank but most of the
development assistance agencies of the Western world to
change their policies. The Swedes, in particular, take the
view that all public aid should be directed to poverty
groups—either poor countries or poor people in poor
countries.

It will be clear that such changes in direction run against
many people's ideas of what is appropriate for the World
Bank as a *bank*. However, the bank's ability to affect
conditions in borrowing countries always depends on the
countries themselves. In order even to start a project directed
at the poor in a given country, the bank must be able to find
an agency in that country whose aims are sympathetic (and
which has a minimum degree of effectiveness). If the

government of that country has no desire to improve the welfare of the poor, the bank's efforts are not likely to change the situation. Here the executive directors who represent the more liberal of the bank's 125 member countries face a dilemma: Part of the liberal philosophy is opposed to intervention in other countries' affairs. ("Who do you think you are, knowing better than country X?") But if the income distribution in country X is visibly getting worse, it is often the more liberal among our directors who are the strongest advocates of intervention. Whether or not to intervene is perhaps the most difficult problem in trying to help from the outside.

Having raised these general issues, I will now say a little about the World Bank's approaches to lending. As yet we do not know the effectiveness of different instruments for reaching the poor, and those we are using now will probably be changed considerably during the next few years as we gain more experience.

There is a large body of literature which urges that the poor must participate in designing whatever project is going to affect them. Though intuitively this may seem an excellent idea, I think that, as with many other ideological approaches to poverty alleviation, success in implementing this theory has been very spotty. But it is clear, at least, that programs of this nature cannot be specified by economists and cannot be centrally administered. For an agency such as the World Bank, which operates in many diverse countries and whose projects are usually large in scale, it is easier—at present—to concentrate on aspects of the poverty problem which can be tackled through rather large implementing agencies, and leave other aspects to governments themselves and to agencies that can work with small groups on diverse small-scale projects. However, because we recognize that our perceptions in, say, five years' time probably will differ from our perceptions now, we are trying to allow flexibility in the design of projects, so that we can take advantage of experience and, if necessary, change the specifications while implementation is in progress.

Doing something for the poorest income groups is not at all easy with the instruments the World Bank has available, since we cannot directly reach people who have no control over productive resources. Thus, we can reach small farmers, but not landless laborers; we can reach the independent small craftsmen in cities, but we cannot reach beggars or people with no employment. We are probably furthest ahead in schemes to help the small farmer. He controls some land, whether he is an owner or a tenant; he knows how to farm. We can supply him with productive inputs, help remove the discrimination against him by giving him access to credit or lowering interest rates, help with his marketing, educate his children and so make his family more productive. Reaching the landless laborer is far more difficult. Even if we could provide him with skills, there is no guarantee that he would ever have the chance to use them.

So far, small farmers have been our main rural target group, and most countries' own antipoverty programs have also focused on that group. Though the settings vary from *ujamaa* villages in Tanzania to more capitalistic environments, the rural development package most commonly desired by governments has been about 70 percent for agricultural inputs, with the remainder for roads, water supply, education, and so forth. We should like to give more emphasis now to other facets in rural development programs and somewhat less primacy to productive inputs, but at the beginning these are the easiest instruments.

Attempts to increase productivity through making inputs available may be self-defeating if the prevailing policies are unfavorable. For instance, if agricultural prices are kept low, perhaps to subsidize wage goods of low-income urban consumers, farmers may have no incentive to increase their output. In such a situation the World Bank will urge the government to make the necessary policy changes.

Experience has also taught us that projects must be replicable: it is necessary to use an approach that fits the income level of the country in question. For example, in a country where per-capita income is $150 and the government collects 12 percent of that in public revenues, $18 per capita indicates the type of public investment projects that should be planned. Very few poor countries are willing to recognize that they have such limited public funds or to admit that the appropriate standard of, say, housing, for that income level is a somewhat modernized version of slums they already have. It is very tempting to knock down the slums that people have built for themselves and to build a few politically advantageous showpieces, which can house very few people. Much of the same sort of thing has been true in irrigation, and in many kinds of agricultural production and manufacturing. One of the most important lessons we can hope to learn from the Chinese experience is how to tailor development projects to existing levels of income so that they can be replicated for the whole population.

I will now comment on our experience in some key areas of inequality: *rural and urban poverty, regional disparities,* and *inequalities between nations.* The World Bank started lending for rural development about three years ago with a very optimistic set of objectives. It was thought that, on a scale suitable for the income level of the country in question, a package could be introduced to enable small farmers to increase their output by 5 percent per year. Recognizing that the average growth of output is less than 4 percent per year for the agricultural sector as a whole in developing countries, and that small farmers are usually less efficient than more-favored producers, to realize this goal would be quite remarkable. Nonetheless, those who are monitoring the projects assert that this is happening. Unfortunately, it takes a very long time before one really knows what has happened in any agricultural project, particularly if it involves building roads, irrigation, and moving people. And we do not yet have much evidence on how much the rural community as a whole is benefiting from these projects— knowledge which is necessary if the strategy is to work.

It is also too early to measure what is sacrificed in basing one's approach on the alleviation of poverty. Will the returns on investment, measured in conventional GNP terms, necessarily be lower? So far the estimated rates of return on good rural development projects have been just as high as those in more conventional projects, agricultural or not. However, I think there is likely to be a trade-off in terms of time: although the poor, who are less well educated and have less access to inputs, will become as productive eventually, increases in production could be realized more quickly if the same resources were made available to people already accustomed to modern technology.

Urban poverty is not yet too urgent a problem for the poorest of the developing countries, where 80 percent of the poor are rural. But at higher levels of development—when incomes reach, say, $400 per capita—urbanization usually takes place so rapidly that not even an ideal society would be able to provide housing, transportation, sanitation, and other facilities quickly enough.

Most Latin American countries now have more than half their populations in cities and towns. Bogota had 2 million people ten years ago; it has 4 million now; it probably will have 8 million in another ten years. São Paulo has 10 million, and it seems inevitable that this figure will double in another twelve or thirteen years. Following the experience of the developed countries, it is likely that in another twenty years the Latin American countries will have become 70-percent urbanized, and that rural-urban migration will then begin to taper off.

Thus, we can expect the problems of cities in developing countries to get worse before they get better. Only a few of the more-advanced city governments have fully realized that they have to accept the squatters and install minimal facilities for them, rather than building middle-class housing and trusting that the poor will not migrate. When the realization comes too late, the result is the worst of both worlds: the facilities are more expensive and difficult to install in squatter communities than if they have been planned from the start. In the end, higher costs are incurred because of lack of planning. For example, many people in São Paulo spend four to five hours each day commuting to work because of the lack of accessible housing. Though for a long time studies of urban migrants showed that these people felt better off, subjectively, in the towns, despite their miserable living conditions, there is some evidence in Brazil that this is no longer the case. The rising infant-mortality rate in São Paulo also suggests that conditions are actually getting worse for the poor, despite the rapidly rising GNP in Brazil.

The World Bank has recently begun work on urban poverty problems, and we are finding it more difficult in urban areas than in rural areas to identify target groups that can be directly assisted. We cannot treat entrepreneurs in the informal or "murky" sector as though they were the urban equivalent of small farmers. Not only are the delivery systems to this sector very diffuse, we do not know how poor urban households behave, what they consume, what they produce. If a large number of producers are supported by a fixed amount of trade, and if some of these are made more efficient, the others will be driven out of business and the income distribution will not be improved at all. If the volume of goods produced by the informal sector is increased, will the market be glutted and will prices fall? Until some of these questions are answered, it is difficult to plan projects directly for particular groups of people.

The income distribution in cities is clearly connected with the distribution of public investment. This being the case, the bank may concentrate for the immediate future on simpler types of urban projects in which it has experience, such as making transportation more efficient, locating work places nearer to where people live, and generally trying to plan the inevitable growth of cities in such a way that the poor do not become poorer after migrating.

A third aspect of the World Bank's work on poverty and inequality concerns backward regions in countries that are otherwise fairly prosperous. The largest pocket of poverty in the Western Hemisphere is Northeast Brazil, where there are 20 million people with living standards very much lower than in the rest of Latin America, let alone the other parts of Brazil. The Brazilian government has channeled a great deal of investment to this area, but its effect on the poor has been relatively small. In addition to rural and urban investment projects to try to reduce such regional imbalances, the bank is doing research on why they exist and are perpetuated.

The growing inequality among nations has received much popular attention. The dramatic changes in the world economy over the past few years—sudden rises and falls in raw materials prices, the rise in the price of oil, and unprecedented rates of world inflation—have had far more disruptive effects on the poor countries than on others. Though the United States has complained loudly, its sufferings are minimal compared to those of most countries in Africa and South Asia. The U.S. and most of Western Europe have managed to adjust to the changed economic circumstances, and of course the OPEC countries have done well. Many of the middle-income developing countries, too, have been able to withstand the recent shocks without a great reduction in growth. But in the poorest countries, where there are large groups of people on the margin of survival, per-capita incomes have been stagnating or actually declining. While this is partly the result of inefficient internal policies, it is largely the result of changes in the international environment.

I turn now to possible remedies. It seems to me unlikely that the developing countries can expect the absolute volume of aid they receive to increase substantially in real terms. The member countries of OECD's Development Assistance Committee, which tries to define aid policies for the market economies as a group, set a target of 0.7 percent of donors' GNP for development assistance on concessional terms. U.S. assistance came fairly close to that target fifteen years ago, and at present several of the West European countries are meeting it. But the U.S. effort has declined drastically, so that it is now only around 0.26 percent of the U.S. GNP. This means that the target for the OECD countries as a whole has less chance of being met now than ten years ago.

If the capital transfers to the developing countries cannot be increased very much, then at least what is available could be allocated more fairly. The OECD has been advocating a distribution of aid which conforms more closely to recipients' needs—with some success outside the U.S., where political criteria predominate. The World Bank Group has been trying hard to improve the distribution of its own lending, so that IDA credits are made only to countries with per-capita incomes under $200. We have doubled the amount of concessional assistance for countries that were hardest hit by recent events in the world economy. We have thus been trying to redistribute concessional assistance both among countries, according to their needs, and within countries, in order to redirect the lending program in favor of poverty groups. This policy involves somewhat higher risks than we should incur in merely maximizing GNP. If our aim were only to raise the growth rate of developing countries as a group, we should have gone on lending mainly to efficient countries such as Brazil, Korea, and Taiwan—which themselves have the resources to eradicate poverty.

3. Growth and Distribution: Trade-Offs or Complements?

Gustav Ranis

If we can count on any underlying certainty with respect to the international economic scene, it is that it is subject to severe shocks—and likely to remain so. It is, nevertheless, possible to recognize that the events of the last few years have been particularly cataclysmic in their impact, especially as far as the LDCs are concerned. These events—including oil, food, and DC stagflation crises—have, among many other consequences, increased the disparity among the LDCs and helped bring into fuller focus the existence of large and growing gaps within and between individual countries of the developing and developed worlds. With respect to the growing gaps between the so-called third and fourth worlds, the political will among both old and nouveau riche to do something meaningful about these gaps still seems to be lacking; perhaps efforts under the still-somewhat-leaky umbrella of the "New International Economic Order," currently under discussion in many quarters around the globe, will eventually begin to bear fruit. It is an important subject, but one we do not intend to deal with here. With respect to the second (and not wholly unrelated) issue, which is the subject of this paper, the answer lies less in the international setting and more in the needs of a "new national economic order." Here, growing awareness of the problem has not as yet been accompanied by either a commensurate increase in understanding or a will to action. As long as this understanding remains incomplete, it is easier for the elites of the developing countries—and others—to leave the matter at the rhetorical level. It will indeed be difficult for those inside the LDCs who would like to change the current state of inequity—or for those outside who would like to help through advice and/or assistance—to be really effective in the absence of further progress on this front.

We could, of course, argue for a long while about whether absolute poverty or the relative within-country distribution of income represents the main problem. Certainly, for populations whose basic needs for food, clothing, and shelter have not yet been satisfied, it is the condition of "low-end poverty" that matters most. But I think it is reasonable to assert that, for the vast majority of the populations of the developing world—certainly once they've started in motion—it is not some Rawlsian lexicographic ordering which affects their level of satisfaction or dissatisfaction, but their own (changing) standard of life relative to that of their countrymen which is now increasingly visible and yet apparently increasingly unattainable. The setting of "poverty lines" at $50 or $75 per capita, or the racking up of "basic needs" with dollar or caloric equivalents, is likely to reflect policymakers' aspirations rather than people's own priorities and perceptions. We readily admit that this is likely to be a less-valid consideration for countries at the low end of the scale, as well as for the truly marginalized members of all societies, rich or poor. For the vast bulk of LDC populations, however, it can be asserted that it is their relative position, either regionally or via the interfamily distribution of income, which weighs most heavily in the welfare function.[1]

Another, and possibly more pragmatic, reason for preferring to concentrate analysis on the relative rather than the absolute poverty issue is that the relative positions of families and/or regions can be more easily integrated within the traditional general equilibrium analysis of the economic system, whether focused on growth, technology, or employment. Poverty at the low end of the income scale, whether in rich or poor countries, is, after all, an arbitrary concept usually tackled by "after the fact" measures; e.g., public employment, fiscal redistribution, food-stamp programs, and other transfers—all "secondary" strategies, if by "primary" strategy we mean the nature of the production process itself. Once we address the question of what happens to the poor, as that is tied to growth, employment, and other aspects of the development pattern itself, it becomes analytically much easier to deal with relative rather than absolute poverty issues. This is because relationships between growth, employment, and the size distribution of income constitute a nexus which is in large part linked up with technology choice and the functional distribution of income, both of which are relative concepts.

With very few exceptions, the LDC development plans of the 1950s and 1960s dealt with employment and regional distribution objectives as part of a secondary strategy which would have to be deployed, if somewhat halfheartedly, after the dust had settled on the primary, output-oriented development program.[2] More recently, public works and nationalization have been added to the list of instruments in the tool kit. The fiscal redistribution of income from upper to lower income groups was expected to pick up secondary demand and employment effects via the impact of a different, more labor-intensive final demand bundle. Finally, making the growth buggy move a little faster was expected to solve the poverty, if not the equity, problem.

However, there now exists a growing consensus that centrally planned public-works programs intended to solve a national underemployment and/or poverty problem are difficult to organize, blueprint, and maintain, and that nationalization—even if its negative-output effects could be overcome—represents a clumsy instrument for redistribution via prices in the mixed economy. Moreover, even if the notoriously low fiscal capacity of LDC governments could somehow be repaired, results of research at Rice University and elsewhere (Soligo and Land, 1974) indicate rather clearly that the changes in final demand composition required to make any real difference would be way out of proportion to what is realistically feasible. "Trickling down" to the poor through higher growth rates is seen as another nonstarter (though only a few years ago Prebisch [1962] suggested this as a solution for Latin America), partly because we cannot expect to have enough development fuel to put into the development tank, and partly because, in any case, the consequences of such a policy are unambiguously bad for distribution.

It is thus a sad but more or less generally accepted finding that, at least for the mixed developing economy, the only reasonable hope of doing something about poverty or distribution is through an attack on the nature of the growth path itself; i.e., changing the rules of the output game, with or without a change in the distribution of initial chips or assets. Even if this conclusion were universally accepted, however, it would only begin to address the central question of this paper: whether growth objectives and distribution objectives, while they need to be viewed together, are by nature likely to constitute trade-offs or complements, and in what types of situations they are competitive rather than complementary. Finally, if these two societal objectives are to some extent competitive, we might want to know how painful the necessary trade-offs are likely to be.

This, it seems to me, is finally the right question: if distribution can be analyzed only in the context of growth, how do we in fact move toward an integration of either neoclassical or classical development theory? For what types of economies? With what measures of equity over time? Regardless of which index of inequality is ultimately preferred—and there are many ways of assessing the various measures available to us (Fields and Fei, 1974)—it is necessary to relate that index to the performance of the system in its other, more familiar aspects. In other words, since income distribution is usually "measurement without theory," linking that measurement to other aspects of growth performance should enable us to ultimately arrive at some approximation of an answer to the aforementioned question. In fact, forging such a link is probably the only way to get from here to there. In an analysis of distribution—and, for that matter, of poverty—is to be more than a measurement effort, it has to become part of our primary understanding of growth.

The Prevailing Evidence: Trade-Off Pessimism

It is fair to say that the overwhelming evidence available to date points in the direction of an inevitable, and rather severe, conflict between most conventional measures of equity for a given society and its growth performance. Working with cross sections, Kuznets (1955, 1963) and

Adelman and Morris (1973) found that LDC distributions
are substantially worse than DC distributions; especially for
the top 20 percent of the population, incomes are clearly
more equally distributed in the relatively rich countries.[3]
Paukert (1973)—though he mixes family and individual
incomes in some of his work—points out that countries
reach a peak of income inequality as they move from $100 to
$200 income per capita. This holds true even if, as Cline
(1975) points out, the inverse U-shape pattern is weaker
within an LDC pattern of countries than when the cross
section is stretched across both DCs and LDCs.

Turning to time trends, these also appear to be generally
favorable to the trade-off hypothesis. For example, Weisskoff
(1970) finds income distribution worsening in Argentina
and Mexico, as does Fishlow (1972) in the case of Brazil.
There is evidence for the Philippines (Ranis, 1974) that
income distribution probably worsened during recent periods of fairly rapid growth.

The point of this paper is not that this overwhelming mass
of evidence can somehow be denied, but rather that there also
exists counterevidence—if admittedly less weighty in terms
of number of countries or their representativeness—which
should also be considered and which should at least give us
pause with respect to the inevitability of a conflict between
the societal objectives of growth and equity. The deviant
countries, mainly Korea and Taiwan, are exceptional in two
senses: their levels of Gini are lower (in the .3 range rather
than in the customary .5 range) and their Ginis have not
risen during the first period of rapid transition growth; i.e.,
things did not have to get worse before they could get better.
These two cases are admittedly special, in that they are the
same countries which previously gave us "deviant" results
with respect to their spectacular (and, by now, well known)
employment and income performance. Ditto for their related
early departures from the general pattern of import-
substitution growth and their moves towards export substitution based on mobilization of agriculture and the absorption of surplus labor in labor-intensive industry (Fei and
Ranis, 1975). It is thus perhaps not surprising that it is again
Korea and Taiwan—and, perhaps, if we had the data, Japan,
historically, as well—which present evidence of unusually
favorable levels and trends of distribution along with rapid

growth performance.

While we recognize that no two countries are ever the same and that the "specialness" of these particular situations must be acknowledged, it nevertheless seems instructive to look at them more closely in terms of what pieces of the lesson are relevant to other LDCs. At minimum, one successful counterexample is worth examining in detail. Moreover, it behooves us to look at other, less-special cases to see whether—at least in certain subphases of development—a similar diminution or elimination of the growth/distribution conflict can be observed. For example, Pakistan between 1961 and 1965, Colombia after 1967, Brazil between 1963 and 1968, the Philippines between 1964 and 1968—all represent historical episodes of deviation from the pronounced import-substitution syndrome, and may also turn out to represent deviations from the generally accepted trade-off phenomenon.[4] If the whys and wherefores of a particular country's favorable growth/distribution performance can be subjected to scrutiny, other countries' observers can judge for themselves its relevance to their own particular situations.

Such an historical approach, if feasible, is, of course, to be preferred to cross-sectional analysis. Hopefully, in addition to the Taiwan case (on which this chapter includes a brief progress report), other longitudinal studies will be forthcoming. Two such are currently well along, on Korea and Pakistan.[5] Others—on Colombia by C. Fields and on Japan by the Hitotsubashi group—may soon be available. At minimum, we would hope that studies for other countries will demonstrate that, at least during periods of time when the overall environment underwent some change, some environments were conducive to a softening or even an elimination of the observed conflict between growth and distribution objectives. Even though a full understanding of the interrelationships between growth and income distribution still eludes us, making a detailed examination of such "special case" deviations from what is assumed to be the common trend may be well worth the effort.

What analysts and policymakers presumably want to discover, in particular, is to what extent the elements of the growth pattern which apparently softened the conflict in, say, Taiwan, are present in other developing countries, and, if they are present, whether it is the lack of political will to make difficult societal choices or something else which is at fault. Of special interest here is the issue of whether, assuming the Taiwan pattern could be imitated, any favorable outcome must be attributed to radical asset restructuring or whether it is possible to achieve these desirable outcomes by merely "tinkering with relative prices." In other words, by letting markets work somewhat better, can we avoid the maldistribution that so frequently results from rapid growth? Or do we need to take some strong measures—including land, capital, and other institutional reforms?

Thus, not only might more analytical light be shed on the pieces in the puzzle of a country like Taiwan, the policy conclusions that might be drawn would be of substantial general interest—even if they are not precisely relevant elsewhere. Government efforts to achieve redistribution by moving directly to replace the market have become more frequent of late. It would be highly instructive to compare—always within the mixed-economy constraint—the results of direct intervention to smooth the conflict between distribution and growth in such countries as India with those of the Korea or Taiwan experiences, which were characterized by less-direct intervention. The situation of the truly socialist countries—e.g., Cuba, China, and some of the less-developed Eastern European countries—is different; they seem to have achieved lower levels of Gini, if with not clearly established rapid growth rates (Chenery et al., 1974). All we want to assert in the context of this paper is that there exists conclusive evidence that for at least one type of system—i.e., the mixed, small, labor-surplus economy represented by Taiwan—rapid growth is compatible with good *levels* and good *trends* in the distribution of income.

Trade-Off Optimism: A Deviant Case

The Taiwanese growth and distribution record, in brief, was one of unusually low levels of Gini (around .3) coupled with unusually high rates of output growth (above 10 percent) during the 1960s.[6] What is even more interesting, for our present purposes, is that the Gini in Taiwan did not follow the Kuznets inverse U-shaped pattern over time. Our data, though sketchier for the 1950s than for the 1960s, indicate that the overall Gini declined from a level of around .5 in 1953 to .4 in 1960 and held in the .3 range between 1964 and 1968, declining markedly thereafter. In other words, if

we accept the notion that Taiwan reached the end of labor
surplus at the end of the 1960s, there was in fact a substantial
Gini decline once wages began to rise significantly. But what
is more interesting is the virtually complete avoidance of the
Kuznets effect prior to the solution of the unemployment
problem during the 1960s.

The growth side of the Taiwan story seems to be as
follows: the typical regime of import-substituting industrialization which characterized Taiwanese policy from 1953
to roughly 1960 was not conducive to employment or to the
related (but not identical) improvement in the distribution
of income in Taiwan, any more than in other developing
countries. The distortion of relative factor and output prices
during an import-substitution policy period yields unneces-
sarily capital-intensive techniques and output mixes. Even
in Taiwan, employment in both rural and urban areas had to
take a back seat as long as capital and imports were under-
valued; and the receipt of an import license or a bank loan, in
the presence of overvalued exchange rates and low official
interest rates, bestowed large windfall profits and represented the major objective of entrepreneurial activity. In fact, the
level of the Gini in 1953 was about equivalent to that of most
contemporary LDCs. We should, however, note that the
basic initial conditions for improvement were laid via land
reforms which took place in three steps during the early
1950s, plus the fortuitous impact of a fairly evenly distributed migrant flow of capital and entrepreneurship from
mainland China in the late 1940s. Moreover, while Taiwan
suffered from a relative neglect of agriculture, as in all
import-substitution cases, the heavy irrigation and institutional infrastructure left by the Japanese colonial system
made it possible for agriculture to nevertheless make substantial progress even during the 1950s. This is one way of
explaining the gradual decline of the Gini even before the
advent of the policy reforms of the early 1960s.[7] We are,
moreover, confident that import substitution of a more
flexible type, as practiced in Taiwan, prevented the economy
from getting into the structural ruts experienced by many
other LDCs. For example, unions never played any important role, and protection, including quantitative controls
and tariffs, was never quite as severe as encountered elsewhere. Most important, in an absolute sense, the agricultur-

al sector continued to enjoy a good deal of favorable government attention.

Turning to the decade of the 1960s, Taiwan early on instituted a series of major reforms, moving her from an import-substitution pattern to an export-substitution pattern of growth.[8] As a consequence of this shift toward an export-oriented industrial growth pattern, it became possible for maturing industrial entrepreneurship to combine with plentiful unskilled labor supplies for industrial production, destined for both domestic and, increasingly, foreign markets. Thus, the important symbiotic relationship between high growth rates and employment was established—culminating, by the end of the decade, in the termination of labor surplus and the coming of the so-called commercialization point (Fei and Ranis, 1964). Fortunately, the good income distribution data becoming available after 1964 place us in a better position to analyze the relationship between distribution and the growth pattern during this export-substitution period. Moreover, since growth accelerated during the 1960s, this is also a period of greatest interest to those who want to analyze why the Kuznets-type pattern of conflict failed to put in an appearance.

If we look more closely at the Taiwanese record on income distribution, we find the overall Gini more or less constant between 1964 and 1968 at .33, and declining substantially thereafter (by more than 10 percent), to about .29. This is strong evidence that the Kuznets effect was entirely avoided before the end of labor surplus had been reached around 1968.[9] In order to get at the growth-related underlying sources of inequality, a decomposition of that overall Gini— in this case, into the various relevant factor Ginis and their relative weights in total family income—can be performed (Fei, Ranis, and Kuo, 1976). From this process, a number of interesting features emerge which permit us to push the causal explanation much further. (However, since this effort represents work in progress, we can only hint at it in the course of this paper.)

One finding was that, as we would have expected, the Gini for the profit share of income was higher than the overall income Gini, while the Gini for the wage share was lower than the overall Gini. Moreover, the wage share itself became increasingly important over the period, rising from .4 of total income in 1964 to .5 by 1968 and to .6 by 1972. The interpretation of this finding is that the wage share rises even during an unlimited supply of labor—which, contrary to the arguments of Lewis (1954) and others, indicates that, even during the so-called unlimited supply of labor phase when wages are more or less constant, labor's share can increase as a consequence of a rapidly increasing total volume of employment and number of hours worked per employee. Kuznets, Lewis, and Marxist and dependencia theorists (Cline, 1975) all have in common the view that, as growth really begins to get under way in earnest, income distribution must worsen as (1) the profit share rises, especially in the modern sector, (2) there is greater asset accumulation by the rich than by the poor in both sectors, and (as especially Kuznets would add) (3) the shift from rural to urban activities enhances the relative size of the more unequal sector. What this argument apparently neglects is the possibility, as demonstrated by the Taiwanese case, that we may simultaneously experience rent reduction in agriculture and a change in the relative position of groups within the laboring class, permitting the overall Gini to be improved by the combination of a rising functional distribution of wage income, falling agricultural income Ginis, and only slightly rising wage Ginis.

Second, if we divide the population into urban and rural households and compute the overall and factor Ginis (and weights) separately, we can see that for rural households the overall Gini declined during the 1960s (from .33 to .29), holding more or less steady thereafter. This development is related to a rapid decline, as we would expect, in the importance of agricultural income relative to nonagricultural income—the share of agricultural income in the total falling from .66 to .42 in the course of six years. This finding indicates that rural family incomes benefit as reallocation from agriculture to nonagriculture activities proceeds *if* that reallocation is, not directed to a distant urban sector and limited to the richer elements of the rural classes, but confined within the rural areas and heavily participated in by the relatively poorer elements of the rural population. Rapid rural mobilization based on improving the efficiency of the relatively poor farmers—both as farmers and as participants in the important and growing rural industries and services—clearly plays a decisive role in the elimination of the Kuznets effect.

Finally, taking the urban families separately, we find that here the Ginis do rise slightly before the 1968 turning point (from .33 to .34) declining rapidly thereafter (to .29). This indicates that here, in fact, the Kuznets pattern does obtain; i.e., equity for urban families under rapid growth can improve only after the turning point when wages begin to rise in a sustained fashion and the growing functional distribution of income in favor of labor once again (but now for different reasons) contributes to an improving size distribution of income.

Looking at the entire development picture from the early 1950s to the early 1970s in Taiwan, we are thus able to make the following general comments at this stage of our understanding: During the 1950s (the import-substitution subphase), land reform prevented the maldistribution of assets—a common feature of LDCs—from becoming part of the landscape. Moreover, early on, the existence of substantial infrastructure, in the form of irrigation, roads, and such institutions as farmers' associations, permitted agriculture to play an important role even during the import-substitution phase and for land to be used rather intensively. Land reform—partly in the form of reduction of rents, partly in the sale of government lands, and partly by transferring "soil to the tillers" (i.e., tenancy reform)—avoided the growth of the large landless rural worker class that often accompanies land reform and agricultural productivity increase in other countries, thus worsening the distribution of rural income. Consequently, as the small owner/operators began to use family labor, larger owners were induced to hire labor, and landless rural workers (and small or poor owner/operators) could be absorbed into the rapidly growing secondary activities in agriculture. These activities included not only rural industries and services but also the growing of such secondary crops as vegetables, mushrooms, and asparagus, which played an important role in the Taiwanese case. Rural works programs generated at the local level by local initiative also played a complementary role, not only in providing additional employment opportunities, but, more important, in clearing the way for the aforementioned increases in directly productive activities: in food-producing agriculture, in secondary crops, and in rural industry and service activities.

In the 1960s, when the growth regime changed to one of export substitution, rapid export-oriented industrialization was accompanied by a substantially enhanced growth of agricultural productivity, especially when high-yielding varieties were superimposed on an already very productive and research-oriented food-producing agricultural sector. Here, as in other countries, the critical issues were (1) who would get the new technology and who could use it, in terms of the availability of other inputs (water, credit, infrastructure, etc.) and (2) what would be the mechanization side effects of high-yielding varieties under labor absorption. In Taiwan, it is quite clear that the unit of cultivation did not change very much as a consequence of increased agricultural productivity; that mechanization was held in abeyance until the end of the decade, when labor surplus began to disappear; and that agricultural income at its source, if we look at the Gini for agricultural income as such, did not worsen. Even more important was the already mentioned rapid growth of rural industries and services and their relatively labor-intensive characteristics. The latter feature (see Ranis, 1973) indicates the important role decentralized industrialization can play in avoiding some of the costs of dualistic growth cited by Lewis, Kuznets, and others. Agriculture is basically a constant-returns industry, with the technology of the high-yielding varieties essentially scale-neutral. Thus, if the normal S-curve of the adoption of new varieties is permitted to play itself out, there need be no fear of a possible conflict between the two societal objectives.[10] Once the problem of who gets the benefits is solved, once the farmers' association type of institutional network provides possibilities not only for generating the agricultural surplus at its source but also for channeling it into rural activities understood and owned by the farmers themselves, the key ingredients for the absence of conflict and maximum mutual reinforcement are present.

It is not possible in this context to present a detailed analysis of the underlying causes of the softening and virtual elimination of the Kuznets effect in the case of the Taiwanese rapid growth experience. This discussion is merely intended to illustrate the main theme of this paper: namely, that the analysis of at least one deviant country in which growth, employment, and distribution were mutually reinforcing, rather than competitive, should give us all some pause—and perhaps lead us to examine particular facets of other country situations more carefully before we accept the inevitability of conflict and heavy trade-offs.

Conclusions

In summarizing the five country case studies included as an annex to the Chenery et al. volume (1974), Jolly presented a number of conclusions which he felt could be derived from these (admittedly sketchy) attempts to look at income redistribution and growth experiences in a number of very different countries. He pointed out, correctly, that in the socialist countries in the sample (in Cuba and Tanzania, at least), whatever income redistribution occurred was the result of conscious government policy directed toward that objective, and that the income distribution results in a market-oriented mixed economy such as Taiwan were essentially by-products of policies aimed at growth. It is important, however, to note that the Gini in Tanzania (.48) and the growth rates in both Tanzania and Cuba compare rather unfavorably, as least as of this date; in fact, as Jolly also points out, the only two cases of very rapid growth accompanied by redistribution seem to have occurred in the Korea and Taiwan cases.

We recognize that all the returns are not in, especially with respect to the mainland China experience. Nevertheless, at this stage of our understanding, we may conclude that the achievement of substantial complementarity between growth and redistribution may be possible in a labor-surplus socialist LDC following the Chinese pattern, with all its implications for total societal mobilization. On the other hand, if a country has chosen a mixed economy pattern— wherever it decides to locate itself along the wide spectrum of available institutional/political choices—it is likely to have a difficult time achieving a happy combination of growth and redistribution via direct intervention by government on behalf of the poor. If there is one thing the Bardhan piece on India illustrates extremely well (in Chenery et al., 1974,

Annex), it is that every time mixed-economy governments intervene on behalf of the poor, the poor find themselves worse off. We do not wish to get into the question of whether this is due to an imperfect understanding on the part of the elite of how the system really works, or to an all-too-perfect understanding. Be that as it may, one positive conclusion is that, just as the market mechanism can be (and has been) used as an instrument for growth in some Eastern European socialist countries, it may be the only reliable device for minimizing the conflict between growth and redistribution in a mixed developing economy.

Second, while we are willing to accept the "specialness" of the Taiwanese experience in terms of Taiwan's peculiar combination of good initial conditions (inherited from the Japanese) and subsequent political realities, it seems foolish to wave aside this deviant case as being irrelevant. Certainly the argument that Taiwan's spectacular growth was related to the singularly heavy inflow of U.S. capital is factually incorrect.[11] The point that can and should be made instead is that the Taiwan experience demonstrates that market allocations do not have to work on behalf of the rich; they can be made to work on behalf of the poor—if two conditions are met: if assets, in both agriculture and nonagriculture, are not very unequally distributed at the outset, and if relative prices are reasonably realistic indicators of resource availabilities. It is thus incorrect to say that we tried our best for growth in the 1960s and that we must now try our best for distribution, or that we tried liberal reforms in the 1960s and must now try to reach for the radical medicine bottle. Both judgments seem premature, since we have seldom really tried "tinkering with relative prices" in the presence of relatively favorable initial asset conditions.

The LDC record of the last two decades, in short, is a poor basis for assessing the inevitability of a conflict between employment, distribution, and output objectives. Attempting to do so may be seriously misleading with respect to the future, given the policy package that obtained in most of the developing world during the 1950s and 1960s, and which, in fact, continues to dominate the landscape to this day. Especially in the labor-surplus economy context, it is easy to document at least the theoretical possibility that both output and employment can be increased at the same time that income distribution remains constant and possibly even improves. The case of Taiwan proves that this circumstance is factually possible to achieve as an LDC moves into its export-substitution subphase of transition growth.

In our view, the problem is not mainly a technical one. On the basis of our understanding of the Taiwanese case, we see no reason why, with the proper set of policies, many LDCs could not have their cake and eat it too—perhaps even twice over, by choosing a more labor-intensive and participatory growth path. In the case of Taiwan, this meant gradually shifting from a relatively enlightened and flexible import-substitution regime to a trade-oriented industrial export regime. It also meant paying early attention to agricultural infrastructure and productivity increase and to a decentral-ized rural industrial growth pattern, with output mixes and technologies continuously responsive to changing factor endowments. Effecting such changes requires, of course, political agreement among the various major parties to the social contract; and change is much easier to accomplish when the resistance offered by vested interests, which have grown up under import substitution, is relatively small and/or the government is relatively strong. Both conditions were met in Taiwan. That landless rural workers, small farmers, and other target groups are bound to benefit from such changes in strategy is clear enough. But it is often less clear that, if landlords or large-scale industrialists are to be penalized, they would not necessarily be penalized perma-nently. Rather, the penalty is likely to come in the form of changes in the way incomes are earned; e.g., in the case of industrialists, a shift from windfall profits derived from government-induced restraint of competition, cheap capital imports, and low interest rates to profits earned by partici-pating in the expanding industrial export markets.

As has been pointed out elsewhere (Ranis, 1974), the alternative of "business as usual" in most of the developing countries is likely to lead to a continuing buildup of social and political pressures by those who take the current rhetoric seriously. Also—and this is a point less well understood—the ultimate soaring of private rates of return in narrowly constrained LDC industrial sectors, as domestic markets continue to dwindle and the process of fueling import substitution becomes increasingly expensive, is likely to boomerang on the elite classes. Even bonanzas of oil and other traditional natural resources, unless indefinitely and generously sustained, may serve only to put off the day of reckoning.

In spite of the increasing atmospherics of confrontationism between North and South, as well as between the rich and poor within each hemisphere, this observer is not yet ready to accept the theory that "vested interests do not intend to change anything but their rhetoric." I am, rather, more inclined to the interpretation that it is understandable and human for such interests to try to avoid unpleasant decisions *if* there is a ready-made alternative at hand—such as a boom in traditional exports or success in the search for new ones— and/or if foreign capital flow permits the maintenance of the present narrow structure of growth. Growth rates can be maintained in this fashion—as the record of the 1950s and 1960s indicates—but it is doubtful how long the increasing disparity between what is said about equity and what is done about it can be tolerated. We recognize that only a few donors and a small minority of the spokesmen of the developing world are now insisting on a more equity- and poverty-oriented development pattern. Developing societies such as ours are polycentered and complicated. All we can do as political economists—which we are forced to be, whether we like it or not—is improve our understanding of the causal relationships between growth and equity and point out the extent to which societies that are not yet on the frontier could, in fact, improve their position with respect to both objectives.

Notes

1. When we assign different weights to the achievement of GNP gains by different groups (as proposed by Ahluwalia and Chenery in chapter 11 of *Redistribution with Growth*, Chenery et al., we are acknowledging just that.
2. One exception was Ceylon (now Sri Lanka).
3. The gap is probably even understated, since in the rich countries there are more independent low-income house-

holds both at the very young and very old end of the spectrum than in poor countries (Kravis, 1960).

4. In fact, Ahluwalia (in Chenery et al., 1974) is quite candid about finding not really strong association, in either direction.

5. See Adelman and Robinson's forthcoming book on Korea, and Ayub's Yale Ph.D. dissertation in progress on Pakistan.

6. This section, describing the record in Taiwan, represents a preliminary sketch of some findings of a study being carried out, with John Fei and Shirley Kuo, for the World Bank.

7. It should be noted, however, that the data for this period are much less adequate, and that Ginis of any reliability are available only for agricultural income.

8. See Fei and Ranis (1975) for more detail.

9. This turning point around 1968 has been independently identified in other work (see Fei and Ranis, 1975) and is linked to a substantial change in the growth pattern of real wages, unskilled and skilled, around that time.

10. It would certainly be the height of folly to curb further diffusion of technology because of avoidable deleterious distributional effects.

11. Foreign capital may have been strategically important, especially to facilitate the transition from import to export substitution. But its quantitative impact has been exaggerated (for details, see Fei and Ranis, 1975). Moreover, the question of why U.S.-assisted growth should have had particularly egalitarian effects in Taiwan and not elsewhere has never been satisfactorily addressed.

References

Adelman, I., and C. T. Morris (1973). *Economic Growth and Social Equity in Developing Countries.* Stanford, Calif.: Stanford University Press.

Atkinson, A. B. (1970). "On the Measurement of Inequality." *Journal of Economic Theory* 2.

Chenery, H., et al. (1974). *Redistribution with Growth.*

    London: Oxford University Press.
Cline, W. R. (1975). "Distribution and Development."
    Journal of Development Economics 1.
Fei, J. C. H., and G. Ranis (1964). *Development of the Labor
    Surplus Economy*. Homewood, Ill.: Richard D. Irwin.
Fei, J. C. H., and G. Ranis (1975). "A Model of Growth and
    Employment in the Open Dualistic Economy: The
    Cases of Korea and Taiwan." *Journal of Development
    Studies* 11, no. 2 (January 1975).
Fei, J. C. H., G. Ranis, and S. W. Kuo (1976). "Growth and
    the Family Distribution of Income by Factor Compo-
    nents." Economic Growth Center, Yale University,
    New Haven, Discussion Paper no. 223.
Fields, G., and J. C. H. Fei (1974). "On Inequality Compari-
    sons." Economic Growth Center, Yale University, New
    Haven, Discussion Paper no. 202.
Fishlow, A. (1972). "Brazilian Size Distribution of Income."
    American Economic Review, May 1972.
Kravis, I. (1960). "International Differences in the Distribu-
    tion of Income." *Review of Economics and Statistics* 42,
    no. 4 (November 1960).
Kuznets, S. (1955). "Economic Growth and Income Inequal-
    ity." *American Economic Review* 45, no. 1.
Kuznets, S. (1963). "Quantitative Aspects of the Economic
    Growth of Nations: Distribution of Income by Size."
    Economic Development and Cultural Change 11, no. 2
    (January 1963).
Lewis, W. A. (1954). "Economic Development with Unlim-
    ited Supplies of Labor." *The Manchester School*, May
    1954.
Paukert, F. (1973). "Income Distribution at Different Levels
    of Development: A Survey of Evidence." *International
    Labor Review* 108, nos. 2 and 3 (August/September
    1973).
Prebisch, R. (1962). "The Economic Development of Latin
    America and its Principal Problems." *Economic Bul-
    letin for Latin America* 7, no. 1 (February 1962).
Ranis, G. (1973). "Industrial Sector Labor Absorption."
    Economic Development and Cultural Change 21, no. 3.
Ranis, G. (1974). "Employment Equity and Growth: Les-
    sons from the Philippine Employment Mission." *Inter-
    national Labor Review* 110, no. 1 (July 1974).

Ranis, G., and Associates (1974). *Sharing in Development: A Programme of Employment, Equity and Growth for the Philippines.* Geneva: International Labour Organization.

Soligo, R., and J. Land (1974). "Consumption Patterns, Factor Usage and the Distribution of Income: A Review of Some Findings." Program of Development Studies, Rice University, Houston.

Weisskoff, R. (1970). "Income Distribution and Economic Growth in Puerto Rico, Argentina, and Mexico." *Review of Income and Wealth* 16, no. 4 (December 1970).

4. Development and Distribution in Tanzania

Kassim Guruli

According to Tanzania's philosophy, not only is the human being the center of economic development, but all human beings are equal and hence ultimately entitled to equal shares of the total domestic product. Equality also implies that no one person or group shall exploit another.

Income distribution itself depends, all other things being equal, on the level of economic growth. Thus, in an underdeveloped country like Tanzania, however fair or equal the income distribution may be, it cannot eliminate poverty entirely.[1] If anything, equal income distribution per se may only redistribute poverty equally among the citizens. In the context of development, however, whether income distribution is equal or not is crucial.[2] The importance of an egalitarian income distribution lies mainly in the following effects.

1. *It acts as the main incentive for rapid development.* A rapid rate of development necessitates total mobilization of the country's natural resources, especially human resources. The masses will enthusiastically support their government if they see the fruits of their work returned to them equitably. In a country where there are sharp differences among the population, where wealth is being concentrated in the hands of a few elite, it is almost impossible to arouse the enthusiasm of the bulk of the population.

2. *It expands the overall market potential of the country, and hence acts as an incentive for investment.* One of the problems of developing countries, including Tanzania, is

the narrowness of the market. Such narrowness can be seen from two angles. First, the market may be narrow in the sense that overall purchasing power is low because per-capita income is very small. In Tanzania, average per-capita income is about Shs800 ($100). But the market in developing countries is also narrow in the sense that real purchasing power—hence, the real market—is concentrated in the elites, who form less than 1 percent of the population. For instance, in Tanzania actual (not average) per-capita income in 1967 varied from Shs934 ($116) in Arusha Meru District to Shs207 ($28) in Tunduru District.[3] A more equitable distribution would expand overall purchasing power. This is especially the case in Tanzania, where income earners spend mostly for consumer goods, since very few own property (enterprises).

3. *It opens possibilities of increasing the volume of investment.* In developing countries, equal income distribution presumes that (a) there is no foreign domination and (b) at least the most important and leading means of production are under public ownership; i.e., nationalized. Only under such conditions is it possible to achieve an egalitarian distribution. This step would put a stop to the colossal outflow of money in terms of profits and dividends. The governments would therefore have this money at their disposal, and it could be used to increase the amount available for investment.[4]

We have pointed out elsewhere that economic growth, all other things being equal, is in the last analysis determined by the level of the productive forces—such elements as (a) objects of labor; i.e., raw materials, semifinished goods, (b) instruments of labor, (c) means of labor; i.e., the specific conditions necessary for the existence of productive processes, which include, in the wider sense, roads and buildings, (d) the worker himself, and (e) experience, skill, and knowledge. The productive forces are in turn determined by a complex set of factors consisting of the average level of workers' skills, the level of technical development of science and the extent of its application, the social relations of production, the extent and efficiency of the means of production, and, finally, natural conditions.

In Tanzania, as in other developing countries, the productive forces are not only underdeveloped but also unevenly distributed, a fact which contributes to "technological dualism." The hoe, for instance, is still the main instrument in agricultural production. Lack of skilled labor and technicians is still the order of the day. Such a low level of productive forces is a stumbling block to quick development.

The development of natural productive forces was blocked first by slavery and later by colonialization. The subsequent creation of the colonial economy established an economic mechanism which made the free development of productive forces impossible. Division of labor in the colonial economies (whereby the developing countries became specialized mainly in the production of agricultural and mineral products for export) and the domination of these economies by foreign monopolies made these countries entirely dependent on the advanced capitalist countries.[5] Apart from underdeveloping their productive forces, these countries also became sources of exploitation and hence sources of surplus value exploitation. It became impossible for them to develop freely and to have an equitable income distribution.

Economic development in Tanzania, therefore, means much more than economic growth. It means the creation of an independent economy—independent of the advanced countries. Economic independence here means the destruction and removal of the present division of labor, whereby we specialize mainly in the production of one or two—or any number, for that matter—agricultural commodities for export and hence are doubly dependent on the advanced countries, both for selling our products and for buying capital and consumer goods.[6] Economic independence means the creation of a home-centered economy, so that we can produce what we want and consume what we produce. By establishing an independent economy we can also create the prerequisite foundation for rapid promotion of productive forces. Within this context, the Arusha Declaration called for self-reliance and an independent, self-centered economy, with a complete and developed productive process. To be more specific, economic independence means developed, well-integrated agricultural and industrial sectors.

Economic independence means also that the economy must be controlled by the nationals themselves in a developing country. If the economy, especially the leading sectors, is

controlled by foreign monopolies, it will inevitably be
dependent upon the highly developed countries. Such social
relationships of production will hamper quick development
of the productive forces and hence retard the growth of
national income. In other words, economic independence
entails first and foremost the destruction of the center-
periphery relationship.[7] This can only be done through the
transformation of foreign private ownership into a national
ownership of the major means of production. As our President Nyerere has pointed out, since we in Tanzania did not
and do not have our own indigenous capitalists, national
ownership can only mean collective-cum-state or socialist
ownership. In Tanzania then, social transformation of
ownership is a prerequisite of both economic growth and
equitable income distribution.

Collective or socialist ownership has taken two forms in
Tanzania. The first is social (or state-cum-public) ownership. This consists mainly of the industrial sector and the
state farms. Second, the rural sector is being transformed into
collective (*ujamaa*) ownership. The difference between the
two forms is that, whereas the state (parastatal) sector
belongs to the entire nation, collective ownership is restricted to the collective concerned; i.e., the particular group of
people forming it. The Arusha Declaration, which called for
the transformation to a socialist economy, also formulated
the strategy for such a transformation.[8]

By 1974 the parastatal sector, the main instrument of
public ownership, accounted for an estimated 90 percent of
total capital formation and 75 percent of value added in the
manufacturing or industrial sector. Out of about 500 industrial establishments (the total in 1974 of all registered companies with more than 10 employees), there were only 70
public companies. The remaining 430 were privately owned.
This means that the public corporations are large and
capital intensive. This relationship also means that the
public companies, though numerically fewer, nevertheless
dominate in capital formation and value added. However,
total employment is evenly distributed between public and
private sectors. The leasing role of the public sector can also
be seen in the fact that nearly all important industrial
projects since 1967 have been undertaken by the public
sector; private foreign investment has been limited to minor-

ity participation in some of these projects.

A transformation of the dominantly foreign private ownership takes place in transitional stages, depending at each stage on internal and external relationships. The first stage, which is still going on, consists in the transformation of the public sector, which until 1967 was mainly limited to public services, into the leading productive industrial sector, thus eliminating the leading role of the private sector. The aim, at least for the foreseeable future, is not to remove the private sector but to make it play a secondary role.

The transformation of the parastatal sector into a leading sector of the economy is being done in two major ways: through nationalization and through partnership or joint ownership by government and foreign private investors. Nationalization is carried out with full compensation. Of the total public sector, at present, only about one-tenth is 100 percent owned by government. Joint ownership makes up the major share of public enterprise. To ensure its own control, the government has acquired majority shares (51 percent) in most joint enterprises.

On the regional and district levels, public ownership occurs through district development corporations (DDCs). These DDCs are potentially powerful methods of promoting productive investments.

Almost all the import and export trade, as well as domestic wholesale distribution, is now in the hands of public-sector institutions. Retail trade, however, is still under private ownership, although in the *ujamaa* villages and, to some extent, in towns parts of it have been taken over by consumer cooperatives. Thus the aim is for the public sector to take the leading role in export and import trade and in wholesale distribution, and hence be in a position to control the rate of economic development.

Last, but not least, the government has embarked on an ambitious socialist rural transformation. This transformation will culminate in two main forms of ownership: state farms and *ujamaa*, or collective, farms.[9] The importance of socialist rural transformation lies in two factors: first, it is the only prerequisite for equal income distribution, as it eliminates differences in land ownership; and second, collective ownership, especially in Tanzania, enables the peasants to pool resources and buy modern tools and inputs, such as oxen plows, tractors, and fertilizers, which are beyond individual reach. What is perhaps most important for achieving equitable income distribution is that the *ujamaa* villages make it easier and cheaper for a poor government such as Tanzania to supply public services—including water, education, and medical care—to rural areas.

Although the creation of a home-centered economy is the goal of economic independence for Tanzania, this can be achieved only through transitional stages. The first stage after the Arusha Declaration called for (a) using agriculture as the basis of achieving this goal and (b) creating light industry as the leading dynamic sector. This means that, within industry, emphasis in investment was to be on consumer goods. To some extent, such policy was no different from general import substitution. But it was not a blind, wholesale import substitution, since luxury goods were by and large avoided. However, this development happened under social and economic conditions different from those in other developing countries.[10] It occurred under circumstances characterized by a simultaneous change in social relations of production; i.e., a change of ownership relations. In other words, the first stage in the creation of an independent economy is the formation of self-sufficiency in basic consumer goods. The extent to which Tanzania has achieved this first goal can be seen in Table 1. Although the ultimate goal is to place more emphasis in the capital-goods sector, nevertheless in the transitional stage it grew slowly. The necessity for such a stage is mainly due to the extreme poverty of Tanzania (per-capita income is about U.S. $100), the complete lack of wealthy indigenous entrepreneurs, and the need to be self-reliant.

The growing self-sufficiency of domestic production has given rise to the growth of a domestic market, which is illustrated by the changes in Tanzania's commodity imports shown in Table 2. The creation of a home market, as this table demonstrates, has substantially reduced the relative imports of consumer goods, while substituting intermediate and capital goods. The period of easy substitution (the first transition stage) is coming to an end, however. The relative increase in the volume of intermediate goods and capital goods during a time of growing world inflation means also a big importation of inflation, especially in this period of high oil prices. The situation has been aggravated by the fact that between 1973 and 1974, mainly because of droughts, Tanzania was forced to import millions of shillings' worth of grain, a move which has worsened our balance of payments. This naturally affects our income distribution policy adversely, as it reduces the cake which we all expected to share.

TABLE 1

PERCENTAGE OF GOODS AVAILABLE THAT WERE DOMESTICALLY PRODUCED

	1961	1965	1971
CONSUMER GOODS	56%	67%	85%
(A) FOOD PRODUCTS	(100%)	(100%)	(100%)
(B) NON-FOODS	(36%)	(50%)	(77%)
INTERMEDIATE GOODS	24%	37%	35%
CAPITAL GOODS	16%	13%	15%

SOURCE: Extracted from
      (a) Census of Industrial Production, Tanganyika 1961
      (b) Survey of Industries 1965 - Tanzania Central
                                 Statistical Bureau
      (c) E.A. Customs & Excise Department - Annual Reports
          of Uganda, Kenya, and Tanzania

TABLE 2

STRUCTURE OF TANZANIA'S COMMODITY IMPORTS

	1961	1965	1971
CONSUMER GOODS	54%	39%	27%
INTERMEDIATE GOODS	32%	33%	43%
CAPITAL GOODS	14%	28%	30%

SOURCE: Annual Economic Surveys

The creation of home market self-sufficiency implies a deepening of the division of labor between agriculture and industry and involves a gradual disengagement from absolute dependence on advanced countries as markets for our agricultural raw materials in the first stage. Conversely, it creates the possibility of the steady growth of an internal market for these products. This growth can be illustrated by the statistics about the cotton crop in Table 3. Note that since independence (1961), while the cotton crop was growing at

TABLE 3

COTTON CROP*

YEAR	TOTAL	USED BY DOMESTIC INDUSTRY (INCLUDING INVENTORY CHANGE)	EXPORTED
1958	169		168
1959	203	8	195
1960	189	2	187
1961	168	-3	171
1962	214	14	200
1963	263	4	259
1964	293	-2	295
1965	369	6	363
1966	436	13	423
1967	N.A.	N.A.	N.A.
1968	283	30	253
1969	386	44	342
1970	402	53	349
1971	363	58	226
1972	427	60	367
1973	430	62	368
1974**	400	63	337

*In thousands of bales, at 181 kg per bale
**Estimated

about 3 percent per year, domestic use of cotton expanded from almost nothing to about 16 percent of the total crop.

The creation of a fairly extensive division of labor between agriculture and industry has resulted in the restructuring of different sectors, particularly in regard to their growth rates. These rates affect not only income distribution in general but especially equitable income distribution. For example, although Tanzania's GDP real growth rate between 1964 and 1973 was 5.2 percent per year, agriculture grew 4.1 percent between 1964 and 1967 and only 2.7 percent from 1967 to 1973. (The droughts between 1973 and early 1975 and the acceleration of worldwide inflation were also factors.) Population has been increasing at the rate of 2.7 percent per annum. The manufacturing sector, in contrast, has been growing at an average rate of 7.5 percent since 1967. Up to 1969, employment in the manufacturing sector grew at an annual rate of about 11.4 percent. After 1967, however, employment grew at a very fast rate (about 60 percent faster than the actual value-added rate). The average growth rate of value added by the manufacturing sector was 9.8 percent from 1964 to 1972.

While the manufacturing sector developed at a much higher rate than the agricultural sector, there were some important differences in the rate of structural change within the former:

1. The strongest growth in value added took place in the nonconsumer-goods industries, which increased their share from 22 percent in 1965 to 41 percent in 1971.
2. With the exception of meat canning for export, which declined, the second-strongest expansion was recorded by the food-processing industry.
3. Capital-goods industries, although the smallest at present, expanded rapidly from 2.7 percent in 1965 to 4.4 percent in 1971. Their share in value of total manufacturing output increased from 1.3 percent to 7.5 percent between 1965 and 1971. Most of this expansion took place in goods that are heavily import dependent.

These structural changes, in combination with other factors, have led to the following problems:

1. Annual growth of agricultural production has not kept
   pace with that of industrial production, causing a
   deteriorating balance of payments. The lagging of
   agricultural production was particularly negative in
   regard to the supply of food materials to the industrial
   sector. This situation became even worse during 1973
   and 1975, when droughts hit Tanzania and it became
   necessary to import millions of shillings in cereal
   grains. Thus, within 1973 and 1974 alone, food imports
   rose from Shs115.8 million in 1973 to Shs834.0 in 1974,
   an increase of 620.2 percent.
2. Because of (1), the national income, especially that of
   the rural population, could not improve, particularly
   since the population was growing at a high rate of 2.7
   percent.
3. The relatively greater role of imports of capital goods
   (imports of intermediate and capital goods rose from 46
   percent of total imports in 1961 to 73 percent in 1971),
   especially under conditions of world inflation, re-
   strained the balance of payments.
4. In spite of the impressive growth rate of the manufacturing sector, the output of many industrial goods has
   not been keeping pace with domestic demand. Mostly
   because of better income distribution, demand for basic
   consumer goods (e.g., salt, cooking oil, and clothing)
   expanded tremendously during this period. To implement the policy of equitable income distribution, the
   government has granted significant wage increases to
   lower income groups over the past four years. For
   higher income groups, however, both direct and indirect income taxes were sharply raised. Because of all
   these measures, disposable monetary income in the
   hands of the public increased by about 20 percent in
   1973 and again in 1974. Consumer-goods production,
   on the other hand, increased only marginally. Since
   imports of consumer goods were heavily curtailed to
   encourage domestic production, the result has been
   rapid domestic inflation.
5. Within the agricultural sector, the production of both
   food and raw materials for export slowed down. The
   decline in production occurred, as in shown in Table 4,
   essentially in the leading export crops: cotton, coffee,

and sisal.

As we have already pointed out, deterioration in Tanzania's trade balance was heavily influenced by the high cost of oil imports, by large imports of food grains, and by the effects of the worldwide price inflation on other imports. Whereas for the year 1974 the value of total exports rose by only Shs406.8 million, or 15.8 percent, to Shs2,987.8 million, total imports increased by as much as 56.3 percent to Shs5,435.8 million. As a result, Tanzania's overall trade deficit deteriorated from Shs897.9 million in 1973 to Shs2,448.0 million in 1974. This deterioration had serious implications for the concept of self-reliance in Tanzania—a concept that goes further than the achievement of a self-centered economy. In the international context (i.e., as far as the relationships between Tanzania and developed countries are concerned), self-reliance also means attaining a self-centered economy mainly through Tanzania's own resources. Self-reliance means that Tanzania's resources must play the primary role and foreign resources the *secondary* role. In other words, foreign resources are intended to act only as a catalyst. Hence the emphasis on rural development—since this is Tanzania's main resource, in both human and natural terms.

The policy of self-reliance makes it imperative that the major means of ownership be shared by the whole nation. However, because of the country's abject poverty, it is difficult, if not impossible, to increase public investment or capital accumulation without foreign help in the broadest sense, including both foreign aid and private capital investment. Thus, while it was possible to nationalize what we already had (which was very little), any further expansion of the public sector requires new investment. This is why the government's strategy is to emphasize the agricultural sector as the basis of development and to stress light industry in the industrial sector. Agriculture is the backbone of the economy. Light industry requires relatively little capital investment, and its gestation period is shorter than that of heavy industry. Moreover, most of the light industry being developed already has an initial market, albeit small.[11]

Nonetheless, it is necessary for the government to seek foreign assistance in order to be able to expand light industry. So the government seeks both joint ownership with foreign

TABLE 4

PRODUCTION OF MAJOR EXPORT CROPS – BASE 1966-67 = 100

COMMODITY	66-67	67-68	68-69	69-70	70-71	71-72	72-73	73-74
COTTON	100.0	89.9	65.1	88.1	97.0	82.9	97.6	81.7
COFFEE	100.0	77.3	99.2	88.8	95.6	88.2	99.3	81.5
SISAL	100.0	97.8	87.5	93.0	89.8	80.5	69.7	69.0
TEA	100.0	105.3	116.5	129.1	124.9	153.8	186.8	185.3
CASHEW NUTS	100.0	91.8	142.7	138.4	135.6	148.2	148.8	170.7
PYRETHRUM	100.0	151.3	106.5	85.0	52.2	82.2	96.6	78.4

SOURCE: Bank of Tanzania, Economic Bulletin vol. 6, no. 3, Dec. 1974, p. 44

capital and outright foreign assistance. Joint ownership, although a necessity, has proved to have many disadvantages:

1. In order to go in for joint ownership, the government has to acquire shares, normally majority shares, through loans or borrowing. This means that the more the public sector grows through joint ownership, the heavier the loan burden grows. Given the relatively high rate of interest and the worsening balance of trade, the country becomes more and more indebted every year. The extra earnings which would have gone to increase the income of the population are spent to service ever-growing debts.
2. The outflow of capital in terms of profits, which now assumes the form of dividends and interest charges, has not been eliminated.
3. Because of a lack of technical knowhow and skilled manpower, Tanzania is forced to enter into management agreements and hire skilled manpower. These agreements are in most cases, if not in all cases, disadvantageous to Tanzania. They have become another source of income drain.
4. Tanzania's ownership share does not amount to effective control. Mainly because of (1) and (3), Tanzania does not effectively control the public sector. To begin with, a public enterprise can be established only if foreign capital is willing to go into joint ownership with the government. In most cases, therefore, it is the foreign private owner who determines the type of enterprise to be established. This effectively means that the allocation of resources is still determined by foreign capital. Again, owing to lack of technical manpower, feasibility studies and project appraisals are still done mainly by foreign expertise. This again limits the effective control of the economy. Because the real management of Tanzania's industries is still in Western hands, it is difficult to implement the policy of equitable distribution.

The transformation of ownership to socialist production has not been really accomplished in Tanzania. Therefore, the existing relationships of production are still a stumbling block to free development of the forces of production. Economic growth is thus still retarded. Other difficulties with the transformation of ownership relations arise from problems caused by poor management of the economy by our own people, who still lack experience.[12] It should, therefore, not be surprising that the proportion of the population earning less than $50 per capita is still somewhere around 60 percent in Tanzania.

The government has taken several important steps to equalize the income of the masses:

1. Wages were increased for the lower levels. The minimum urban industrial monthly wages were raised from Shs180 to Shs240 in 1973, and to Shs340 in 1974.
2. Salary scales for the middle- and high-level public sector remained substantially frozen.
3. Public-sector citizen wage/salary now runs, in most cases, from Shs3,600 to Shs58,000 per year. Since the public sector is now the dominant form of ownership, this wage differential reflects that of a large part of the economy.
4. The pretax income range has narrowed between the highest-paid public-sector worker and the lowest-paid, from more than seventy to one at independence to about eighteen to one. The after-tax range (or effective range in terms of consumption) has fallen from sixty to one to about thirteen to one.
5. The share of recurrent and public investment expenditure directed to rural areas has increased sharply. This has altered the balance significantly toward poor farmers.
6. The government has introduced free universal primary education and has substantially altered the education system so that theory and practice are harmonized. Furthermore, instead of entering the university immediately after secondary school, a student is required to work in the field for a minimum of two years. One of the requirements for admission is a good recommendation from the place where the field work was done.
7. On the other end of the scale, adult education is being promoted vigorously. Tanzania now is one of the few

African countries where illiteracy has been reduced substantially.
8. Participatory democracy through decentralization of decision making, workers' participation, and more independence for the *ujamaa* villages is being urged.

In this paper we have tried to highlight, in general terms, the reciprocal relationship between economic development and income distribution in Tanzania. We have stressed the facts that the basis for an equitable income distribution lies in socialist or common ownership, and that common ownership is the prerequisite for free development of productive forces and the economic growth on which income distribution depends. We have also tried to show that equitable income distribution cannot be considered separately from educational and cultural development that is freely available and accessible to all. This paper was also intended to illustrate that, for Tanzania, economic development essentially means transformation of ownership relations. The measurement of development must be seen within this broader context.

Notes

1. This observation has led some conservative economists to assert that it is pointless to worry about redistribution of income until there is something to distribute.
2. Indeed, income distribution is proving to be the central research concern of development economists.
3. In Tanzania as a whole, income distribution in 1972 was as follows: the poorest 40 percent of the population had per-capita incomes over $190. The pretax range between the highest-paid and the lowest-paid public sector was just over 70 to 1 in (1962). There is no doubt that under such conditions of income distribution private capitalism in general and private foreign capital restricts itself to the richest 20 percent of the population.
4. While one school of thought advocates that inequality stimulates growth by increasing the rate of saving and

capital formation, in developing countries inequality has been shown to lead to (a) luxury consumption, or investment in luxury goods, and (b) outflow of surpluses to the advanced countries in form of profits to foreign private investors.

5. The dominant role can be demonstrated by the fact that even as late as 1970 40 percent of GDP, and about 40–75 percent of the total export value came (and still comes) from agriculture, with three main products—coffee, cotton, and sisal—contributing more than 40 percent. The industrial sector, on the other hand, contributed only about 10 percent to GDP in 1970 (R. Hofmeier, *Transport and Economic Development in Tanzania* [Munchen: Weltfrum Verlag, 1973], pp. 29–32).

6. The disadvantages of specialization in the production of agricultural raw materials or even processed materials by the developing countries are now widely known and even accepted by many development economists. Such disadvantages include the following:

a. Although there is, theoretically speaking, a world division of labor between the developed and developing countries (wherein the developed countries are specialized essentially in the production of industrial goods and the developing countries in the production of agricultural raw materials), in practice the developed countries are to a great extent both industrial and raw-material producers. This is the case especially with the U.S. But even European countries are nowadays volume producers of food, including dairy products. This kind of division of labor naturally is disadvantageous to the developing countries, because it effectively—except, perhaps, for oil-producing countries—reduces the world market for these export products.

b. The development of technology, especially in the chemical industry, has made it possible for advanced countries to introduce synthetic materials which are replacing natural raw materials and hence further reducing the markets.

c. The development of science and technology has permitted the more-efficient use of raw materials; e.g., if 10 years ago one needed 10 units of raw materials in order to produce 1 unit of output, now only about 5 units of raw materials are required to produce the same output. Hence the importance of raw materials, except for oil, is relatively declining.

    d. Since the market for raw materials is primarily in advanced countries, they have a monopoly of this market. This keeps them in a situation in which they can lower raw-material prices at will.

    7. Although it is outside the scope of this paper to go into the details of dependence relationships between advanced capitalist and developing countries, the primary effects of the present economic mechanism in developing countries are: (a) distortion of the normal economic structure, which hampers development and creates income inequality; (b) income drain, as a result of domination by foreign private capital investment and dependency on advanced countries' markets for the sale of raw materials; and (c) creation of a dependent petty-bourgeois class.

    8. For full details of Tanzania's policy on socialism and self-reliance, see the Arusha Declaration and Nyerere, J. D., *Freedom and Socialism* (London: Oxford University Press, 1968).

    9. For a full and detailed explanation of the policy on socialist rural transformation in Tanzania, see "Socialism and Rural Development" in Nyerere, *Freedom and Socialism*. To evaluate the actual rural transformation which has so far taken place would require a very lengthy paper.

    10. Most of the discussions among Western development economists, radical or otherwise, usually ignore the social relations of production and tacitly assume a given capitalist economic structure. But strategies of economic development cannot be discussed in a vacuum, as these depend essentially on the economic institutions under which they are supposed to operate. Thus the policy of import substitution (or, what is almost the same thing, putting an emphasis on light industry) has effects under socialism different from those such a policy would have in a free-market economy.

    11. This is, in fact, one of the major reasons why private investment in general and foreign private investment in particular are interested in the light-industrial sector for investment in developing countries.

    12. It must also be pointed out, in all fairness, that not all

the top 5 percent of the high income group in Tanzania, which is mostly composed of the petty bourgeois and the bureaucrats, are in favor of the socialist transformation, although they do not oppose it openly. Thus, some of the difficulties are deliberately engendered. Such difficulties include shortages due to hoarding and economic sabotage, including deliberate misallocation of resources.

References

Adelman, I. and C. T. Morris (1973). *Economic Growth and Social Equity in Developing Countries.* Stanford, Calif.: Stanford University Press.

Amin, S. (1974). *Accumulation on a World Scale.* New York: Monthly Review Press.

Baran, P. "On the Political Economy of Backwardness," in Wilbur, C. K., ed. *The Political Economy of Development and Underdevelopment.* New York: Random House.

Chenery, H., et al. (1976). *Redistribution with Growth.* London: Oxford University Press.

Dobb, M. (1966). *Soviet Economic Development since 1917.* N.p.: International Publishers.

Dos Santos, T. (1970). "The Structure of Dependence." *American Economic Review* 60.

Emmanuel, A. (1974). "Myths of Development versus Myths of Underdevelopment." *New Left Review,* no. 85 (May/June 1974).

Frank, A. G. (1969). *Latin America: The Development of Revolution.* New York: Monthly Review Press.

Seers, D. (n.d.). "The Meaning of Development." *International Development Review.*

Tanzania. "Surveys of Economic Reviews." Bank of Tanzania Economic Bulletin.

World Bank (1973). *World Bank Atlas: Population, Per Capita Product and Growth Rates.*

Part 2: Who Are the Poor?

The really poor get little aid
From Revolution, Grants, or Trade
Because, no matter how we fiddle,
Everything flows towards the middle.

It seems we should not be afraid
To monitor both Loans and Aid,
Although the task is very stiff
To find what would have happened if!

The policies of I.M.F.
Are not, we hope, completely deaf
To Social Claims, but still, it gets
Upset when banks default their debts.

To make new riches Trickle Down
People must move from farm to town,
And this produces Urban Blight,
So Bubbling Up may make things right.

If growth is not to hurt the poor,
Of certain things we must be sure:
No rural gains should be betrayed
By falling rural terms of trade.

Migration must be organized
Or cities will get oversized,
And one conclusion must prevail:
All piecemeal policies will fail.

Kenneth Boulding

5. Exports, Entrepreneurs, and Equity: A Solution to the Problems of Population and Poverty in Southeast Asia?

Robert A. Hackenberg

What has gone wrong? We were confidently told to take care of the GNP and poverty will take care of itself; that a high GNP growth target is the best guarantee for eliminating unemployment and redistributing incomes later through fiscal means. . . . We went wrong in assuming that income distribution policies could be divorced from growth policies and could be added later to obtain whatever distribution we desired. . . . We also know that once production has been so organized as to leave a fairly large number of people unemployed, it becomes almost impossible to redistribute incomes to those who are not even participating in the production stream (ul Haq, 1972, p. 6).

Sustained fertility decline even in urban areas is problematic at best unless urban living conditions vastly improve within the next decade or two. I am aware of no evidence of sustained fertility decline—either spontaneous or induced through a family planning program— ever having taken place in the absence of significant socioeconomic development and modernization that considerably altered the lives of most of the population (Kocher, 1973, p. x).

Progress Is Not Welfare: Thoughts on Economic/Demographic Transitions

Since Malthus, the dynamics of economic and population growth have been inseparable. In today's LDCs, economic prospects rest in part on hopes for fertility control (Schultz, 1971; Demeny, 1971); conversely, the goals of population programs incorporate assumptions about necessary gains in living standards (Freedman and Berelson, 1976). These reciprocal concerns converge on a subject of immediate interest to both economists and demographers: *income distribution.*

Certainly, if economic growth is to promote the aims of development and not merely to solidify the position of existing elites, income distribution is a key requirement (Adelman and Morris, 1973; Chenery, 1974). It also appears that gains in GNP, brought about through urban-industrial growth, are necessary but not sufficient conditions for the promotion of population control. In the recent literature, an increasingly prominent role is given to income distribution, rather than to gains in total GNP alone, as the trigger variable which promotes acceptance of family planning. The evidence for this position is summarized in two recent studies by William Rich (1973) and James Kocher (1973).

Rich (1973, pp. 2-3) states the income-distribution hypothesis as follows:

> There is . . . striking new evidence that in an increasing number of poor countries . . . birth rates have dropped sharply *despite* relatively low per capita incomes and *despite* the absence of relative newness of family planning programs. . . . The countries in which this has happened are those in which the broadest spectrum of the population has shared in the economic and social benefits of significant national progress to a far greater degree than in most poor countries—or in most western countries during their comparable periods of development. Family planning programs have generally been much more successful in those countries where increases in output of goods and social services have been distributed in such a way that they improved the way of life for a substantial majority of the population rather

than just for a small minority.

The record also shows that those countries which continue to sustain high rates of population growth despite their achievement of relatively high *per capita* income figures have wide disparities in income and little access to social services. Only a small group within these countries has started to practise fertility control; this group generally consists of the favored minority.

Later in this monograph, he makes a specific comparison between Taiwan (a country with evenly distributed income) and the Philippines (where income remains concentrated in the hands of a small upper class. The figures given by Rich (1973, p. 24) below are for 1964–1965:

[In these years], the *per capita* income in Taiwan was approximately $246, or similar to that of the Philippines, which was $235. There was, however, a considerable discrepancy between the distributions of income in the two countries. The highest 10 percent of the population in the Philippines was significantly wealthier than the same group in Taiwan, but the lowest 20 percent was more than twice as well off in Taiwan. Moreover, there also is evidence in Taiwan that income distribution has improved markedly over time, whereas in the Philippines it has become more and more concentrated among the wealthiest 20 percent of the population. These two factors help to explain why a much greater share of the population appears to have reached the socioeconomic level conducive to reduced fertility in Taiwan than in the Philippines.

In a similar argument relating income distribution to fertility decline, Kocher (1973, pp. 64–65) constructed a table which presents two groups of third world nations, classified in terms of degree of income distribution and fertility. Data from the table are abstracted below.

Kocher's data illustrate the very significant impact of economic growth on fertility under conditions of equitable income distribution, such as are found in South Korea and Taiwan. On the other hand, in Thailand and the Philip-

TABLE 1
ECONOMIC AND DEMOGRAPHIC INDICATORS AMONG EQUAL AND UNEQUAL
THIRD WORLD NATION INCOME DISTRIBUTIONS

COUNTRY	YEAR	PER CAPITA INCOME DOLLARS	RELATIVE INCOME INEQUALITY*	CRUDE BIRTH RATE PERIOD	BEGINNING	END
A. EQUAL INCOME DISTRIBUTION COUNTRIES						
S. KOREA	1961	106	38	1950-60	45	42
	1969	210		1960-70	42	30
JAPAN	1961	383	45	1920-55	36	19
	1969	1,430				
TAIWAN	1961	116	47	1932-47	45	41
	1969	300		1963-70	36	26
W. MALAYSIA	1961	368	52			
	1969	340		1956-70	47	32
B. UNEQUAL INCOME DISTRIBUTION COUNTRIES						
PHILIPPINES	1961	188	74	1960-70	45	45
	1969	210				
THAILAND	1961	101	76	1960-70	43	43
	1969	160				
MEXICO	1961	297	82	1950-60	44	44
	1969	580		1960-70	44	41
BRAZIL	1961	268	99	1950-60	41	41
	1969	270		1960-70	41	38

*Sum of decile deviations from 10%

pines, where economic gains have been significant but distribution remains highly asymmetrical, the population problem shows no substantial improvement. These observations tend to confirm the much-earlier assertion of British political economist J. S. Furnivall concerning Southeast Asia: "Progress is not welfare."

However, it is theoretically possible for progress to be associated with welfare in both its economic and demographic consequences. All that is necessary is that the terms of the "twin transition" models be observed in Southeast Asia where they are presently absent; e.g., Thailand and the Philippines. Both economic and demographic transition models, furthermore, place central emphasis on the role of the entrepreneur and, through him, on the dynamic position of the peasant market (bazaar) economy. The economic transition model will be introduced first.

Having characterized the societies of the region as having "open dualistic economies," a prominent group of economists, presently or recently associated with the Yale Economic Growth Center, has outlined a transitional sequence of steps leading upward from the evils of agrarian traditionalism and stagnation which are the heritage of colonialism. Key publications are those of Paauw (1966, 1970), Pauuw and Fei (1973), Ranis (1974), and Ranis and Associates (1974).

Such economies are said to be *open* because a substantial share of their GNPs (even in colonial times) came from external trade; they are *dual* because of the sharp organizational partitioning of agricultural (traditional) sectors from industrial (modern) sectors. Their capacity to experience transformation rests upon the capital-formation potential inherent in the economy's capacity to continue to engage in the export of primary products (copra, sugar, timber, copper ore, rubber, palm oil, tin).

The transition envisioned incorporates two stages. In the first, presently advocated for Malaysia and Thailand (Paauw and Fei, 1973), intensification of primary exports leads to *import substitution* (the replacement of imported manufactures with domestically produced goods), accompanied by heavy protectionism and financing from profits generated by the raw-materials trade. The achievement of this stage in the transition is marked by the training and promotion of a substantial group of indigenous entrepreneurs who learn about production technology and finance, distribution, and marketing at this time. However, agriculture remains essentially backward, and its low productivity—associated with high manpower absorption and microscopic wage and profit margins for small producers—represents a "purchasing power" brake on the prospects for continuing growth based on import substitution. The narrow domestic market soon becomes exhausted.

As stagnation once again approaches, the second stage of the transition, *export substitution* (represented in Southeast Asia by Taiwan and the Philippines), is introduced. This phase take its name from the replacement of production for protected domestic markets by the manufacture of exports for world consumption. The advantage, of course, is that industry replaces agriculture as the primary foreign-exchange earner, with greater growth potential, prospects for improved stability, and much larger returns to both capital and labor.

In this phase of development, the entrepreneurs who have gained experience as producers for domestic markets during import substitution now introduce labor-intensive production processes, absorb surplus rural manpower at low wages, and compete successfully in foreign markets. As population pressures decline in rural areas, mechanization and increased production become possible. Crop diversification permits production of food and fiber for industrial processing, so that backward linkages are established between agriculture and export-oriented industry.

At the end of the development cycle, labor becomes scarce (as in Japan), wages rise commensurately to reward skills and worker productivity, and income distribution is achieved through sharing in the wages, profits, and services which are the gains realized through successful development. In Southeast Asia, both Taiwan and South Korea are following Japan into this final phase, according to Paauw and Fei (1973). The "commercialization of labor" (Paauw and Fei, 1973, p. 250; Fei and Ranis, 1964) reflects the termination of labor-surplus conditions, signaling the completion of the economic transition.

From the standpoint of income distribution, rather than of mere increases in GNP, the critical phase in the growth process incorporates the rise of small- and medium-scale industries based on regional entrepreneurship and the absorption of surplus farm population into localized growth centers with high concentrations of industry, rather than into primate cities (Manila, Bangkok, Djakarta). These decentralized urban-industrial communities stimulate the diversification and modernization of agriculture and channel its participation in the export market for manufactures (Clawson, 1967).

The *economic transition* model, for which empirical support may be found throughout Southeast Asia, incorporates many parallels with the *demographic transition* model for anticipated fertility declines in developing areas (Stolnitz, 1964). Since improvement in income distribution is frequently postulated on the assumption that explosive population growth can be curtailed, the partial congruence between the two hypothesized processes is hardly surprising.

During the colonial period, mortality control unaccompanied by fertility reduction produced gluts of unassimilable population in traditional rural communities, with resultant land pressures, underemployment, and income declines. Because, under *minifundia* conditions, high fertility is equated with free farm labor and old-age security (Mamdani, 1973), a change in life style must take place before fertility reductions can be expected. These changes parallel many components of the economic transition.

The key is urban-industrial growth in decentralized regional locations which permits simultaneous changes of residence and occupation, drawing rural people from surrounding farm areas and shifting the basis of their support from subsistence to wage-earning activities. In the urban cash economy, children become a liability rather than a capital asset, especially when costs of education required to prepare them for employment are included.

Furthermore, opportunities for self-improvement in the urban environment are available to those who accumulate savings for investment in small business enterprises. As capital formation is perceived to compete with the cost of children, a choice is forced between social mobility and expanding family size. Thus economic modernization creates a favorable environment for fertility control, and a merger is completed between the models of economic and demographic transition with the consequences of each contributing to the success of the other.

Entrepreneurship in the Philippines

A key role in this convergence is that of the *entrepreneur*— the small- and medium-scale businessman and industrialist. He is the chosen instrument for negotiating the shift from import to export substitution, with a subsequent drive toward full employment and higher wages. The entrepreneurial role as a channel of upward mobility, with attendant fertility reduction, is equally significant. Since it is unlikely that income distribution can be improved without rapid deceleration of population growth, the two functions are interlocked.

For these process models to become predictions, and for the predictions to become realities, the number of entrepre-

neurs must be substantial and capable of increase, according
to conditions specified in detail by Leibenstein (1957, pp.
120–146) and Hoselitz (1967). Such a situation already exists
in the Philippines, with which the rest of this discussion will
be concerned.

> Only a small number of highly skilled entrepreneurs is
> required to make the investment decisions in large-scale
> industry in the Philippines. In medium-scale and
> small-scale industry the situation is drastically differ-
> ent, with thousands of entrepreneurs required. Each
> will have to make a rather lonely decision to risk his
> family's capital in a new or an expanded enterprise. . . .
> The potential entrepreneurs so essential for industrial
> growth already exist in the outlying areas of the Philip-
> pines. For a number of reasons the human resources
> potential of the Philippines is substantially better than
> that of the country's probable competitors (Ranis and
> Associates, 1974, p. 548).

In a thoughtful assessment of ". . . some half-dozen studies
of Filipino industrialists," Anderson (1969) has pieced together a natural history of entrepreneurship in the Philippines; the primary source for his summary is the substantial
investigation of Carroll (1965). The following points are
drawn from Anderson's summary:

1. All available case material indicates a familiar course of
   organizational evolution from single proprietorship to
   family firm and thence to hiring nonfamily personnel.
2. Entrepreneurs tended to be generalists—broadly experienced in a number of occupations—and therefore,
   more willing and able to innovate and "open to numerous strategies."
3. Sociopolitical competence and technical skills were
   important, and these were acquired equally often
   through formal education and through informal training (apprenticeship, on-the-job training).
4. Manipulation of financial and social capital was
   necessary to create opportunities. A personalistic network was usually exploited to raise investment capital.
   Savings or earnings from trade were usually insuffi-

cient.

5. "Finally, the backgrounds of a high proportion of Filipino entrepreneurs include various experiences in trade and frequently in petty buy-and-sell. . . . Cases analyzed reveal that, although many entrepreneurs did use their operations to provide for day-to-day needs, they did *not* only seek a fast profit. . . . Some petty entrepreneurs reinvested regularly to build for the future despite the increasing risks and anxieties of expansion. They demonstrated a willingness to have their capital and resources tied up on long-term fixed investments and to hire large staffs of employees" (Anderson, 1969, p. 666).

The supply of entrepreneurs—small- and medium-scale businessmen and industrialists—arises primarily from the class of street merchants and petty tradesmen ("buy-and-sell businessmen") found in the *bazaar market:* the traditional Asian form of exchange, involving trade in small lots for negotiated prices with a "complex balance of carefully managed credit relationships" and "an extensive fractionation of risks and, as a corollary, of profit margins" (Geertz, 1963, p. 32).

Entrepreneurs arise from the bazaar market because only buy-and-sell businessmen are in a position to earn incomes sufficient to accumulate savings and develop "the complex balance of credit relationships" which provide access to other funds. Both economic-transition theory and government wage policies determine that the earnings of industrial labor should be kept to a minimum to (a) entice foreign investors and (b) provide a competitive advantage in the export markets.

It follows, according to both economic and demographic transition models, that the industrial workers should be the lowest socioeconomic stratum in LDC society, and have the highest fertility rates as well. This prediction is based on both their low earning capacity and their restricted social mobility. It receives empirical support at both national and local levels. In the Philippine Bureau of Census and Statistics Survey of Households for 1971 (the most recent year), production workers and manual laborers (urban) appeared with farmers and farm workers (rural) at the bottom of the income pyramid. In our baseline study of Davao City (Hack-

enberg, 1974) and in the smaller industrial center of Iligan
(Ulack, 1975) factory workers had the lowest earnings and
the highest fertility.

Conversely, both economic and demographic transition
theory would predict that a middle class of potential entrepreneurs (based on bazaar market activities in the Philippines), characterized by moderate incomes and reduced
fertility, should be visible in regional growth centers or
secondary cities. The data from Davao and Iligan also
support this conclusion.

The critical position occupied by the entrepreneurial
group, although widely recognized, is not matched by a
commensurate level of research. There are two critical areas
in which additional Philippine information is needed: one
such area is the structure, function, capacity for expansion,
and growth potential of small *market systems*.

It is widely recognized (Davis, 1973; Cook, 1976) that
bazaar markets are the primary conduit for the exchange of
mass-consumption goods and services through Southeast
Asia and Latin America. It may well be, as the task force
studying the market system in Oaxaca (Mexico) under Ralph
Beals reported, that their importance will increase in the
immediate future because of the rising unemployment in the
urban-industrial sector:

> If the present trend toward high unemployment and
> underemployment in the urban-industrial sector of the
> Mexican economy continues, then . . . the volume of
> traders and of commodities circulating through the
> marketing system will expand. The . . . peasant-artisan
> population—faced with diminished possibilities for
> migration—will turn increasingly to the marketing
> sector for remunerative employment (Cook and Diskin,
> 1976, p. 279).

But this hypothesis advanced by the Oaxaca study group
poses a question which deals not so much with market
organization as with labor force participation. A second
focus for research is suggested: the proportion of *market
workers* (the source of potential entrepreneurs) in the labor
force, the probability of upward mobility within the group,
and the trends in numbers of persons seeking to enter this

occupation and the impact on remuneration to participants. Recent data from the Philippines reviewed by Ranis and Associates (1974, p. 12) documents, during the decade of the 1960s, a reduction of 10 percent in farm labor and an addition of approximately the same proportion to the commerce and services sectors. Meanwhile, the urban-industrial sector, unable to absorb workers displaced from rural areas, declined by .6 percent. These data confirm that, as the urbanization process continues, displaced farm workers are utilizing the market economy as the source of entry occupations when joining the urban labor force.

Other information in the Ranis report (1974, p. 12) confirms that this shift of the labor force into commerce and services is not the result of economic growth in this area of the economy. The 1960-1970 comparison discloses that value added per worker by each sector of the labor force increased for agriculture and industry—the two areas in which proportion of employment declined; in commerce and sales, however, increased worker participation was accompanied by a reduction in value added.

These scattered observations, while insufficient to draw conclusions, raise some troublesome questions. Entrepreneurs emerge from a marketing system which is erected on the traditional conception of the Asian bazaar. Can they modernize their procedures sufficiently to participate in the import-substitution phase of economic development? Can they absorb the additional members of the labor force seeking employment in the tertiary sector? And will this expansion of workers diminish the returns from the bazaar trade to the subsistence level?

If the answer to the first question, concerning participation in import substitution, is affirmative, the remaining questions pose no serious threats. An expanding market structure can absorb additional workers at improved rates of compensation, while actually increasing the potential for accumulation of savings. These assertions are premised on some assumptions propounded by Leibenstein (1957, pp. 126-127):

The growth of entrepreneurship depends on (a) the *size* of the entrepreneurial group, (b) the *level* of per capita income, and (c) the rate of *growth* in per capita income.

. . . The size of the entrepreneurial group determines the extent of the contacts [with other members]. . . . and may determine the extent of the potential bandwagon effect as the group grows. . . . The lower the level of per capita income, the smaller the supply of entrepreneurship in response to the demand that may exist. . . . A continuing state of income growth enables the inexperienced to become experienced, the experienced to continue in their field and to grow in perceptiveness and technique, and tends to create a situation in which entrepreneurship becomes profitable and attractive.

The evidence from economic indicators using aggregate data at the national level is not encouraging when matched against Leibenstein's assumptions. The Ranis report confirms that the size of the entrepreneurial group is growing, but reveals that the trend in per-capita income (as represented by real wages) is downward:

The information available on earnings shows a generalized fall in real urban earnings for the most occupational groups during the 1960s. Thus the Central Bank index of common laborer's wages indicates an 8 percent fall in real terms from 1960 to 1971 . . . especially in the years after 1969 when consumer prices accelerated. The Central Bank statistics show that semi-skilled and skilled earnings fell even more than unskilled (Ranis and Associates, 1974, pp. 10–11, 353–356).

These circumstances mitigate against the success of the "economic transition" strategy for Philippine development, since the position of the prospective entrepreneurs appears to be undermined during the present stage of import substitution.

Emergent Entrepreneurship in Davao City: 1972–1974

The dynamics of these adverse trends may be better understood within the context of a particular community where the interplay of forces may be seen as a sequence of discrete events. The concepts as well as the quantitative relationships between them may be more minutely examined with some measurements obtained from two cross-sectional surveys of Davao City completed in 1972 and 1974 (Hackenberg, 1975). As the second-largest city (1975 pop. 486,000) and third-largest metropolitan community in the Philippines, Davao exemplifies the objective of regional industrial concentration as a stimulus to diversified economic growth. It is the timber-processing center of the Philippines and the nucleus of an agribusiness zone exporting bananas, sugar, and copra. In earlier decades, it served and administered the largest abaca-growing region in the world (Hackenberg and Hackenberg, 1971).

The major contribution of the baseline (1972) study was to establish the spatial, social, and economic class configuration of the community with the associated characteristics shown in Table 2.

TABLE 2

SOCIOECONOMIC, ECOLOGICAL AND DEMOGRAPHIC CHARACTERISTICS OF DAVAO CITY: 1972*

	LOCATION WITHIN THE CITY	% OF URBAN POPULATION	MEAN HH INCOME PER MONTH	PRIMARY ECONOMIC ACTIVITY	POPULATION GROWTH RATE
UPPER CLASS	IN AND NEAR CENTRAL BUSI- NESS DISTRICT	28.5	812	GOVERNMENT, PROFESSIONS, MANAGEMENT	LOWEST CBR = 20
MIDDLE CLASS	IN AND NEAR CENTRAL CITY MARKETS	33.5	491	SELF-EMPLOYED IN TRADITIONAL SALES AND SERVICES	MEDIUM CBR = 34
LOWER CLASS	PERIPHERAL LOCATIONS OUT- SIDE POBLACION	38.0	335	WAGE WORK IN INDUSTRIAL OCCUPATIONS	HIGHEST CBR = 41

*The analysis of the 1972 survey was completed by the classification of individual enumeration districts (of which there were 23 in the entire sample) into 3 groups according to central tendencies in income. Each of the 3 sets of EDs was then discovered to occupy a region of the city: the 9 upper-class EDs clustered near the central business district, the 6 middle-class EDs were located on the edge of the CBD adjacent to the principal urban markets, while the 8 lower-class EDs were all outside the *poblacion* to the north and south in the vicinity of the industrial estates, i.e., factory locations. In addition to highest rates of industrial employment, lower-class EDs contained the highest concentrations of unskilled labor and the highest rates of employment by private enterprise and large-scale industry (more than 50 employees). The tables describing these relationships are in the published report (Hackenberg, 1974, pp. 32-34). The technique of describing the characteristics of an area so that they may be attributed to its residents is known as *ecological correlation*.

The combination of highest population growth rate and lowest income among the largest sector of the population (the lower class) was an explosive mixture from which an accelerated rate of income decline could be expected.

The second survey (1974) was expected to confirm this gloomy prediction because of (a) the accumulation of the foregoing negative forces acting to depress income within the city and (b) inflationary trends within the national economy which accelerated sharply in the months following the completion of the 1972 study. That the prediction was more than accurate is shown by the comparisons of real income by social class in Table 3.

TABLE 3
1972 AND 1974 MONTHLY HOUSEHOLD INCOME IN DAVAO ADJUSTED FOR
LOSS OF PURCHASING POWER

	ACTUAL PESOS 1972	PURCHASING POWER IN 1965 PESOS[1]	ACTUAL PESOS 1974	PURCHASING POWER IN 1965 PESOS[2]	1972-74 % LOSS
A. TOTAL POPULATION					
MEAN INCOME	523	282.4	603	186.9	-33.8
MEDIAN	343	185.2	409	126.7	-31.6
B. LOWER CLASS					
MEAN INCOME	335	180.9	523	162.1	-10.4
MEDIAN	269	145.3	345	107.0	-26.4
C. MIDDLE CLASS					
MEAN INCOME	491	265.1	526	163.1	-38.5
MEDIAN	342	184.7	393	121.8	-34.1
D. UPPER CLASS					
MEAN INCOME	812	438.5	824	255.4	-41.8
MEDIAN	558	301.3	613	190.0	-36.9

[1]In mid-1972 the peso had sunk to .54 of its 1965 value.

[2]In mid-1974 the peso had lost an additional .23 of its 1965 value and its purchasing power was quoted at .31.

SOURCE: Business Division, National Census and Statistics Office, quoted from p. 166 of the 1975 PHILIPPINE YEARBOOK (an NCSO publication), Manila.

The household income figures from the second survey, when adjusted for decline in purchasing power by conversion to 1965 pesos, disclosed an average loss of 34 percent over the two-year period! The remainder of this section will present an examination of this phenomenon and of the efforts to compensate for losses in earning power sustained by each class level. The first of several salient points is that purchasing-power losses struck each class not equally but, rather, inversely. The highest income group lost the most, while the lowest income group lost the least.

The interclass comparison clearly reveals that those households most severely threatened by losses of purchasing power resulting from inflation made the greatest efforts to offset them. The next relevant finding from the 1972–1974 comparison concerns individual (rather than household) income and is presented in Table 4. In comparison with Table 3, the distribution of losses in wages appears in Table 4 to be much more evenly distributed across class levels; the lower-class decline in mean individual income was 2.5 times greater than the decline in mean household income, for example. This fact is consistent with earlier data from the Ranis report stating that a real decline in urban wages had taken place in recent years (Ranis and Associates, 1974, pp. 10–11, 353–356).

TABLE 4
1972-1974 INDIVIDUAL INCOMES ADJUSTED FOR LOSS OF PURCHASING POWER

	ACTUAL PESOS 1972	PURCHASING POWER IN 1965 PESOS[1]	ACTUAL PESOS 1974	PURCHASING POWER IN 1965 PESOS[2]	1972-74 % LOSS
A. TOTAL POPULATION					
MEAN INCOME	321	164	336	104	-36.6
MEDIAN	243	124	253	78	-37.1
B. LOWER CLASS					
MEAN INCOME	231	118	280	87	-26.3
MEDIAN	219	112	222	69	-38.4
C. MIDDLE CLASS					
MEAN INCOME	303	155	307	95	-38.1
MEDIAN	236	120	244	76	-36.6
D. UPPER CLASS					
MEAN INCOME	436	222	459	142	-36.0
MEDIAN	316	161	338	105	-34.8

[1] In mid-1972 the peso had shrunk to .54 of its 1965 value.

[2] In mid-1974 the peso had lost an additional .23 of its 1965 value and its purchasing power was quoted at .31.

SOURCE: Business Division, NCSO, 1975 PHILIPPINE YEARBOOK, p. 166, Manila.

Expressing the results of Tables 3 and 4 somewhat differently, the following generalization emerges: wages paid to individuals were reduced almost equally across the board by inflation, meaning that their peso value changed very little over the two-year period. Therefore, the reasons for the relative success of lower-class households in coping with inflation must be sought in features of the urban economy other than wage fluctuations.

The first alteration of significance was found in the area of labor-force participation. Table 5, which examines changes

TABLE 5
LABOR FORCE COMPOSITION BY ECONOMIC CLASS: 1972 AND 1974**

	LABOR FORCE AS % OF TOTAL POP.		% OF LABOR FORCE ACTUALLY EMPLOYED		EMPLOYED PERSONS PER HH	
	1972	1974	1972	1974	1972	1974
LOWER CLASS	49.3	48.4	47.2	60.4	1.44	1.74
MIDDLE CLASS	52.4	51.0	49.5	56.7	1.52	1.64
UPPER CLASS	59.8	54.7	46.0	55.0	1.75	1.66
TOTAL POPULATION	53.4	50.9	48.2	57.6	1.56	1.68

**The labor force is defined as the population between the ages of 15-54.

Total number of persons in sample actually employed, 1972.......1,555
(25.7% of study population).

Total number of persons in sample actually employed, 1974.......1,768
(29.3% of study population).

Absolute increase in 1974 in sample employed as % of 1972.......213
(13.7% of 1972 base).

in patterns of urban employment, contains a substantial part of the answer. Because of unfavorable changes in the age structure, the actual size of the labor force diminished by 2.5 percent over the two-year period (see the left-hand column in Table 5). Despite this, the proportion of the labor force actually employed increased by an astonishing 9.4 percent. As might be expected from the household-income comparisons, the greatest gains in labor-force participation were posted by lower-class households (see Table 5, middle column). Among these households, the rate of employment was raised by 13.2 percent. In other words, among the low-income households of Davao, eight persons were employed in 1974 for every seven person at work in 1972.

TABLE 6
EMPLOYED MEMBERS OF THE HOUSEHOLD BY ECONOMIC CLASS

(PER 100 HOUSEHOLDS)

	HH HEADS		SPOUSES		CHILDREN		OTHERS	
	1972	1974	1972	1974	1972	1974	1972	1974
LOWER	87	93	17	30	23	36	16	15
MIDDLE	94	94	24	33	20	33	12	15
UPPER	93	94	31	34	28	26	23	13
TOTAL	91	94	23	32	24	29	16	15

Across the entire city, employment per household increased from 1.5 members in 1972 to 1.7 members two years later. Once again, the most significant gain appears among the lower-class households. The nature of the additions to the labor force is revealed in Table 6. While the employment of household heads showed little change across the two-year interval, the number of working wives increased by 40 percent. And when interclass differences are compared, the greatest increments in the employment of both wives and children appear among lower-class families.

The conclusion to be drawn from Tables 5 and 6 is that people of Davao City who were unable to meet the costs of inflation by obtaining increased wages responded instead by increasing the number of wage earners. Utilization of this mechanism, however, implies some assumptions about the elasticity of the demand for labor. Since the local labor force grew by almost 10 percent in only two years, it might appear that a commensurate expansion of local industry and the creation of new jobs also took place. This assumption may be tested by examining the occupational structure at the date of each survey, as has been done in Table 7. This table presents eight major occupational groups arranged in rank order by frequency of employment in 1972. This arrangement calls attention to the predominant role of sales and services in the occupational structure of a community better known as an industrial center. These two categories, comprising the first and second ranks in Table 7, included 43.4 percent of the labor force in 1972.

Of particular interest is the subcategory containing "market vendors, buy-and-sell merchants, peddlers, and sari-sari storekeepers," which was the largest single occupational class within the city. This cluster of occupations represents the traditional bazaar market from which the emergent entrepreneurs may be expected to differentiate themselves through successful competition.

The bazaar economy functions, according to Geertz (1963), by distributing both risks and microscopic profits among a very large number of participants. Since small inventories can always be subdivided, and there is always space on the street for "one more pushcart," *the labor-absorptive capacity of the bazaar economy appears to be infinitely expandable.* The capital and skills required for entry are minimal and the technology involved is primitive. Yet through the bazaar markets moves the bulk of the

TABLE 7
OCCUPATIONS CLASSIFIED BY INDUSTRY, TRADE AND PROFESSION: 1972 AND 1974

(ARRANGED IN RANK ORDER BY INDUSTRY)

RANK		1972 NO.	%	1974 NO.	%
1.	SALES				
	MARKET VENDORS, PEDDLERS, BUY AND SELL				
	MERCHANTS, SARI-SARI STOREKEEPERS	178	11.5	285	16.2
	OWNER, SMALL OR MEDIUM BUSINESS	96	6.3	117	6.6
	SALES REPRESENTATIVES	39	2.5	50	2.8
	SALESPERSON	29	1.9	14	.8
	BUSINESS MANAGERS	19	1.2	18	1.0
	COLLECTORS	5	.3	8	.5
	PURCHASING AGENTS	0	0.0	11	.6
		366	23.7	503	28.5
2.	SERVICES				
	MECHANIC/AUTOMOTIVE	79	5.1	56	3.2
	TAILOR-DRESSMAKER	64	4.2	50	2.8
	MAINTENANCE/SECURITY	63	4.1	57	3.2
	PERSONAL SERVICES	59	3.8	103	5.8
	FOOD SERVICES	39	2.5	62	3.5
		304	19.7	328	18.3
3.	MANUFACTURING/CONSTRUCTION				
	FACTORY WORKERS	174	11.3	156	8.9
	BUILDING TRADES	98	6.4	139	7.9
	FOREMAN; CONTRACTORS	20	1.3	35	1.6
		292	19.0	330	18.4
4.	CLERICAL				
	OFFICE WORKERS	134	8.7	148	8.4
	ACCOUNTANTS/AUDITORS	44	2.9	31	1.8
	OFFICE SUPERINTENDENTS	13	.9	21	1.2
		191	12.5	200	11.4
5.	PROFESSIONAL/TECHNICAL				
	EDUCATION	97	6.3	98	5.6
	ENGINEERS	11	.7	8	.5
	ATTORNEYS	9	.6	6	.3
	CLERGYMEN	7	.5	2	.1
	MEDICAL TECHNICIANS	6	.4	13	.7
	DOCTORS	5	.3	3	.2
	EXECUTIVES	4	.3	3	.2
	OTHER	0	0.0	3	.2
		139	9.1	136	7.8
6.	TRANSPORTATION/COMMUNICATIONS				
	TRUCK, BUS AND A/C DRIVERS	115	7.5	115	6.4
	COMMUNICATIONS AND GRAPHICS	13	.8	3	.2
		128	8.3	118	6.6
7.	AGRICULTURE AND FISHING				
	FARMING	49	3.2	83	4.7
	FISHING	13	.8	23	1.2
		62	4.0	106	5.9
8.	SHIPPING				
	STEVEDORES	27	1.8	34	1.9
	SAILORS	2	.1	7	.4
		29	1.9	41	2.3
9.	UNCLASSIFIED	27	1.8		
TOTAL		1,538	100.0	1,762	100.0

foodstuffs consumed by the resident population of Davao City. Textiles, building materials, and household goods utilized by the vast majority of low- and middle-income households are also provided by the traditional sector.

Inspection of the 1972 and 1974 figures in Table 7 confirms that the sales sector was the only expanding category of employment in Davao City. And within the sales sector, occupational expansion was limited further to jobs within the bazaar economy. Over the two-year period, the proportion of workers engaged in sales grew from 23.7 percent to 28.5 percent; the market vendors' group expanded from 11.5 percent to 16.2 percent, accounting for almost the entire gain in the sales sector.

Further evidence of change is disclosed by an examination of the interclass occupational dynamics of the 1972–1974 period regarding sales personnel. The proportion of sales employment among the lower class over the two years increased from one-fourth in 1972 to one-third in 1974. Conversely, the share of the middle-class households remained constant at two-fifths of the total. Upper-class participation, however, was reduced from one-third in 1972 to one-fourth in 1974.

TABLE 8
DISTRIBUTION OF SALES OCCUPATIONS BETWEEN CLASSES: 1972-1974

(% OF TOTAL LABOR FORCE BY CLASS)

	LOWER CLASS	MIDDLE CLASS	UPPER CLASS	LABOR FORCE TOTAL %
1972	6.2%	9.8%	8.2%	24.2%*
1974	9.0%	12.2%	7.2%	28.4%*

*Percent figures do not agree precisely with Table 6 because of differences in rounding.

Because of the critical position of the traditional sales group in the city's economy, a subschedule of the 1974 survey asked a number of questions concerning workers in the bazaar trade. In addition to their growth in numbers and redistribution between classes, the subschedule recorded the socioeconomic characteristics of these self-employed salespersons, representing one-sixth of the workers of Davao:

1. *Traders in the bazaar market were middle-aged, married women.* Almost three-fourths (72 percent) of all market

workers were women, with a median age of 40.7 years. While there were no notable age differences, the sex composition of this category changed by social class. The male proportion of those employed in trading was 10 percent among the lower class, 37 percent among the middle class, and 33 percent in upper-class districts. Nonetheless, the group was overwhelmingly female and represented 43 percent of all employed spouses.

2. *Women engaged in the bazaar trade were undereducated.* Analysis of the female labor force published elsewhere (Hackenberg, 1975) confirms that the jobs sought by married women are confined to the sales-and-services and clerical-professional categories. Only among upper-class women did the latter group equal the former in size, but at all three class levels the education of saleswomen in the bazaar market fell below the average for their group, as disclosed by Table 9. The education of women in the bazaar economy was 2.26 years below that of all other employed women.

TABLE 9
EDUCATIONAL LEVELS OF WOMEN TRADITIONAL SALES WORKERS BY ECONOMIC CLASS

(MEAN YEARS OF EDUCATION COMPLETED)

	TRADITIONAL SALES WORKER	ALL WOMEN WORKERS
LOWER CLASS	5.91	7.37
MIDDLE CLASS	5.94	7.55
UPPER CLASS	7.52	10.62
ALL WOMEN	6.17	8.43

3. *Women market traders received relatively high incomes.* While there were substantial class differences in earnings (see Table 10), the mean income received by women bazaar workers was 78 percent of that for all women workers. Curiously, the proportion of the average income received by female employees was the same for women bazaar traders at each class level.

It seems clear, then, that the bazaar economy has been utilized in recent years as a source of supplementary income

TABLE 10
MEAN INCOMES OF TRADITIONAL SALES WORKERS BY SEX AND ECONOMIC CLASS
(PESOS)

	TRADITIONAL SALES		ALL WORKERS	
	MALE	FEMALE	MALE	FEMALE
LOWER CLASS	534	126	347	161
MIDDLE CLASS	333	197	363	216
UPPER CLASS	464	237	552	319
TOTAL	384	175	392	227

to provide the lower-class households of Davao with a hedge against inflation. As such, however, its major positive function is to preserve the marginal "subsistence urbanization" position of the poor within the city. It would be difficult to link these events to the concept of "emergent entrepreneurship" associated with the economic transition model. Neither do they seem to be akin to the social relationships described in the earlier Philippine literature (Anderson, 1969; Carroll, 1965). It may well be that the present level of population growth, coupled with declining purchasing power, obviates the prospects for capital formation and entrepreneurial behavior.

The spurt in the size of the working population, without the creation of a number of new jobs in the western sector of the urban economy, meant that the pool of wages available for distribution (including the profits from market and street sales) remained essentially fixed (subject to inflationary adjustments) during the interval between 1972 and 1974.

Consequently, the outcome of adding the new women to the work force was a reduction in the shares of previous sales workers and the redistribution of these shares, in smaller portions, to both old and new members of the group. Since the largest increment of workers came from lower-class households, their relative gain was greatest; since the income was drawn from those previously receiving it, the loss was primarily sustained by the middle class. By adding its own household members to the sales force, however, the middle class cushioned the loss by increasing the number of shares of traditional sales income it received.

Therefore, the gap existing in income and employment terms between lower- and middle-class households was partly closed over the two-year period. Instead of reporting that low-income households benefited from this develop-ment, it might be more appropriate to say that poverty was distributed more equitably among the lower 60 percent of the urban population.

There have been substantial changes in the composition and size of the working population of Davao since 1972, but these changes have left income distribution unaltered. While there has been significant change in the size of incomes received by many households within the city, these changes do not signify any reallocation from the upper two-fifths, who hold more than 70 percent of the personal income, to the lower three-fifths, with less than 30 percent.

Exports, Entrepreneurs, and Equity: Solution for Whom?

Thoughts differ about what ought to be. Many people have ideas about a just income distribution, which of course is fine, but these ideas sometimes trip them up when trying to explain the existing state of affairs. It usually makes a difference whether you want to explain a phenomenon or pass ethical judgment on it; and yet the two are often confused, with the result that both the explanation and the judgment may suffer (Pen, 1974, p. 110.)

In Southeast Asia, both economic and demographic tran-sitions are essential to the avoidance of the Malthusian specter. Each assigns an important role to income distribu-tion and to entrepreneurship as a mechanism for attaining it. Entrepreneurs, in the Philippines and elsewhere, emerge from the street trade associated with the bazaar economy. In both economic and demographic transition models, entre-preneurship is associated with upward social mobility. To the population theorist, the important by-product of mobili-ty achieved is fertility decline; to the development economist, the primary gain is seen in the production of exports leading to expanded trade and eventual socioeconomic equity.

Both national and local data from recent Philippine (and Davao City) experience, however, indicate that the commercial sector from which entrepreneurs are to emerge is being glutted with surplus workers from two sources: displaced farm labor ejected from agriculture and housewives forced to seek employment to supplement declining real household income. As the real earnings of the middle-class households in cities like Davao continue to spiral downward while employment increases, it appears that the profit margin from the street trade, which might have been invested in the import-substitution phase of economic transition, is going instead to subsistence purchases.

Rather than progress with welfare, the outcome of the process outlined earlier in this chapter may be merely redistribution of a fixed (and adequate) profit margin from trading among an ever-larger number of recipients:

> The fact that profit-making opportunities and profit-seeking individuals exist does not imply that their combination will yield economic growth. . . . There are zero-sum games and non-zero sum games. . . . Translating this notion into the economic environment makes it clear that enterprising individuals can make money either by "exploiting" their fellow men or by the creation and marshaling of resources in more productive combinations. . . . In the zero-sum enterprise there is only a distributive effect (Leibenstein, 1957, p. 113).

Leibenstein's comment seems to seal the fate of entrepreneurship as it has been described on the basis of recent surveys of Davao City. But other critical issues have been addressed with reference to the economic transition model as a vehicle for generating both employment and income distribution at a suprapoverty level of living.

Tyler (1976), in a thought-provoking article, argues that an increase of 50–100 percent in the level of LDC exports would be needed to reduce unemployment to the 10 percent level in the developing world. He asserts that the Western world is unqilling to absorb this volume of exports, even if it is able to do so. He concludes that the practicality of the export-substitution route to employment with equity is restricted to such small countries as Hong Kong and Taiwan:

Small developing economies would appear to have a greater ability than large countries to use manufactured-export expansion to resolve their unemployment problems. Beginning with a few manufactured exports, rapid export growth in a small country results in exports becoming proportionately large relative to output and employment earlier than in a large country. Furthermore the smaller amount of export production required to absorb large proportions of labor is less likely to trigger protectionist reaction in the world economy. . . . For the larger countries in our sample, industrial export promotion offers little promise of eliminating unemployment and underemployment in the reasonably short run. This pessimistic finding is not mitigated by the fact that manufactured exports may be growing very rapidly. It is paradoxical that Brazil, while enjoying one of the fastest rates of growth for manufactured exports, has the furthest to go before such exports will substantially contribute to alleviating its labor-surplus problems (Tyler, 1976, pp. 361, 367).

One of the major conclusions regarding economic trends which emerges from our Davao City studies is that there is a tendency ". . . toward a dichotomous division into relatively undifferentiated high-income and low-income areas. . . . The middle-income districts which could be clearly differentiated in 1972 are, today, inseparable from the lowest-income groups of 1972 on the basis of statistical tests" (Hackenberg, 1975, pp. 51–52). This finding is consistent with the conclusion reached by Adelman and Morris (1973) that:

> . . . economic growth brings greater inequality and "typically" an absolute decline in real income for most of the population. Furthermore . . . their study suggests that, in an average country going through the earliest phases of economic development, it takes at least a generation for the poorest 60 percent to recover the loss in absolute income associated with the typical spurt in growth (De Gregori, 1974, p. 612).

The recent trend of events in the Philippines appears to

bear out Kuznets' prediction that the rich will benefit more from economic development opportunities than the poor because they are favored by savings ratios and, thus, better enabled to invest. But what of the import-substitution phase, now alleged to be nearing conclusion in the Philippines, and the florescence of local entrepreneurship which it was supposed to facilitate?

The "Western" sides of the central business districts of all Philippine provincial cities are aglitter with displays of locally manufactured (or assembled) appliances, hardware, furniture, farm equipment, and motor vehicles. However, the large corporate enterprises in Manila responsible for the manufacture of these goods have learned the "vertical integration" principle from the multinationals (Japanese, American, British, and German) with whom they are frequently in partnership.

To extract maximum profit while protecting established markets, the multinational manufacturers have sought to expand "backward" into ownership of raw-material producers and "forward" into the distributing and retailing phases of business activity (Vernon, 1973). It is conventional in the Philippines for a company which manufactures a line of appliances to diversify into related products and then establish a marketing company to handle both credit and sales at the local level. What chance is there for local entrepreneurs, with their background in the small-business sphere of the street market, to engage in competition with the industrial giants of the Philippines and their multinational affiliates?

As Powelson (1975) has stated, the consequence of this pattern of development is an intensification of dualism: the returns to the modern sector are advanced at the expense of the traditional sector. However, both he and Ranis (Ranis and Associates, 1974) have argued that this pattern has built-in limitations which will force alterations in the directions desired:

> Dualism has a built-in constraint, however. Even with import substitution, the modern sector's demand for imports grows each year, primarily for capital goods but also for a few consumer goods which the domestic sector cannot supply. This demand ultimately reaches an

amount that cannot be financed by traditional exports.
. . . Nontraditional exports are needed. . . . An agonizing
reappraisal of the nation's economic policies follows, to
force manufacturing enterprises in the modern sector to
become efficient enough to export. It is with this
reappraisal that dualism begins to end; the poor become
favored because they are needed as workers; and the
balance begins to swing (Powelson, 1975, p. 104).

These predictions offer hope for the long run. But one is
tempted to quote Keynes' rejoinder, "Yes, but in the long run
we are all dead." For meanwhile, the population bomb keeps
ticking, social mobility is paralyzed, the polarities of social
class become intensified, and present income-distribution
patterns become rigidified by the progressive elimination of
the bazaar market system from a competitive role and a share
in the growth process. Furthermore, and perhaps worst of
all, the whole pattern becomes bulwarked by assumption of
authoritarian political power.

When acknowledged, these considerations lead development analysts to invoke the bottom line: overthrow of the
present elite and replacement by social, economic, and
political institutions more favorable to social equity. The
Ranis report (1974, p. 13), for example, affirms the following
message:

Clearly the particular growth path chosen in the past
has tended to be adverse to the interests of the average
worker, and still more so to that of the below average
worker. A developmental process that nurtures and
sustains trends in the structure of earnings that result in
steadily increasing inequality cannot expect to continue
for very long, or, at any rate, to continue without
profound and painful political change.

In a *Times Journal* (Manila) release of December 27, 1975,
David Sycip, a respected private business analyst, put the
issue in emphatic terms:

. . . the next five to ten years will see our society evolving
into a substantially more egalitarian one—more egalitarian in terms of income and wealth, and in terms of

opportunities to seek to improve one's personal circumstances . . . in the event the goals of the New Society [the
Marcos dictatorship] do not seem likely to be fulfilled in
the reasonably near future, the egalitarian society will
evolve as a result of major political changes which
impatient people may precipitate or directly bring
about.

The incipient threat of revolution in the event that wealth is
not effectively redistributed is accepted as a reality by perhaps the majority of social scientists, planners, politicians,
and historians.

It sounds logical, but it is simply not true. Neither
continuously declining living standards, nor diminishing
resources, nor explosive population growth, nor the simultaneous accumulation of wealth in undreamed-of amounts
by a privileged few will, *of themselves*, alter the course of
future events by forcing revolutionary social change. While
this is one of the fondest dreams of the twentieth century—
especially in the formerly colonial regions that gained
freedom after World War II—recent history does not support
it.

The cases of Indonesia and Brazil come easily to mind.
Both are vast regions with huge, ill-distributed populations
that have been subjected to continuously declining real
incomes in the face of massive population growth for the
past three decades. Both are stable, two-class systems in
which the elite has never been seriously threatened. Granted,
coups d'etat are not unknown in either country. The changing of the pictures on the palace walls is the major result of
such a "revolution" as far as the average citizen is concerned.
Pareto, whose nineteenth century mind has proven peculiar-
ly appropriate to our twentieth century society, designated
such events as "the circulation of the elites." His point was
that the mere replacement of the exploiters by a few of the
exploited does not change the nature of the social system.

It is not the intention here to draw a close analogy between
the Indonesian peasant and the Philippine farmer, the
Indonesian bazaar market and the city of Davao, or the
Indonesian military dictatorship and Philippine martial
law. It can apparently continue to expand endlessly, like the
universe itself, with ever-increasing socioeconomic distances

between its inner (upper-class) and outer (lower-class) members. It does not cross an imaginary threshold and suddenly disintegrate, despite the fond wishes of the liberal philosophers.

Like the belief in eternal salvation or immanent justice, the conviction that there are "inevitable historical processes" is comforting to those who consider themselves to be "on the side of history." The recent history of the developing countries provides little comfort, however, to those who believe that the systems containing the greatest measure of inequity or maldistribution of wealth will be the first to fall of their own top-heavy instability. As Karl Wittfogel argued so cogently in *Oriental Despotism*, the reverse is much more likely to be true.

As Jan Pen observed in the quote that began this section, "It . . . makes a difference whether you want to explain a phenomenon or pass ethical judgment on it." It may be the ethics rather than the explanation that invokes the prediction of the inevitability of more equitable income distribution brought about by political means. Geertz (1966), in his now-classic presentation of economic involution in Indonesia, bases his gloomy assessment of the future on the pattern of wastage of human resources which is already irrevocable. His contrast of Java and Japan is still instructive:

> The most striking—and the most decisive—is the contrast between the way Java utilized its rapid population increase and the way Japan utilized hers. Between 1870 and 1940 Java absorbed the bulk of her increase in numbers—about thirty million people—into her village social systems of the sort already described, but in the first century of modernization, Japan maintained a relatively unchanging population in agriculture while the total population increased two and one-half fold. Practically all the increase in the labor force was absorbed in non-agricultural activities. . . . Almost all the natural increase of the national population was absorbed in urban areas. . . . The dynamic interaction between the two sectors which kept Japan moving and ultimately pushed her over the hump to sustained growth was absent in Java. . . . To a great extent, Japan maintained it and Java lost it in the four critical decades

of the mid-nineteenth century: 1830-1870 (Geertz, 1966, pp. 131–135).

This paper was begun on one Malthusian note, and, unfortunately, it must end on another. Teitelbaum (1975), among others, gives a recent and cogent recapitulation of the position Geertz developed more than a decade ago: it is possible for population growth to outrun the capacity of the economy to achieve what must be *simultaneous*, rather than *sequential* goals: increased GNP and more equitable income distribution. Or, as Mahbub ul Haq (1971, p. 6) put it:

We ... know that once production has been so organized as to leave a fairly large number of people unemployed, it becomes almost impossible to redistribute income to those who are not even participating in the production stream.

We are coming to realize that the very pattern and organization of production itself dictates a pattern of consumption and distribution which is politically very difficult to change.

Acknowledgements

The baseline data from the 1972 Davao City survey were collected with support from contract NIH-NICHD-72-2797 provided by the Center for Population Research, National Institute for Child Health and Human Development. The 1974 Davao City survey was financed by a grant from Philippine Business for Social Progress.

References

Adelman, I. and C. T. Morris (1973). *Economic Growth and Social Equity in Developing Countries*. Stanford, Calif.: Stanford University Press.

Anderson, J. N. (1969). "Buy-and-Sell and Economic Personalism: Foundations for Philippine Entrepreneurship." *Asian Survey* 9, no. 9.

Carroll, J. J. (1965). *The Filipino Manufacturing Entrepreneur: Agent and Product of Change.* Ithaca, N.Y.: Cornell University Press.

Chenery, H. (1974). *Redistribution with Growth.* London: Oxford University Press.

Clawson, M. (1967). "Implications of Urbanization for the Village and Rural Sector," in Ward, R. J., ed. *Challenge of Development.* Chicago: Aldine.

Cook, J. (1976). "The Market as Location and Transaction," in Cook and Diskin, eds. (1976).

Cook, J. and M. Diskin, eds. (1976). *Markets in Oaxaca.* Austin: University of Texas Press.

Davis, W. G. (1973). *Social Relations in a Philippine Market.* Berkeley: University of California Press.

De Gregori, T. (1974). Review of *Economic Growth and Social Equity*, by Adelman, I., and C. T. Morris. *Journal of Developing Areas* 8, no. 4.

Demeny, P. (1971). "Economics of Population Growth," in National Academy of Sciences. *Rapid Population Growth*, vol. 2. Baltimore: Johns Hopkins Press.

Fei, J. C. H., and G. Ranis (1964). *Development of the Labor Surplus Economy.* Homewood, Ill.: Richard D. Irwin.

Freedman, R. and B. Berelson (1976). "The Record of Family Planning Programs." *Studies in Family Planning* 7, no. 1.

Geertz, C. (1963). *Peddlers and Princes: Social Development and Economic Change in Two Indonesian Towns.* Chicago: University of Chicago Press.

Geertz, C. (1966). *Agricultural Involution: The Processes of Ecological Change in Indonesia.* Berkeley: University of California Press.

Hackenberg, R. A. (1974). "The Poverty Explosion: Population Growth and Income Decline in Davao City, 1972." *Philippine Planning Journal* 5, nos. 1 and 2.

Hackenberg, R. A. (1975). *Fallout from the Poverty Explosion: Economic and Demographic Trends in Davao City, 1972-1974.* Davao Action Information Center, Davao, Philippines, monograph no. 2.

Hackenberg, R. A. and B. Hackenberg (1971). "Secondary Development and Anticipatory Urbanization in Davao, Mindanao." *Pacific Viewpoint* 12, no. 1.

Hoselitz, B. F. (1967). "The Entrepreneurial Element in Economic Development," in Ward, R. J., ed. *Challenge of Development*. Chicago: Aldine.

Kocher, J. (1973). "Rural Development, Income Distribution, and Fertility Decline." Population Council Occasional Paper, New York.

Leibenstein, H. (1957). *Economic Backwardness and Economic Growth*. New York: Wiley.

Mamdani, M. (1973). *Myth of Population Control: Family, Caste and Class in an Indian Village*. New York: Monthly Review Press.

Paauw, D. S. (1966). "The Role of Agriculture in National Development Planning." Philippine-American Rural Development Workshop, University of the Philippines, Los Banos, Laguna.

Paauw, D. S. (1970). "Strategies for the Transition from Economic Colonialism to Sustained Modern Growth." *Development Digest* 8, no. 4.

Paauw, D. S., and J. C. H. Fei (1973). *The Transition in Open Dualistic Economies: Theory and Southeast Asian Experience*. New Haven: Yale University Press.

Pen, J. (1974). *Income Distribution*. Baltimore: Penguin Books.

Powelson, J. P. (1975). "Why Are the Poor so Poor in Less Developed Countries?" *Human Organization* 34, no. 1.

Ranis, G. (1974). "Employment, Equity, and Growth: Lessons from the Philippine Employment Mission." *International Labor Review* 110, no. 1.

Ranis, G. and Associates (1974). *Sharing in Development: A Programme of Employment, Equity and Growth for the Philippines*. Geneva: International Labour Organization.

Rich, W. (1973). "Smaller Families through Social and Economic Progress." Overseas Development Council, Washington, Monograph no. 7.

Schultz, T. P. (1971). "An Economic Perspective on Population Growth," in National Academy of Science. *Rapid Population Growth*, vol. 2. Baltimore: Johns Hopkins Press.

Stolnitz, G. (1964). "The Demographic Transition: From High to Low Birth Rates and Death Rates," in Freedman, R., ed. *Population: The Vital Revolution*. Garden City, N.Y.: Doubleday.

Teitelbaum, M. S. (1975). "Relevance of Demographic Transition Theory for Developing Countries." *Science* 188, no. 4187 (May 2, 1975).

Tyler, W. G. (1976). "Manufactured Exports and Employment Creation in Developing Countries: Some Empirical Evidence." *Economic Development and Cultural Change* 24, no. 2.

ul Haq, M. (1971). "Employment and Income Distribution in the 1970s: A New Perspective." *Development Digest* 9, no. 4.

Ulack, R. (1975). "Impact of Industrialization on the Population Characteristics of a Medium-sized City in the Developing World." *Journal of Developing Areas* 9, no. 2.

Vernon, R. (1973). *Sovereignty at Bay*. Baltimore: Penguin Books.

Wittfogel, K. A. (1957). *Oriental Despotism*. New Haven, Yale University Press.

6. Operating in
a Complex Society

John P. Powelson

Obstacles to more-equitable income distribution in any country may be divided into three broad classes:

- *structures* that deny the poor equal access to resources, including feudal land tenure, biased credit institutions, lack of good schools and infrastructure in rural areas (or in core cities in the United States), and lack of communication networks concerning opportunities;
- *policies*, such as those governing interest and exchange rates, taxation, government spending, investment incentives, and price and wage controls, which may be biased against maximum employment of labor or against the production of traditional and export goods, or which may turn the terms of trade against the poor; and
- *personal qualities of the poor themselves*, such as lack of experience, cultural characteristics that are disadvantageous in "equal" bargaining with more sophisticated counterparts and adversaries, and naivete about how to function advantageously in a complex, modern economy.

Each class of obstacles has its champions. Marxist literature stresses the structural, to the virtual exclusion of the other two. Where Marxists do relate to policies, these are thought to emanate from structure, in that a capitalist society behaves in one way and a socialist society in another. Among the non-Marxist literature, writers on land tenure are the most voluminous. A typical argument is this: "The land tenure system of Chile, coupled with the operation of credit institutions, has made it virtually impossible for the great bulk of the farm population to acquire the knowledge and other inputs essential to a modern, technically evolving agriculture" (Crosson, 1970). The Inter-American Committee on Agricultural Development (CIDA) has demonstrated that large feudal farms in Latin America have high marginal productivity of land and low marginal productivity of labor, while small subsistence farms show the opposite configuration (Barraclough, 1973). The implication is that a more rational distribution of laborers over the land would promote both increased production and a more-equitable income distribution. Other studies have shown a similar situation in Asian countries (Lele, 1972). The benefits of the "green revolution" have accrued mainly to large landowners, who alone can afford the necessary irrigation and fertilizer (Frankel, 1971; Datt and Sundharam, 1971; Agarwal and Kumawat, 1974). A number of writings demonstrate that small farms and small-scale businesses have less access to credit and other inputs (including advice) than large operations (Lele, 1972; Bosa, 1969; United Nations, 1970; Society for Social and Economic Studies, 1959; Ames, 1975; Jodha, 1971). All the sources cited in this paragraph are, in each case, representative of a much-larger body of literature.

   Policy has been the principal target of another group of economists, who argue that import substitution and capital-intensive development have led to dualism, which in turn is a principal factor in poverty (Adelman and Morris, 1973; Chenery et al., 1974; Nelson, Schultz, and Slighton, 1971; Powelson, 1975). Import substitution has been brought about in many countries by a set of policies which includes lower-than-market interest rates, high protection for consumer goods combined with low duties on intermediate and capital goods, such incentives for investment as tax holidays and accelerated depreciation, encouragement to urban unions and other policies leading to wage rates higher than the marginal productivity of labor, capital-intensive methods in such development projects as highways, overvalued currencies, and emphasis on urban rather than rural development.

Bela Balassa (1971) has examined the impact of tariff policies. To this policy set, one may add price controls that favor urban growth centers, encouraging capitalization according to the Fei and Ranis model (1964), and the manipulation of marketing boards, principally in Africa, to the detriment of poor farmers (Bauer, 1954).

Economists have paid little attention to the third type of obstacle: the personal qualities of the poor. To the extent that these have been studied at all, the task has been undertaken by anthropologists, sociologists, and social psychologists. Lewis (1961) developed the theory that the "culture of poverty," or mutual interactions among the poor, destroys their capacity to overcome degradation. Erasmus (1961) pointed to the experiential nature of learning by primitive peoples, which prevents them from acquiring second-hand knowledge. Foster (1967) developed the concept of the "limited good" (or "zero-sum game," as economists would call it), by which the poor apply social sanctions to those who succeed economically and who are believed to have "robbed" the others (see Stoller, in the present volume). Hackenberg (1973) showed how large size may benefit an individual family, while population growth endangers the affluence of all. McClelland (1961) wrote about the "need for achievement" as a factor in developing entrepreneurial ability. Inkeles and Smith (1974) defined "modern man" and attempted to show the forces that transform a person from traditional to modern.

Factors That "Produce" Equity

Let us consider that three factors "produce" income equity: economic structure, economic policies, and the personal qualities of the poor. These factors are not homogeneous (any more than land, labor, and capital are), and they are difficult to measure. Yet many of their component parts (e.g., land-tenure systems, exchange-rate overvaluation, belief in the limited good) can indeed be measured. It is possible to conceive of these factors as combining to cause greater (or less) equity in income distribution. Each pair would then have a marginal rate of substitution. If the cost of achieving different quantities of each factor could be calculated, there would be an elasticity of substitution as well. The question could then be approached as to whether it is possible to improve equity under the existing structure by changing policies, or whether a change in the personal characteristics of the poor might improve their position even under existing structure and existing policies. Complementarity would also become a point of argument: Does a certain structure lead to certain policies (as Marxists would contend)? Would certain changes in the personal characteristics of the poor bring about reinforcing policy changes, perhaps because policymakers would then find it more advantageous to incorporate the poor into their plans?

This way of thinking might open up avenues which advocates of the poor have not previously explored. For there are, indeed, many possibilities for the poor to improve their status *under existing structures and policies* (onerous though these may be).

I will concentrate on the most neglected of the "factors of production of equity"—the personal characteristics of the poor. This factor has been neglected by economists as being "outside economics." Others neglect it because it is not easily defined or measured—a shortcoming which does not, however, diminish its importance. Sensitivity is a third reason; nationals of LDCs in particular may not want to accept the idea that underdevelopment stems primarily from personal inadequacies and not from structures or policies, which may be more easily controlled.

At this point I will present a hypothesis only, along with a plea for further investigation. The hypothesis is that a society placing a high value on materialism (or the elimination of poverty) can share its material benefits only with those people who (a) adopt materialism (or avoidance of poverty) as a principal goal, (b) appreciate the necessity for certain policies, attitudes, and behavior patterns that are conducive to affluence, and (c) learn to put these policies, attitudes, and behavior patterns into practice. The patterns referred to are those of a society of increasing complexity, and they are generated after many years of experience. Just as a child attempts at his peril to walk without learning to crawl, a sudden jump from the primitive and traditional to the modern and complex may be a factor underlying the current malaise of unemployment, overpopulation, and dualism.

Each set of policies, attitudes, and behavior patterns is occupation specific, in that one set is appropriate for business managers, another for employed laborers, another for farmers, and so on. There will doubtless be common elements among them, however.

This hypothesis in no way disputes the contention that poverty is often primarily caused by an unjust economic structure or by unfortunate policies, nor should it be interpreted as an attempt to shift the "blame" from the elites to the poor. I do, however, suggest that it is easier for governing elites to adopt structures and policies that ignore the poor if the behavior patterns of the poor themselves make it difficult for the elites to incorporate them into a productive, materialist society. If this hypothesis proves correct, then decisions about intermediate technology and simple forms of organization should not be made on the basis of economic criteria alone. Rather, such decisions should take into account the development needs of social groups in transition.

Coping with Complexity

Inkeles and Smith (1974) defined "modern man" as one who is open to new experience, is ready for social change, is disposed to hold opinions on many issues, is interested in acquiring facts about those issues, is future oriented and accepts fixed schedules as desirable, believes he can control his environment, plans, relies on others to meet their obligations, values technical skills, possesses educational and occupational aspirations, is aware of the dignity of others, and understands how production occurs. On the basis of these criteria, and with the use of questionnaires, the authors rated individuals using an OM scale (actually, alternative OM scales) as an overall measure of modernity. They then tested the backgrounds of individuals with different OM ratings in order to determine associated factors. They concluded that schooling and factory experience are highly associated with modernity, but that the following factors are not: ethnic origin and religion, quality of schooling, relative modernity of factory worked in, and urban experience. Experience in a cooperative movement, however, contributed significantly to modernity.

I should like to add a slightly different tack to the general direction in which Inkeles and Smith appear to be heading. A high-production society is complex. To participate in it, and reap its benefits, one must understand its complexities. When Europe and North America developed during the century following the industrial revolution, they did so gradually. Each new complexity (in machinery, social organization, or whatever) was not so far advanced from the previous order that it could not be understood by large numbers of people. From household production to the putting-out system to the small factory were steps that were readily comprehensible, and therefore could be widely followed.

Today's dualism in the third world is, in part, a function of the rapidity with which modern technology and modern organization have been introduced. The jump from traditional to modern technology is so broad that only a few can make it. Those who can have been exposed—through education, travel, or profession—to the functioning of a modern society in other countries. As the modern sectors grow in their own countries, a few more people become introduced to modern complexities. But there is room for only a few.

As Inkeles and Smith have suggested, modernity—or the ability to understand complex societies, as I prefer to put it— is not easy to come by. Indeed, it can be very costly. Since the Inkeles-Smith definition is still subject to discussion (and since, even if it is accepted, the means of bringing about modernity are also controversial), obviously no one yet knows the cost of making one person modern—or how the cost function advances as numbers of modern persons are increased. The relative costs of relying on schools or factories (as alternative "factors" producing modernity), or on combinations of the two, have likewise not been worked out.

The most frightening prospect, however, is that, if the costs are eventually worked out, the venture may turn out to be uneconomic no matter what method is applied. No doubt there is already some intuitive grasp of the costs of converting traditional (mostly illiterate) people into participants in modern industrial complexes. It may well be that the *social* cost of doing this (which would include schooling) is greater than the cost of the machinery that would render such people unnecessary. If this is so—and no one yet knows whether it is so—there is indeed a conflict between maximization of output and income distribution.

The rapid increase in population makes it all the more likely that the social cost of modernizing people is too high. In country after country, large amounts of investment will obviously be necessary just to keep the per-capita amount of capital from declining. If the cost of modernizing people is added to this, it may well be that the economic calculus alone would call for marginalizing the new people—leaving them in rural areas or city slums and attending to them as well as possible—because incorporating them into the productive process would be too expensive, compared to alternative (modern) technologies.

In January 1976, I interviewed the management of an advisory service for small-scale businesses (hereinafter referred to as AS) in a heavily populated, though essentially rural, district in an African country. AS has approximately 300 clients, about 30 of whom are manufacturers and the rest retailers and wholesalers. All are family firms, very few having more than six or eight employees. After six years of operations, the AS management believes it is only now beginning to understand the motivations of its clients. Improvement in business practices was deemed very slow during these six years, with only one or two clients materially better off as a result of the relationship with AS. Optimism was expressed, however, because of a few promising events now unfolding.

Virtually every client looks upon his business as an adjunct to the family whose purpose is to provide a minimum of consumable income. The enterprise is not a source of capital, and the idea of expanding is a rarity. Most clients are illiterate and nonnumerate; they neither keep accounts nor see any need to do so. They do not distinguish personal assets from business cash or inventory; it is considered quite proper for the family to use cash in the till or stock on the shelves.

Most clients are engaged in several activities, some of them ventures (such as speculation in maize), others continuing businesses. Only a very few remain in business for more than six months; in the great majority of cases, an AS adviser will discuss the conduct of a business with its manager only to discover on his next visit that the manager has disappeared

and a new one has taken over. Rarely are the full costs of any
venture or merchandise known, especially in the case of
manufactures. Often the profits of one venture subsidize the
losses of another, and the owner does not know which one is
profitable. AS management cited a hotel which they believed
was running at a loss, but which was subsidized by the
owner's garden. (He could have earned more by closing the
hotel and selling the food from the garden in the market.)
Perhaps the hotel was a prestige item or provided social
satisfaction, but it was not good business.

Very few clients understand the rudiments of marketing—
how to decide which merchandise to sell and how to seek
customers. Few know how to fill out applications for bank
loans. Obtaining a loan is, however, a matter of prestige—an
end in itself. The proceeds of loans are often spent on
extrabusiness activities. Frequently, borrowing occurs with
the bona-fide intention to devote proceeds to business, but a
funeral will intervene, or the borrower will decide to buy a
car. Spur-of-the-moment decisions about how to spend
money are often made on the basis of the availability of
funds.

Hiring practices are usually unrelated to production. A
cousin in need of school fees for his son will work until the
fees are earned, then disappear. Thus, labor may be even
more temporary than management. The same is true of other
resources. Supply of inventory stock is not necessarily geared
to needs of production or sales, but may depend on when the
owner wants (for personal reasons) to make a trip to town to
buy it. The cost of overstocking is not appreciated. Nor do
most owners understand how much cash they need in the till.
Often a shop will be closed while the owner seeks change for
a customer—possibly losing two or three customers in the
meantime.

The concept of seeking customers through advertising is
usually not understood. Shops will open with the naive
belief that customers will materialize from somewhere; the
owner sits inside to await them. When they don't come, he
closes. Competition through quality is also rare. Few business people grasp that word-of-mouth information about
better services or higher-quality merchandise will bring
more business.

One AS client reached the verge of great success, then

failed. AS personnel (not the client) arranged to have his product displayed in tourist shops in the capital city. The product was a big hit, and from there it traveled to other tourist centers and even to specialty shops in foreign countries. The client, however, did not understand how this had happened, and doubtless he did not know what foreign cities were like nor how to cater to tourist preferences. He took inventory from his shelves for his personal use and for his friends and family, despite the fact that he did not own the factory outright but shared it with partners. He also took cash from the till, and invited his friends to make long-distance calls on his newly acquired telephone (still a novelty in the area). He did not pay his debts. A factory that showed promise of making its owners wealthy thus went bankrupt.

Since interviewing the AS management, I have been assembling a bibliography of materials on small businesses in developing countries. There are approximately 200 such items, many of them small tracts not readily available in American libraries. In virtually all of these, there is very little reference to small-scale rural retailers and producers. More material is available on how some of them advanced to become manufacturers, relying on credits from government-sponsored financial institutions.

J. J. Carroll (1965) studied ninety-two manufacturing firms in the Philippines in an attempt to discover what had impelled their owners into manufacturing. He found that 79 percent of them had been involved in other businesses first, two-thirds had fathers who were independent businessmen, and 14 percent had mothers in business. He concluded that most of these business owners understood the system of rewards associated with business ownership and responded to economic incentives. They were, in short, a stage ahead of the AS clients.

Marris and Somerset (1971) studied fifty-one small-scale businesses in Kenya which had received loans from the Industrial and Commercial Development Corporation, a government lending agency. He found the entrepreneurs complaining about lack of opportunities, with frustrations that led to driving ambitions. However, many were mistrustful and self-reliant, restricting their businesses to a size over which they could have complete control. Shopkeepers and craftsmen in rural markets were less ambitious, less experienced, and lacked self-confidence. All who succeeded described themselves as isolated from their communities of origin—a finding possibly supported by Foster's concept of the limited good. At the same time, they did not yet belong to the wider society of urban (and more sophisticated) business, a factor which increased their frustration.

Other studies are available, and other theories have been proposed, about how a local business person breaks out of the limitations of his original community—the best-known are perhaps by Hagen (1962) and McClelland (1961). So far, however, I have turned up little or no material that deals specifically with the problem mentioned by AS management: the producers who are constrained by their inability to cope with the complexities of a modern production and distribution system, and who therefore are unable to take advantage of its opportunities.

The belief that understanding complex socioeconomic systems is a gradual achievement is supported by the histories of shopkeepers and small producers of foreign origin, such as Chinese in Southeast Asia, Indians in East Africa, Lebanese in West Africa, and Portuguese and Italians in Argentina and Brazil. It is sometimes suggested that only the more ambitious people migrate; hence migration alone will predispose toward success. Perkins (1975) denies this allegation with respect to the Chinese, preferring to attribute success to "a prior accumulation of experience with complex organizations or institutions" (p. 3). Among this accumulated experience are more than two centuries of commercialization, premodern banks, commercial networks, civil-service examinations, and the high value placed upon education and literacy. Commercial development was already well advanced before the rash of foreign privileges brought China into contact with the Western world during the nineteenth century.

In contrast to that of China, the Indian experience appears closely tied to conquest by the British. Although many Indians rejected (or were indifferent to) Western ideas, nevertheless, by the turn of the nineteenth century, a large number were ready to adopt the English language and Western notions of utilitarianism, equality before the law, and private property. Although princely India remained traditional, such Western inventions as rail transportation, scientific irrigation, and the factory system were introduced into British India. By the time East Africa was colonized late in the nineteenth century, a large number of Indians had "grown up" with the effects of the industrial revolution; like the British themselves, they had been introduced to complex societies gradually. Naturally, these were the Indians whom the British took to Africa—to help build the Uganda railroad, to serve in the Queen's rifle corps, and to perform other tasks that the British themselves did not want to do. These Indian immigrants became the basis for commercial development in Kenya and Uganda.

We hardly need reminding of the many years of commercialization to which the Lebanese had been exposed, as major traders, bankers, and middlemen in their strategic location between the Mideast and Europe. Similar experiences befell the Portuguese, Germans, and Italians who migrated to South America. All these groups—Chinese, Indians, Lebanese, and Europeans—had been gradually introduced to complex societies over more than a century before they assumed their commercial dominance in Southeast Asia, East Africa, West Africa, and certain South American countries, respectively.

It seems, however, that something more than exposure to complex organization is needed for the initiation of modern industrial growth. Why were the Chinese still premodern in the early twentieth century? Why did not the Incas, the Aztecs, and the Mayas—whose civilizations were more complex and commercial than those, say, of the Chibchas or the Araucanians—develop into "modern" societies? I do not propose that "certain personal characteristics" are a sufficient explanation of growth, nor do I denigrate the factors of structure and policy, which I believe were all-important to the failures of the South and Central American Indians, the Chinese before 1949, or the (Asian) Indians. I share with Perkins, however, the belief that development and equitable distribution of income in Taiwan, South Korea, and the People's Republic of China have certain common origins, just cited, which were later ignited by the Chinese revolution, World War II, and American influence. Indeed, post-1949 Taiwan and the People's Republic show great similarities that are hard to explain in terms of the difference between capitalist and communist development.

Much more literature is available for small-scale farms than for small-scale businesses, and again I have not culled it all. In an investigation of agricultural credit in Nicaragua, Loehr (1971) discovered that after several years of participation in credit programs, many farmers had lower net worths than before. They had used their loan proceeds for consumption and, failing to increase production, had ended up with roughly the same assets as before, but they now were additionally burdened by the debt.

I have not found other studies demonstrating that the net worth of small-scale farmers actually *decreases* as a result of their use of agricultural credit. Nevertheless, several studies imply that this is so. There is evidence of the widespread failure of small-scale farmers to pay their debts (Nisbet, 1971; Williams and Miller, 1973; Tinnermeier et al., 1968; Bottomley, 1975). When farmers cannot pay their debts, they have most likely lost rather than gained by using credit.

In its *Spring Review of Small Farmer Credit* (AID, 1973), the Agency for International Development brought together a number of studies indicating that most credit programs for small farmers do not achieve their objectives, and that often the credit is lost. The principal reasons, AID concluded, were structure and policy related, in that markets, technology, and controlled prices in LDCs usually are not attractive to small-scale farmers; under favorable circumstances, farmers would respond to incentives and invest in new technologies. Farmers also wondered whether the institutions that loaned them money were going to last.

A study undertaken in Sri Lanka (Agrarian Research and Training Institute, 1974), on the other hand, uncovered attitudes among borrowing farmers reminiscent of those found by AS. Rural indebtedness, the study concluded, "is a major economic, social, and cultural problem." It found a "scale of sin" to be associated with different kinds of debt, in which nonrepayment of loans for consumption, pilgrimages, sickness, and marriage were considered very sinful; it was believed that such sins would be punished in the next incarnation. Loans for agricultural development, house construction, or capital-goods purchases were considered less sinful, however.

None of the studies that I have so far encountered recognizes, much less confronts, problems in farming analogous to those of the small-scale business cited in the interview with the management of AS. Surely small-scale farmers must need to know their costs just as much as small-scale business people need to know costs, and surely they have similar problems in selecting products, employing labor, and marketing. Possibly the entire system of small-scale farm production (including credit) and marketing is simpler than that of small-scale business, and perhaps therefore the constraints of structure (e.g., land tenure) and policy (e.g., price controls on inputs and products) weigh more heavily than cultural limitations. Despite the wealth of literature on agriculture in developing countries, this particular facet appears to have received inadequate attention.

In both small-scale business and small-scale farming, it would appear that cooperation is a useful vehicle for gaining experience in complex organization. AS launched a market cooperative in which approximately fifteen merchants in a rural market received joint credit and bought inputs cooperatively, in order to take advantage of discounts. The loan was, however, parceled out to individual participants. Peer pressure caused substantially greater performance of contract, including repayment of debt, than was found in AS experience with individual clients. All members were aware that if any participant failed, the scheme would be imperiled for all.

After examining the elements of success in Latin American peasant cooperation, T. F. Carroll (1971) concluded that factors of cohesion are neither spontaneous nor voluntary, but come about when they represent the only possibility of survival for the group. He found distrust and the concept of limited good to be cultural constraints, along with the structural constraints of inappropriate land-tenure arrangements. Group purchasing, he concluded, can be an opening wedge where cooperation meets distrust. Marketing and credit are other areas in which farmers can see advantage in cooperation. Group farming with individual land parcels has also worked. Nevertheless, Carroll expressed a pessimism which—as I read it—would support my contention that participation in complex organization comes about slowly, and cannot be achieved in a single generation.

Specification and Promotion of Practices

The business practices discovered by AS indicate (by contrast) the policies, attitudes, and behavior patterns required if the poor are to function successfully in a complex, materialist society. It is now necessary to specify those patterns precisely and to determine ways by which to promote their adoption. (I do this only for small-scale business persons, as an example. Other practices would need to be derived for persons of other occupations.)

Promotion might be accomplished either directly or indirectly: directly, through schooling, small-scale business advisory services, farm extension, on-the-job training, and the like; indirectly, through structural changes (such as agrarian reform) or policy changes (such as those mentioned above) aimed at stimulating labor-intensive technology or the output of traditional goods. (Creation of an opportunity is a prerequisite to someone's perceiving that opportunity.) If it is to be pursued rationally, so that direct and indirect methods will complement each other, the concept of "functioning in a complex society" needs to be understood and measured; the extent to which failure to so function is a constraint upon production needs to be known; and the cost effectiveness of different approaches needs to be determined.

Inkeles and Smith are on the right track in their identification of "modern man" and the way he behaves. Their concept, however, is not easily adapted to policy. Instead, I would prefer to identify discrete types of behavior with small-scale business persons, small-scale farmers, wage laborers, professionals, government functionaries, and as many other classifications as seem pertinent. Policies are more easily structured when they are behavior specific.

I prefer the term "functioning in a complex society" to "modern man." The usual opposite of "modern" is "traditional." A modern person is open to change, while a traditional one does what he has always done (Shils, 1971). It seems to me that the question is, rather, one of perceiving both the opportunities presented by complexity and the possible ways of taking advantage of them. Also, "functioning in a complex society" is a relative concept. A society itself is more or less complex, and an individual may be more or less aware of its opportunities.

I recognize the cultural bias of assuming that perception leads to acceptance. It is possible both to be aware and to reject. Still, it seems to me that more material wealth is wanted by a great many people, if only in order to escape abject poverty, and that their major constraint lies in lack of awareness of what must be done to achieve more wealth. I take issue with my Marxist friends who argue that the poor are powerless in a hostile structure, for my own observations in visiting small production centers disclose that there are many ways of increasing income under existing structures. The experience of AS alone confirms this conclusion.

Small-Scale Business Persons—An Example

AS has drawn up a list of business practices about which it advises small-scale business persons (SBPs). Its advisers record progress (or lack of it) on the basis of monthly or quarterly visits to clients. These practices are related to the degree of complexity of the economic environment, which is no longer confined to the household production/village market stage. New modes of communication and transport, family remittances from men who have migrated to the city, and similar developments open up possibilities for expanding to new lines, which in turn requires new production and marketing methods. SBPs able to perceive these implications are, presumably, the ones willing to adopt the necessary procedures (which I have adapted, below, from the AS list). Let us postulate that a SBP who is aware of the opportunities provided by the current stage of complexity of his society (the one in which AS operates) will do the following:

- keep a cash change fund;
- record cash receipts, disbursements, and balances;
- adopt inventory-control procedures and keep stock purchase records;
- keep a debtors' ledger and a creditors' ledger;
- open a bank account;
- undertake security measures;
- keep his premises neat and organized and his stock properly displayed;

- price-mark his inventory displays;
- keep stock records and know the optimum stock (and how to determine it) as well as appropriate turnover;
- use advertising and sales promotion;
- develop a system for measuring manufacturing costs;
- introduce new products;
- prepare a profit-and-loss statement and balance sheet;
- keep a budget;
- institute a customer follow-up system;
- use quality-control procedures;
- pay attention to customer relations; and
- use consultant services as required.

If we have selected the proper practices, the extent to which those practices are adopted can be deemed to be the degree to which that SBP functions well in a society of the degree of complexity found in his environment.

Another set of practices might be drawn up for laborers, measuring such items as willingness to arrive at and leave work on time and job tenure. Another set would be appropriate for small-scale farmers, and so on. Research needs to be performed to determine whether there is indeed a high coefficient of regression of adoption of these practices (or clusters of them) upon the rate of return of SBPs.

When I discussed this idea with the AS management, they raised the question of whether a high rate of return was the principal objective of most of their clients. Community prestige seemed to rank at least as high (as I mentioned earlier, approval for a loan was in itself a matter of prestige). Furthermore, a society may become more complex, not only in the ways material goods are produced and exchanged, but also in the ways in which prestige is obtained. If this is so, a different behavioral set might evidence perceptions of the opportunities in a complex society.

I therefore amend my definition so as to express my concern only for a *producing and exchanging* society, which with increasing complexity offers more opportunities for material reward. We are concerned with material poverty, not lack of prestige; hence the ability of a SBP to earn profits ought to be related to his behavioral set, as a measure of his understanding of the opportunities available in his society. Likewise, the ability of a worker to keep a job and earn

higher pay would reflect his understanding of social opportunities, and the same, *mutatis mutandis,* for other actors.

The task of determining how much profit has been earned
by an illiterate and nonnumerate SBP, or how much investment he has made, is hindered by enormous obstacles: to do
so, it is necessary to reconstruct a balance sheet and a profit-
and-loss statement. The matter at first seemed easy. As I
walked around the shops and factories of AS clients, I
thought I could jot down their balance sheets just by looking
and asking a few questions. However, the amounts of debts
(receivable and payable) and cash are crucial, and these are
not always known even by the owner himself. To the extent
that he does know these totals, he will not reveal them to a
stranger—even one from his own tribe. The multiplicity of
ventures undertaken simultaneously by many business
owners makes an allocation of accounts difficult. Through
patient cultivation of friendships as well as some heroic
suppositions, AS has been able to compile much information. The prospects for further research into other situations,
where similar advisory services do not exist, are, however,
bleak.

Policy Capture

Let us suppose that the relationship between behavioral
practices and rates of return can be established. What next? It
is then necessary to determine what forces underlie the
policies of SBPs. What causes a SBP to adopt a certain
practice? Policy is defined as the weighted set of reasons
which would lead the SBP to adopt (or intensify his adoption of) a particular business practice. Let us assume a
sample of n SBPs, of which we are investigating the ith ($i = 1$
... n). Assume a set of m business practices similar to the
ones listed previously (in that list, $m = 18$); let X_{ij} be the
degree to which the ith SBP adopts the jth practice. If X_{ij} can
be adopted "more or less," there will be certain reasons
causing SBP_i to adopt it "more," and these reasons themselves might be expressed in "more" or "less." Let us refer to
these reasons as *cues* to the behavior of SBPs: we label them
W_h ($h = 1 ... k$). W_{jh} refers to the hth cue which might lead to
the adoption of the jth business practice. We then postulate

the following relationship:

$$X_{ij} = a + \sum_h b_h W_{jh}.$$

This says that the extent to which the ith SBP will adopt the jth practice depends on the set of cues W_{jh}, j being fixed for each equation.

The policy functions of each SBP^i with respect to each X_{ij} could be obtained in various ways. The most direct way would be through a questionnaire (probably verbal) in which each SBP would be asked which cues influence him. There would be enormous difficulties in doing this. AS has already discovered that subjects are mistrustful and that months of patient cultivation are necessary in order to gain their confidence. Any operation out of the ordinary, or whose immediate usefulness is not perceived, is looked upon with caution, and the true answers may not be given. Tentatively, another method is suggested: the Hammond policy-capture tests (Hammond, 1975). This method is based on the assumption that the SBP either does not know or will not express his policy in the form of an equation. This "inability to express" has nothing to do with whether or not he is literate. In other applications, Hammond tests have been successful in capturing policies which even the most sophisticated subjects were unable to express independently. The supposition is that the subject knows how to *apply* his policy, even though he cannot express it. He is therefore presented with several hypothetical situations—how much of X_{ij} would he adopt, given a certain set of cues and weights (which are then explained)? Thus, by such statistical means as regressions, his policy is derived.

The most common method of presenting hypothetical situations is through bar diagrams, which can be viewed either on a computer-related television screen or on cards. Let us take a hypothetical X_j: Suppose X_3 = the degree to which an SBP will adopt a system of inventory control. This can be measured in varying ways, from the simple counting of inventory from time to time (low value for X_3) on to comparing actual inventory at a given time with expected inventory (materials bought minus those used—medium value for X_3) up to the extreme of a complete cost-accounting and internal-control system of the sort adopted in the most modern factories (highest value for X_3). Suppose that, after an exhaustive questioning of knowledgeable persons (the SBPs themselves, the staff of AS, other residents of the area), it is agreed that the following set of cues, W_3, influences the degree to which *any* SBP will adopt X_3:

Typical reply	*Implied cue*
A SBP should use inventory controls if . . .	
. . . he has a large inventory.	W_{31} = size of inventory
. . . he doesn't trust his employees.	W_{32} = trust for employees
. . . he is interested in minimizing his costs.	W_{33} = degree of interest in cutting costs
But he should not use them if . . .	
. . . by so doing he would offend his employees (whom he ought to trust).	W_{34} = degree of offense felt by employees

More cues may be selected. Theoretically, any number is possible. The total number depends on a balance between (a) more cues being more explanatory and (b) more cues muddying the reliability of the results (i.e., loss of degrees of freedom). Probably the investigator would select no more than five or six cues which are agreed upon as being generally the most influential.

The test is then run as follows: Fifty hypothetical situations are determined, in which the cues are given various values (weights) ranging from "very little" to "very much." These values are expressed by the length of the bars in fifty different diagrams, all similar to the one presented in Figure 1. Values are assigned randomly to the cues, except that adjustment is made so that no two cues are correlated closely with each other. (If they are, the result is as if they were the same cue.)

If the test were to be run in Colorado, a television screen might be used to flash the fifty hypothetical situations. The viewer (judge) would rate the degree (from 1 to 20) to which he would adopt inventory controls (X_3) in every situation. As he punched his judgments into the computer terminal, the

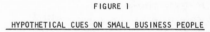

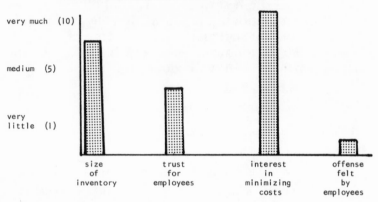

computer would immediately calculate his policy function as well as his multiple R^2 (his degree of consistency, or his ratio of explained-to-total variation from the mean). If the test were being administered elsewhere in the U.S. or in Europe, the bar diagrams could be typed out automatically by a portable terminal connected to the computer by telephone. For clients of AS, the tests would probably be given by interview and the results later fed into the computer.

Table 1 shows the results of a simulated test in which hypothetical SBPs gave their individual judgments of thirty hypothetical situations in which cues $W_{31} \ldots W_{34}$ were relied upon for determining the extent of inventory control (X_{i3}). The following symbols were used:

INVENTORY = size of inventory,
TRUST = the degree of trust expressed by each SBP in his workers,
COST/MIN = the degree to which the SBP was interested in minimizing costs,
OFFENSE = how offended the SBP believed his employees would feel if inventory controls were instituted.

The computer generated thirty cases randomly. In each case, each cue was weighted by a number of Xs from 1 to 10, 1 indicating "very low" and 10 indicating "very high." For example, the first case represented the following situation:

TABLE 1

SAMPLE COMPUTER PRINT-OUTS
FOR POLICY-CAPTURE TESTING

CASE 1

```
INVENTORY      ..........
TRUST          XXXX
COST/MIN       XXXXXXXXX
OFFENSE        XXXXXXXXX
               X
               ..........
JUDGE: 1
? 10
JUDGE: 2
? 15
```

CASE 2

```
INVENTORY      ..........
TRUST          XXXXXXXXXX
COST/MIN       XXXXXXXX
OFFENSE        XXXXXXXXXX
               XXX
               ..........
JUDGE: 1
? 9
JUDGE: 2
? 20
```

CASE 3

```
INVENTORY      ..........
TRUST          XX
COST/MIN       XXXXXXXXX
OFFENSE        XXXXXXXXXX
               XXXX
               ..........
JUDGE: 1
? 10
JUDGE: 2
? 16
```

CASE 4

```
INVENTORY      ..........
TRUST          XXXXXXXXX
COST/MIN       XXXX
OFFENSE        XXXX
               XXXXXXX
               ..........
JUDGE: 1
? 12
JUDGE: 2
? 10
```

The firm had a moderate sized inventory (4). The owner expressed great trust in his employees (9). If he decided to institute inventory controls, he expected his employees to feel little or no offense (1).

The two SBPs (referred to as Judge 1 and Judge 2) responded to this situation as follows: Judge 1 declared 10; he would enforce inventory controls about "half way" (the scale being 1 to 20, inclusive). Judge 2, on the other hand, would enforce inventory controls frequently (15). Only the first four cases are presented in Table 1. Similar computer printouts were generated for cases 5 to 30 inclusive.

By following the remaining thirty cases, it is possible to determine the cues on which the two judges relied most as well as the extent (coefficients) of their reliance, whether it was linear or nonlinear, and how consistent were their responses (i.e., how closely one would rate two similar situations, seeing them at two different times). Consistency is measured by the multiple R^2.

After examining the scores, the computer made the following analysis of the two judges: Judge 1 was a "humanist," who was primarily concerned with how his employees would behave as a result of his instituting inventory controls. If the situation were such that he trusted them, he would not need to install the controls. If he believed his employees would be greatly offended, he likewise would not install them. He paid no attention to the other two cues.

Judge 2, on the other hand, was a "pure businessman." He paid no attention to his trust for his employees, or to how offended he expected them to feel. Rather, he would institute controls if his inventory were large (the larger the inventory, the more need to control it) and if he wanted to minimize his costs (inventory control is a way of minimizing costs).

In Table 2, AAAA refers to Judge 1 and BBBB to Judge 2. Judge 1 gave zero weight to inventory size, Judge 2 gave it a weight of .36, and so on. POSLIN means that the function was positive linear, and NEGLIN that it was negative linear. The computer would also have picked up a nonlinear function had such been the result (e.g., where a judge would install inventory controls if he had either little or much trust in his employees, but would not do so if he had a moderate amount of trust). Nonlinear results would not make much sense in the present analysis, however.

TABLE 2

COMPUTER PRINT-OUT OF RELATIVE WEIGHTS IN POLICY-CAPTURE TESTS

A: JUDGE: 1
B: JUDGE: 2

0.0 -----------0.5------------1.0

		WEIGHT	FUNCT FORM
INVENTORY			
A		0.00	POSLIN
B	BBBBBBBBBBBBB	.36	POSLIN
TRUST			
A	AAAAAAAAAAAAAAAAAAAAAAAAAAA	.69	NEGLIN
B		0.00	POSLIN
COST/MIN			
A		0.00	POSLIN
B	BBBBBBBBBBBBBBBBBBBBBBB	.64	POSLIN
OFFENSE			
A	AAAAAAAAAAAAA	.31	NEGLIN
B		0.00	POSLIN

0.00------------0.5------------1.0

TABLE 3

COMPUTER PRINT-OUT OF JUDGMENTS IN POLICY-CAPTURE TESTS

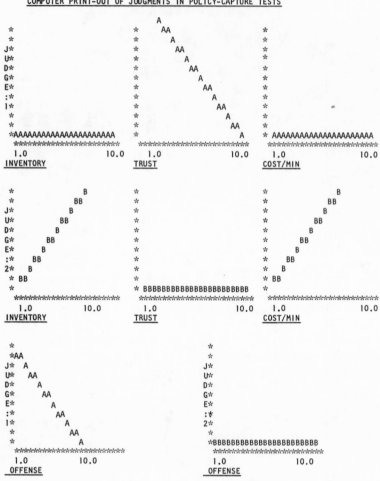

```
                              A
  *                    *    AA                        *
  *                    *     A                        *
 J*                    *      AA                       *
 U*                    *       A                       ✫
 D*                    *        AA                     *
 G*                    *         A                     *
 E*                    *          AA                   *
 :*                    *           A                   *
 1*                    *            AA                 *
  *                    *             A                 *
  *                    *              AA               ✫
 *AAAAAAAAAAAAAAAAAAAAAAA   *         A          * AAAAAAAAAAAAAAAAAAAAAAA
 ✫✫✫✫✫✫✫✫✫✫✫✫✫✫✫✫✫✫✫✫✫     ✫✫✫✫✫✫✫✫✫✫✫✫✫✫✫✫✫✫✫✫✫     ✫✫✫✫✫✫✫✫✫✫✫✫✫✫✫✫✫✫✫✫✫
  1.0               10.0    1.0               10.0    1.0               10.0
 INVENTORY                 TRUST                      COST/MIN


  *            B          *                          *              B
  *            BB         *                          *              BB
 J*          B            *                          *             B
 U*          BB           *                          *            BB
 D*         B             *                          *           B
 G*        BB             *                          *          BB
 E*        B              *                          *         B
 :*       BB              *                          *        BB
 2*      B                *                          *       B
  *     BB                *                          * BB
  *                       * BBBBBBBBBBBBBBBBBBBBBBBB  *
 ✫✫✫✫✫✫✫✫✫✫✫✫✫✫✫✫✫✫✫✫✫     ✫✫✫✫✫✫✫✫✫✫✫✫✫✫✫✫✫✫✫✫✫     ✫✫✫✫✫✫✫✫✫✫✫✫✫✫✫✫✫✫✫✫✫
  1.0               10.0    1.0               10.0    1.0               10.0
 INVENTORY                 TRUST                      COST/MIN


  *                                                  *
 *AA                                                 ✫
 J*   A                                             J*
 U*    AA                                           U*
 D*      A                                          D*
 G*       AA                                        G*
 E*         A                                       E*
 :*          AA                                     :✫
 1*            A                                    2*
  *             AA                                   ✫
  *               A                                 *BBBBBBBBBBBBBBBBBBBBBBBB
 ✫✫✫✫✫✫✫✫✫✫✫✫✫✫✫✫✫✫✫✫✫                              ✫✫✫✫✫✫✫✫✫✫✫✫✫✫✫✫✫✫✫✫✫
  1.0               10.0                             1.0               10.0
 OFFENSE                                             OFFENSE
```

Finally, the computer typed out the functions generated by the scores of each judge (see Table 3). Once again, AAAA refers to a function for Judge 1 and BBBB to a function for Judge 2. Where AAAA and BBBB are horizontal, they indicate that no attention was paid to this cue. The coefficient of consistency (multiple R^2) showed .88 for Judge 1 and .93 for Judge 2. Each judge was therefore highly consistent in his scores, Judge 2 a little more so that Judge 1.

Illiterate SBPs, of course, are not familiar with bar diagrams. Therefore, the Hammond tests might fail to capture their policies adequately. If this is believed to be the case, the investigator might describe each situation verbally, looking at the bar diagram himself but not necessarily showing it to the respondent, or he might show it to the respondent, in conjunction with a verbal explanation.

Cost Effectiveness

We return to an earlier comment: Planners and policy-makers in LDCs may believe, intuitively, that the social costs of orienting SBPs, small-scale farmers, laborers, and others to successful functioning in a complex economy are so great that it is more economic to concentrate on "modern" methods that do not require widespread participation of the poor. But how can we know whether this is so? Better yet, how can we know the cost effectiveness of different methods of approach?

The problem is outlined in Figure 2. By "economic efficiency," we mean maximum output from a given quantity of national resources. There are two separate routes for achieving this (the capital-intensive on the right, and the labor-intensive on the left). It is often believed that LDCs tend to adopt the right-hand route as a result of mistaken or irrational policies, or because the social structure (e.g., land tenure) is politically difficult to change, or because if the social structure is not changed, ruling classes benefit at the expense of the poor. I suggest, instead, that the social costs of using the left-hand method may be so great that less output will be achieved with given resources; hence, a lower degree of efficiency will be the result.

As is shown in the diagram, structural changes (e.g.,

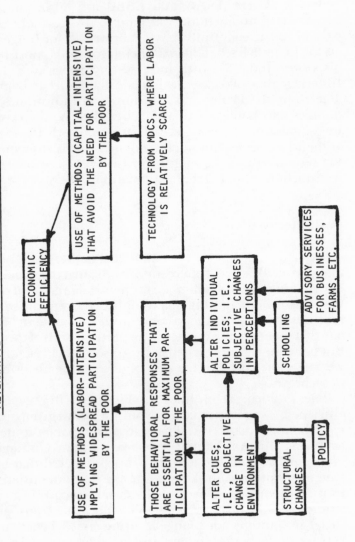

FIGURE 2

ALTERNATIVE ROUTES TO ECONOMIC EFFICIENCY

agrarian reform) and policy changes (e.g., withdrawal of investment incentives) would objectively change the environment in which the poor operate. These changes might in themselves (1) alter an individual's policy (see sideways arrow) or (2), because the objective values or the cues have been changed, affect his behavioral response. On the other hand, schooling and advisory services (such as AS) may alter the weights (b-coefficients) that individuals assign to cues, and thus change behavioral responses even if the objective values of the cues themselves are unchanged. Considering that any one of these routes has costs (political opposition to changes in structure and policy, the economic costs of schooling and advisory services), the question is how to achieve maximum change in behavioral response at minimum cost. Even if this could be calculated, it may turn out that the social cost of goods and services produced may be minimized by using the right-hand route. If that is so, society would have to make a choice between economic growth, on the one hand, and social development and equitable income distribution, on the other.

Further studies need to be done in order to determine (a) whether the practices rated by AS are indeed associated with a greater rate of return on investment, (b) what cues influence whether or not a SBP will adopt particular practices, and (c) how AS goes about suggesting that its client SBPs change their policies, and how successful its methods are. Efficiency in achieving appropriate policy changes, measured against the cost of operating a service such as AS, would determine the cost effectiveness of this method of altering the behavior patterns of SBPs. If this cost were extrapolated to cover the institution of small-business advisory service throughout a given country, and if the resulting increase in income could be projected, one might obtain some crude estimate of the cost of incorporating this section of the poor into the productive economy—a cost which could then be compared with that of an alternative method, such as "modern," capital-intensive technology.

References

Adelman, I., and C. T. Morris (1973). *Economic Growth and Social Equity.* Stanford, Calif.: Stanford University Press.

Agarwal, N. L., and R. K. Kumawat (1974). "Green Revolution and Capital and Credit Requirements of the Farmers in Semi-arid Region of Rajasthan." *Indian Journal of Agricultural Economics* 29, no. 1.

Agency for International Development (AID) (1973). *Spring Review of Small Farmer Credit.* Washington: U.S. Department of State.

Agrarian Research and Training Institute (1974). *Socio-Economic Factors in Rural Indebtedness.* Colombo, Sri Lanka, Occasional publication series, no. 7.

Ames, G. C. W. (1975). "Who Benefits from Credit and Who Repays?" University of Wisconsin *Land Tenure Newsletter,* January/March 1975.

Balassa, B. A. (1971). *The Structure of Protection in Developing Countries.* Baltimore: Johns Hopkins Press.

Barraclough, S. (1973). *Agrarian Structure in Latin America.* Lexington, Mass.: Lexington Books (D. C. Heath).

Bauer, P. T. (1972). "The Operation and Consequences of the State Export Monopolies of West Africa." *Journal of the Royal Statistical Society,* part 1 (1954), reprinted in Bauer. *Dissent on Development.* Cambridge, Mass.: Harvard University Press.

Bosa, G. R. (1969). "The Financing of Small-Scale Enterprise in Uganda." Makerere Institute of Social Research, Makerere University, Kampala, Uganda.

Bottomley, A. (1975). "Interest Rate Determination in Underdeveloped Rural Areas." *American Journal of Agricultural Economics,* May 1975.

Carroll, J. J. (1965). *The Filipino Manufacturing Entrepreneur.* Ithaca, N.Y.: Cornell University Press.

Carroll, T. F. (1971). "Peasant Cooperation in Latin America," in Worsley, P. M., ed. *Two Blades of Grass.* Manchester: Manchester University Press.

Chenery, H., et al. (1974). *Redistribution with Growth.* London: Oxford University Press.

Crosson, P. R. (1970). *Agricultural Development and Pro-*

ductivity: Lessons from the Chilean Experience. Baltimore: Johns Hopkins Press.

Datt, R., and K. P. M. Sundharam (1971). "The Green Revolution," in Chen, K., and J. S. Uppal. *Comparative Development of India and China.* New York: Free Press.

Eramus, C. J. (1961). *Man Takes Control.* Minneapolis: University of Minnesota Press.

Fei, J. C. H., and G. Ranis (1964). *Development of the Labor Surplus Economy: Theory and Policy.* New Haven: Yale University Press.

Foster, G. M. (1967). *Tzintzuntzan: Mexican Peasants in a Changing World.* Boston: Little, Brown and Co.

Frankel, F. R. (1971). *India's Green Revolution: Economic Gains and Political Costs.* Princeton, N.J.: Princeton University Press.

Ghosal, S. N. (1973). "Farm Financing by Commercial Banks: A Strategy." *Prajnan* 2, no. 4 (October/December 1973).

Hackenberg, R. A. (1973). "A Developing City in a Dual Economy." Davao Action Information Center, Davao, Philippines.

Hagen, E. (1962). *On the Theory of Social Change: How Economic Growth Begins.* Homewood, Ill.: Dorsey Press.

Hammond, K. R., et al. (1975). "Social Judgment Theory," in Kaplan, M. and S. Schwartz, eds. *Human Judgment and Decision Policy.* New York: Academic Press.

Hoselitz, B. F. (1968). *The Role of Small Industry in the Process of Economic Growth.* The Hague and Paris: Mouton.

Hunter, G. and A. F. Bottrall (1974). *Serving the Small Farmer: Policy Choices in Indian Agriculture.* London: Croom Helm.

Inkeles, A., and D. H. Smith (1974). *Becoming Modern.* Cambridge, Mass.: Harvard University Press.

Jodha, N. S. (1971). "Land-based Credit Policies and Investment Prospects for Small Farmers." *Review of Agriculture,* September 1971.

Lele, U. (1972). "Role of Credit and Marketing Functions in Agricultural Development." International Conference on Agriculture in the Development of Low-Income Countries, Bad Godesberg, Germany (mimeographed).

Lewis, O. (1961). *The Children of Sanchez: Autobiography of a Mexican Family.* New York: Random House.

Loehr, W. J. (1971). "Toward a Comprehensive Evaluation of Development Institutions: The Institutional Effectiveness of the Nicaraguan Rural Credit Program." Ph.D. thesis, University of Colorado.

Marris, P. and A. Somerset (1972). *The African Entrepreneur: A Study of Entrepreneurship and Development in Kenya.* New York: African Publishing Corp.

McClelland, D. (1961). *The Achieving Society.* Princeton, N.J.: Van Nostrand.

Nelson, R. R., T. P. Schultz, and R. L. Slighton (1971). *Structural Change in a Developing Economy: Colombia's Problems and Prospects.* Princeton, N.J.: Princeton University Press.

Nisbet, C. R. (1971). "Money-Lending in Rural Areas in Latin America." *American Journal of Economics and Sociology* 30, no. 1.

Perkins, D., ed. (1975). *China's Modern Economy in Historical Perspective.* Stanford, Calif.: Stanford University Press.

Powelson, J. P. (1975). "Population Growth and Unemployment in Africa." *Cultures et Développement* 7, no. 1.

Shetty, M. C. (1963). *Small-Scale and Household Industries in a Developing Economy.* New York: Asia Publishing House.

Shils, E. (1971). "Tradition." *Comparative Studies in Society and History* 13.

Society for Social and Economic Studies (1959). *Capital for Medium and Small-Scale Industries.* New York: Asia Publishing House.

Tinnermeier, R., et al. (1968). "An Evaluation of Selected Supervised Agricultural Credit Programs in Peru." North Carolina State University agricultural mission, Lima, Peru.

United Nations (1970). "Small-Scale Industries in Arab Countries in the Middle East." Report of a group meeting held in Beirut, Lebanon, November 1968.

Williams, S. and J. A. Miller (1973). "Credit Systems for Small Farmers: Case Histories from Mexico." Bureau of

Economic Research, Graduate School of Business, University of Texas, *Studies in Latin American Business,* no. 14.

7. A Review and Critique of Foster's "Image of Limited Good"

Irene Philip Stoller

In 1965 George Foster published his article "Peasant Society and the Image of Limited Good," which brought together several themes important in Foster's earlier work—themes dealing with the nature of peasant personality, world view, and economic organization. He used data from his own field experiences in Tzintzuntzan, Mexico, in addition to that gathered by such other anthropologists working in peasant communities as Banfield (1958), Dube (1958), and Lewis (1951), to construct a model of peasant cognitive orientation which he felt would be useful to explain what he saw as peasant resistance to opportunities for economic development.

The concept has been controversial since the article first appeared. A number of anthropologists have found it useful; others have attacked it on numerous occasions. Through time Foster seems to have modified his position somewhat in response to criticism, but he has basically stood by his model. His critics have attacked, among other things, the logical procedures used to develop the model, the data used to support it, and its general usefulness as an explanatory device. On the other hand, his supporters have found the model useful to explain the apparent inability of some communities to develop economically.

In this chapter I will review the "image of limited good," discuss some of the criticisms directed at it, and offer some of my own ideas about a model adequate to help us understand the factors influencing people to take advantage of opportunities for economic development.

According to Foster's model (reprinted in Potter, Diaz, & Foster, 1967, p. 300), members of a society share a cognitive orientation which provides them with a means to structure their perception of the universe and establish norms for behavior. This cognitive orientation is both unconscious and psychologically real to members of the society. Because this cognitive orientation provides guidelines for behavior, behavior that follows from the cognitive orientation is rational for members of the group; thus all normative behavior is rational when one understands the cognitive orientation underlying it. According to this model, it is possible that behavior which is rational according to a particular cognitive orientation may be out of tune with changes in actual economic situations in a community. Problems in economic development may arise from behavior conditioned by a particular cognitive orientation rather than from irrational rejection of economic opportunities.

Foster was particularly interested in the relationship between economic reality and its perception by what Kroeber called classic peasant societies: ". . . a class segment of a larger population which usually contains also urban centers. . . . They constitute part-societies with part-cultures" (Kroeber, 1948, p. 284). The important part of the definition deals, not with the particular occupations of members of peasant communities, but with the community's position as part of a larger society.

The phrase "image of limited good" was coined as the descriptive and explanatory device which underlies peasant cognitive orientation. It is used to mean

> that broad areas of peasant behavior are patterned in such fashion as to suggest that peasants view their social, economic, and natural universes—their total environment—as one in which all the desired things in life such as land, wealth, health, friendship and love, manliness and honor, respect and status, power and influence, security and safety, exist in finite quantity and are always in short supply, as far as the peasant is concerned. Not only do these and all other "good things" exist in finite and limited quantities, but in addition there is no way directly within peasant power to increase the available quantities . . . there is a primary

corollary to the Image of Limited Good: if "Good"
exists in limited amounts which cannot be expanded,
and if the system is closed, it follows that an individual
or a family can improve a position only at the expense of
others (Foster, 1965, pp. 304–305).

According to this image, peasants perceive that noneconomic goods as well as economic goods exist in limited
supply. Because the model presupposes that peasants see
their system as closed, the corollary to the idea that an
individual or family can improve its position only at someone else's expense is the idea that if someone has improved
his position, it must have been done at someone else's
expense.

When the model was "fed back" to the data which Foster
had collected in Tzintzuntzan, he felt that it pointed out
structural regularities in peasant behavior in Tzintzuntzan
and elsewhere which extended the image of limited good
beyond the economic sphere into social interaction, health
beliefs, and folklore. Evidence was cited from four areas to
back this up—economic beliefs and behavior, and beliefs
about friendship, health, manliness, and honor. In his
discussion, Foster suggested but did not actually state that
the reality of peasant economies is such that perceptions of
economic reality are extended into other spheres of behavior.
This would mean that the concept of limited good in
noneconomic areas is an outgrowth of the reality of limited
good in the economy.

These beliefs about the nature of the peasant universe lead
to mechanisms for maintaining the stability of the system, so
as to ensure that people will not be tempted to advance
beyond the economic position of their fellows in the community. Thus, wealthier people conceal their wealth, or
become subject to formal sanctions or such informal sanctions as gossip and ridicule, or are compelled to participate
in such institutionalized systems of redistribution as con-
signing great sums of money to ritual expenditures (e.g., the
cargo system in Latin America). These sanctions make it
difficult for people to participate when opportunities for
economic mobility do become available to them. Some
authors, such as Cancian (1965), have questioned whether
the cargo system in some Latin American communities

actually redistributes wealth to as great a degree as that implied by Foster or, whether, instead, it actually maintains inequalities.

While he treated peasant economic and social systems as closed systems, Foster was aware that peasant economies—because they are, by definition, parts of larger systems—are not truly closed. By 1960 half the men in Tzintzuntzan had worked as braceros in the United States, and Foster believed that the termination of that program in 1964 had had an adverse social and economic effect on the community because it closed out a major source of income (1967, p. 29). Unfortunately, in that study the effect of the braceros was not considered in any detail; money earned outside the community was treated as a lucky break rather than an economic option (1965, pp. 315–316). This is an inadequate explanation of a crucial issue. One cannot help but wonder what the specific effect of migration was on both those who migrated and those who did not.

According to this model, peasant economies are not stagnant because people lack the drive to achieve, as in McClelland's discussion of a need for achievement (1961). Rather, the need for achievement has remained latent because the lack of economic opportunity has led to the development of an image of limited good which blocks further economic development even when opportunities do become available. Efforts at economic development must be directed toward increasing economic opportunity rather than toward changing peasant cognitive orientations, because lack of economic opportunity is at the base of the image. In other words, Foster believed that peasant resistance to economic development is a rational response based on a cognitive orientation that is an outgrowth of actual economic conditions. This cognitive orientation, he explained, led to the development of informal and formal institutions designed to maintain the system—because Foster saw cultural forms as basically conservative rather than as continually adaptive to changing conditions. Eventually, he concluded, peasant cognitive orientation would change and the peasant would be able to take advantage of economic opportunities.

Foster's paper had not been out long before others began to criticize it. Kaplan and Saler faulted Foster on logical grounds—for using inductive methods to derive theory from a collection of particular facts. They also criticized his use of certain examples as the data base for his argument and subsequently using the model to explain the same data; thus, peasant beliefs about the limited availability of love are used both to formulate the concept and to prove it. They questioned whether one can even talk about the meaning of unlimited quantities of love or honor (Kaplan and Saler, 1966, p. 203). (At this point it might be useful to remember that the jealousy which older siblings feel for newborns— and which Foster used as an example of the extension of the image of limited good into the noneconomic sphere—is not necessarily an expression of their belief that they are being deprived of love, but may instead be an expression of their dismay that their mother's attention, a clearly finite quantity, must now be divided.) Kaplan and Saler further pointed out that Foster did not specify exactly what his model did explain, and that the model was therefore difficult to test—a criticism I will return to again later (Kaplan and Saler, 1966, p. 205).

In the reply to Kaplan and Saler, Foster continued his attempt to consider both cognitive and economic factors without being aware of the circular nature of his combination of the two ideas:

> I see behavior as being a function, in large measure, of a cognitive orientation. . . . If the economic conditions which traditionally have prevailed in peasant communities and which are closely associated with inhibiting forms are changed . . . and if the cognitive view of peasants changes away from the Limited Good orientation . . . then the social forms that constitute negative sanctions will decrease in intensity and in some instances wither away completely (Foster, 1966, p. 214).

Because his is basically a static model, it is difficult to understand how the cognitive orientation would change.

Bennett (1966) criticized Foster's model for its lack of understanding of the realities of agrarian economies, all of which have a tendency to display the zero-sum game behavior described for peasant communities. Bennett attributes this behavior, not to a cognitive orientation peculiar to peasants, but to the difficulty farmers have in controlling either their costs of production or the prices of their products. Because of the specific problems associated with farming, Bennett argued, one must be careful to distinguish between economic and cultural factors. Behavior discussed in the model cannot be understood without considering both these specific economic conditions and the exploitation of peasant communities in economically underdeveloped regions.

Kennedy (1966) saw the peasants' perception that economic good is limited as being no more than the restatement of an economic truism—that goods exist in limited supply and that there is competition for those goods. On the basis of data collected both from his own research and from research conducted by others, Kennedy also questioned the assumption that homogeneity and individualism are traits that exist in all peasant communities. He was also critical of Foster's lack of historical perspective, coupled with his assumption that peasant systems are closed systems.

The last two points—that the model does not consider historical perspective and that it treats peasant systems as closed systems—are particularly telling. Granted that Foster recognized the latter assumption as being contrary to reality, it is still difficult to construct an adequate model if one of the crucial facts of the system is treated as though it were its opposite. Foster's definition of peasants included, as a crucial component, the relationship between the peasant community and the larger society; yet this fundamental characteristic of the social organization of peasant communities was ignored in constructing a model to explain peasant behavior.

Acheson (1972) took a rather different tack. He was interested in the factors which enable individuals to take advantage of economic opportunities and in what sorts of economic opportunities were available to people in another community in the same region of Mexico as Tzintzuntzan. Cuanajo, the community which Acheson studied, had few opportunities available for earning income which were not already being fully exploited. The only businesses open to most members of the community were the operation of mechanized carpentry shops and the sale of furniture produced by the carpenters. There are several prerequisites to opening a mechanized carpentry shop—skill in carpentry and access to electricity, capital, or a partner who has these. Most of those individuals who did not enter carpentry lacked the necessary prerequisites; the remaining people who did not respond to the available opportunity were those who already possessed high prestige in the community or who were heavily involved in local politics. Acheson saw economic factors, rather than social or cultural factors, as the major impediments to economic growth. His particular focus helps illuminate the differences that allow some members of a community to take advantage of economic opportunities while other people are inhibited from taking advantage of the same opportunities. It is an attempt to understand the forces for development as well as the forces that inhibit development (Acheson, 1972, p. 1153). This point of view is particularly valuable because it recognizes that innovation takes place on the level of the individual rather than on the level of the community as a whole.

Gregory tried another approach altogether in his article "Image of Limited Good, or Expectation of Reciprocity?" (1975). He believed that there was no point in arguing about a concept which had already been heavily debated, accepted, and rejected by various anthropologists. Instead, he offered an alternative explanation of the behavior which Foster used to illustrate the image of limited good. Gregory asserted that this behavior could be explained by a model which he called "expectation of circumstantially based reciprocity" (ECBR). He felt that this model allowed for an expanding economy in which individuals could continue to expect that good would be redistributed but would recognize that good is not finite; it is expandable. Gregory saw his explanation as a way of avoiding the pitfalls inherent in assuming that peasant communities operate under the rules of a zero-sum game. His explanation also took into account the fact that change and economic growth had been occurring in the community he studied (Gregory, 1975, p. 74).

Despite the considerable criticism, Foster's concept has achieved widespread popularity—his article has been reprinted in a number of anthologies, the image has been used in several introductory textbooks, and a number of anthropologists have found it a useful explanatory model (Gregory, 1975, p. 73). One of the reasons for its continued popularity is that it provides a seemingly clear explanation for behavior which many people outside the culture have difficulty understanding—the apparent inability of many peasant communities to develop economically. Unfortunately, Foster's model tends to focus our attention on the community today, causing us to ignore the political and economic perspective of history.

One of the difficulties for nonanthropologists (especially quantitatively oriented social scientists, such as economists) in looking at the image of limited good is that this seemingly plausible idea has been accepted by some and rejected by others without any attempt to systematically test (a) whether the image does indeed govern behavior in a number of cultures with similar economic conditions and (b), if it does govern behavior, how it continues to operate and how changes in economic opportunity eventually act to change the image.

The data used to bolster the image of limited good have been gathered as part of Foster's own research and by other anthropologists working under similar circumstances. To my knowledge, no one has operationalized this concept and set out to test it in any sort of systematic way against data from a variety of other rural communities around the world. Nor has anyone tested the concept to see if it operates in certain nonrural contexts as well.

The basic problem here is that those anthropologists who believe that the image of limited good *is* operating in rural communities and *is* a valid concept feel that its usefulness has been proven by Foster's data and their own experiences, while those who do not accept it as a valid model believe that a model based on invalid premises is not worth testing. Thus the controversy continues, while other social scientists become interested in possible applications of the image and wonder why more rigorous research on the topic has not been attempted

Before going any further into the characteristics of a model adequate to explain difficulties in achieving economic growth without increased inequality of income, it might be useful to consider the implications of the model as it exists for economic growth and income distribution.

If the population of a country or a region was composed largely of peasants, if they subscribed to the image of limited good, and if the mechanisms which redistribute wealth actually did keep income equally distributed, then income in that region would be equitably distributed. However, peasants are, by definition, part of a larger social and economic system. People who are active in the larger-scale system do not subscribe to the image of limited good. Thus it is possible that, over time, the larger-scale sector, the "modern" one, would take advantage of growing economic opportunity and become wealthier and wealthier while the peasant population stagnated. Those individuals from the peasant sector who did not accept the image would gradually be drawn into the modern sector, where they would act to maximize their economic advantage. Gradually the society would become less and less equal, as those individuals predisposed to maximize their economic advantage continued to do so, while those who still believed in the image became relatively poorer and poorer. And, indeed, this seems to be occurring throughout the less-developed countries— the poor are not only becoming relatively poorer, they may be getting absolutely poorer. Although the problem seems to fit the model, we still need to question whether there might not be another, better explanation for the problem.

The first premise in the argument is that, in a community where the image of limited good operates, there is indeed an equitable distribution of wealth. This basic assumption— that peasant communities are homogeneous in wealth— presents a clear problem. Peasant systems are parts of larger systems; and, in the countries where the model has been reported, the overall distribution of wealth is not only unequal but seriously distorted. Inequalities of wealth exist on the local level as well as on the national level. Only by eliminating those areas where there are no wealthy representatives of the larger-scale culture can we begin to speak of relative homogeneity of wealth. And even within those communities, some authors, such as Cancian (1965), have reported differences in relative wealth which may appear small to us but which have apparently endured over a number of years.

This brings us to the next point: if there are periodic attempts to keep the distribution of the pie equal via festivals, cargo systems, etc., do these redistributive measures actually accomplish this end? Again, there is evidence that the cargo system may not distribute wealth but may instead reinforce unequal distribution of wealth on the local level. Redistributive measures may also fail when people refuse to participate or to convert to religions which encourage saving, or when people periodically migrate from the region to seek better economic conditions.

A continuing difficulty with the image is that the model developed from the image distorts the essential relationship between the peasant community and the larger system. If one regards the peasant community as closed, it is logical to assume that changes in the image must come from within the community or, ultimately, from within the individual. Thus, the ultimate responsibility for lack of peasant responsiveness to economic opportunity can be found within the individual psyche. Although some supporters—especially those who have not read Foster carefully—have stressed this aspect, even Foster believed that changes in the image of limited good would come about only when the actual opportunity structure changed. For him, as well as for most of his detractors, there is no future in attempts to change individual cognitive orientations; the ultimate road to economic development is through improved economic opportunity.

Another difficulty with the concept has to do with the problem of migration from rural areas into urban areas. Growth in opportunities outside the rural sector may drain off the more ambitious, upwardly mobile individuals from the rural community, leaving the poorer people in the traditional sector. What then appears at first glance to be across-the-board peasant resistance to change may in actuality be merely the response of those who are somewhat poorer and thus less able to risk their meager resources in possibly risky projects. Even so, it is amazing that the record reveals so much willingness to experiment. (Some examples of this willingness are discussed later in this chapter.)

Anthropologists may have a special difficulty in developing a theory adequate to deal with the relationship between the local group and the larger system because anthropology began by studying small, relatively isolated communities as though they existed in a vacuum without contact with other communities. While there are limitations to this approach even in studying hunting and gathering groups, the limitations are magnified when the assumption of closedness is applied to peasant societies which exist as parts of larger traditions. Anthropologists have a particular problem in this regard because anthropology has traditionally focused on cultural systems as independent wholes rather than as parts of greater systems. This approach was further encouraged by the practice of many anthropologists who studied only one community or group of people. Such a practice makes it difficult for the discipline to confront the economic oppression of peasant communities by larger societies. We often prefer to rely on explanations which focus on the inability of peasant communities to accept economic development. In this regard, Acheson's article (1972) is particularly useful because he examines the actual economic and social situations of both people who took advantage of opportunities for growth and people who did not.

The use of the contrary-to-fact assumption that peasant societies are closed systems tends to perpetuate the idea that any culture is a closed system which cannot accommodate conflict or stress without damage to the system. This idea, in turn, makes it easy to see the situation as one which is better left alone. In this regard, the work of some of the conflict theorists, who can help us appreciate the constructive role of conflict, would be useful. Dahrendorf contrasted a structural-functional model of society with a conflict model of society in which change and conflict are seen as ubiquitous rather than as symptomatic of malfunctioning (Dahrendorf, 1973, p. 105). Coser (1957) saw conflict as an essentially creative process producing new norms, new institutions, and new techniques, resulting in new technologies.

Another difficulty with the image of limited good is that it can be used as an easy out by people introducing economic development projects. Although Foster (1967, p. 347) implicated the image in the failure of some of the projects introduced by CREFAL (Centro Regional de Educación Fundamental para la América Latina), the overwhelming impression one receives after reading about the CREFAL development projects is of the almost uniformly poor planning and administration by the change agents. Potters were encouraged to use kilns which could not fire correctly because of poor design; weavers were paid at rates so high that the weaving project could not support itself once the numbers of visitors to the CREFAL demonstration project declined, and the weavers subsequently had to compete in the open market with weavers from other communities whose goods were being sold more cheaply. Yet each time CREFAL introduced another project, people could be found who were willing to try out new methods of raising their incomes. Foster also believed that other communities might be even more willing than Tzintzuntzan to try out CREFAL projects (1967, pp. 330–346).

While Foster was aware of the pitfalls inherent in assigning too much blame for the failures of the CREFAL projects to the image of limited good, the image can obscure the real problems of poorly planned development projects by blaming their rejection on the cognitive orientation of the people rather than on poor planning. If effective economic development projects are to be created, one must look carefully at problems as they occur and try to understand what might be wrong with the project before deciding it was rejected because of a cognitive orientation that discourages innovation. It is important not to use the image of limited good (or any other cognitive model) to explain project failures too hastily.

Although I have been critical of Foster's model, the questions he raised about why some communities grow more readily than others remain to be answered. If we are to develop a more useful model, however, we need to consider more data along with several factors that Foster chose not to consider. By looking at historical, economic, ecological, and demographic variables, we can generate hypotheses which can be tested in many areas and which can help us answer the question, how do the different variables affect economic growth?

The image of limited good is based on data gathered by Foster and several other anthropologists, such as Lewis, Lopreato, and Banfield, all of whom stressed the divisive aspects of peasant communities. To these authors, peasant communities are characterized by a great deal of invidious comparison, gossip, and general dissension. According to Foster, the belief that one man's gain must be at another man's expense is a part of the image of limited good which creates sanctions against people who try to improve their economic situation. According to Robert A. Hackenberg, in a discussion of his own field experiences, gossip is a dominant theme in many communities, but this does not stop people from acting to improve their economic positions: in a community where gossip is rampant, people learn to ignore it and to go on as if it did not exist.

There is evidence that not all peasant communities are as dissension ridden as Foster's data imply. Friedl's work in a Swiss alpine village (1976) demonstrated that the area's harsh ecology and constant threat of avalanches have forced the villagers to engage in many cooperative ventures. Foster also stated that the image of limited good prevents peasant communities from working in cooperative groups. From my own experience in studying an arts-and-crafts marketing cooperative in this country over a period of several years, I can testify that peasants are not unique in having difficulty working in cooperative ventures.

A model which tries to explain differentials in economic development must also consider the history of the group being studied. The history of peasant communities is intertwined with the history of the larger system of which peasant communities are a part. It is interesting that Foster relied heavily on evidence gathered from Italian peasant communities, because Italian peasants have been notably exploited throughout their history. Mexican history over the past four centuries has also been particularly traumatic for that country's rural population, and it is difficult to write about peasant attitudes in these countries without taking this factor into account. Foster's stress on conservatism also obscures the tremendous changes which have occurred in Mexico, and which are still occurring. Not the least of these changes is the growing dependence of Tzintzuntzan on labor migrations to the United States.

Although the history of peasant communities is important, one also needs to remember the present economic and status positions of peasants in the larger society. In stressing the conservatism of peasants, it is easy to forget that peasant economic opportunities are very circumscribed. One result of this is the tremendous worldwide migration of peasants into urban areas in an attempt to improve their economic position. Although Foster reported that migration from Tzintzuntzan to urban areas had not been extensive, at the time he wrote, Tzintzuntenos had the option of working in the United States as braceros and remitting large sums back to their community. With employment of braceros in the U.S. now extremely limited, population pressures on available resources in Tzintzuntzan are likely to be severe.

We also need to consider the specific ecological and demographic conditions in different peasant communities to see what their effects are on economic development. Perhaps, as Friedl noted (1976), severe ecological conditions in the absence of corresponding population pressure can lead to a situation emphasizing cooperation. A situation of severe land shortage coupled with an expanding population and equal division of land among heirs may have very different consequences.

It may also be that, in many ecological and populational situations, peasants know something that we do not when they see economic resources as limited rather than as infinitely expandable. Perhaps some aspects of peasant conservatism may represent a more-realistic appraisal of the world's economic situation than our Western optimism that growth is infinite, and that we need only find new sources to tap in order to continue operating as the industrialized nations have been operating during the last century or two.

References

Acheson, J. M. (1972). "Limited Good or Limited Goods?" *American Anthropologist* 74.

Acheson, J. M. (1974). "Reply to George Foster." *American Anthropologist* 76.

Anderson, R. T., and G. Anderson (1962). "The Indirect Social Structure of European Village Communities." *American Anthropologist* 64.

Banfield, E. C. (1958). *The Moral Basis of a Backward Society*. New York: Free Press.

Bennett, J. W. (1966). "Further Remarks on Foster's 'Image of Limited Good'." *American Anthropologist* 68.

Cancian, F. (1965). *Economics and Prestige in a Maya Community*. Stanford, Calif.: Stanford University Press.

Coser, L. A. (1957). "Social Conflict and the Theory of Social Change," reprinted in Etzioni, A., and E. Etzioni-Halevy, eds. *Social Change: Sources, Patterns and Consequences.* New York: Basic Books.

Dahrendorf, R. (1973). "Toward a Theory of Social Conflict," reprinted in Etzioni, A., and E. Etzioni-Halevy, eds. *Social Change.*

Dube, S. C. (1958). *India's Changing Villages: Human Factors in Community Development.* London: Routledge and Kegan Paul.

Foster, G. M. (1961). "Interpersonal Relations in Peasant Society." *Human Organization* 19.

Foster, G. M. (1962). *Traditional Cultures and the Impact of Technological Change.* New York: Harper.

Foster, G. M. (1965). "Peasant Society and the Image of Limited Good," reprinted in Potter, J. M., M. N. Diaz, and G. M. Foster, eds. *Peasant Society: A Reader.* Boston: Little, Brown.

Foster, G. M. (1966). "Foster's Reply to Kaplan, Saler, and Bennett." *American Anthropologist* 68.

Foster, G. M. (1967). *Tzintzuntzan: Mexican Peasants in a Changing World.* Boston: Little, Brown.

Foster, G. M. (1974). "Limited Good or Limited Goods: Observations on Acheson." *American Anthropologist* 76.

Foster, G. M. (1975). "Comment on Gregory." *Current Anthropology* 16, no. 1.

Franks, V. and V. Burtle (1974). *Women in Therapy.* New York: Brunner/Mazel.

Friedl, J. (1976). "Swiss Family Togetherness." *Natural History* 85, no. 2.

Gregory, J. R. (1975). "Image of Limited Good or Expectation of Reciprocity?" *Current Anthropology* 16, no. 1.

Kaplan, D., and B. Saler (1966). "Foster's 'Image of Limited Good': An Example of Anthropological Explanation." *American Anthropologist* 68.

Kennedy, J. G. (1966). "Peasant Society and Limited Good: A Critique." *American Anthropologist* 68.

Ketchin. A. Personal Communication.

Kroeber, A. L. (1948). *Anthropology.* New York: Harcourt, Brace.

Lewis, O. (1951). *Life in a Mexican Village: Tepoztlan*

Revisited. Urbana, Ill.: University of Illinois Press.

Lopreato, J. (1961). "Interpersonal Relations in Peasant Society: The Peasant's View." *Human Organization* 19.

Lowenthal, M. F., M. Thurnher, and D. Chiriboga (1975). *Four Stages of Life.* San Francisco: Jossey-Bass.

McClelland, D. C. (1961). *The Achieving Society.* Princeton, N.J.: Van Nostrand.

Nash, M. (1961). "The Social Context of Economic Choice in a Small Society." *Man,* no. 219.

Nolan, M. L. (1974). "The Realities of Differences between Small Communities in Michoacan, Mexico." *American Anthropologist* 76.

Piker, S. (1966). "The Image of Limited Good: Comments on an Exercise in Description and Interpretation." *American Anthropologist* 68.

8. Dualism and Productivity: An Examination of the Economic Roles of Women in Societies in Transition

Elise Boulding

Recent work in development research suggests that industrializing countries may enter a prolonged state of economic dualism (Adelman and Morris, 1967, 1973). This dualism is characterized by the coexistence of a low-productivity subsistence agriculture sector and a high-productivity agribusiness and industrial sector in the developing society. This compartmentalization generates income inequalities of such magnitude that many persons in the developing society are worse off during "development" than they were in the preindustrial stage. The capital-intensive character of the industrial sector, including industrialized agriculture, coupled with the complex knowledge and skill structures that join the human being to the machine, pushes a society that does not already have powerful mechanisms for guaranteeing free flow of information and skills to every corner of that society, into enclave development. The faster development takes place within the enclave, the harder it is to cross the information barrier for those on the outside. This leaves a mass of subsistence farmers for whom enclave technology is useless, since it cannot be utilized to increase their productivity. Neither can it be used to draw them into the industrial sector, because of the latter's small labor requirements. The industrial sector thus has nothing to offer them, since they cannot afford to consume its products either. Programs

This chapter is a shortened version of chapter 4 of Elise Boulding's *Women in the Twentieth Century World* (1976).

designed in the enclave to improve the agricultural productivity of the small farmers on the outside are preempted by the middle-size farmers, who expand their holdings at the expense of small peasant holdings. Such programs leave previously self-sufficient subsistence farmers landless and poverty-stricken, with no new source of income in sight.

The coexistence of a low-productivity subsistence sector and a high-productivity market-oriented enclave is not a new phenomenon of industrialization, however. From the time of the earliest clustering of towns in the Middle East and Mesoamerica (9000 B.C. or earlier), such dualism has existed. To a considerable extent it has been based on another type of dualism, a gender-linked division of labor that left women with the subsistence tasks of growing and processing food and babies and engaging in domestic manufacture for home consumption, while men entered the market economy of the new city-based production, trade, and service networks. While women have never been totally confined to the subsistence sector in any society, they have always been far more active in it than men once urbanism developed. Because the resultant income inequalities operated within family units rather than between economic or class-interest groups, they were socially invisible. These inequalities have also been partially mitigated by intrafamily grants (men sharing some of their earnings with the women of their households). At the same time, the partial, private, and voluntary nature of the within-family income transfers and the lack of alternative economic opportunities for women contributed to the crystallization of a lower social and political status for women in relation to men, both within families and in society generally.

One way to conceptualize the traditional gender-based dualism is to think of the women's sector as a labor-intensive subsistence sector with minimal access to the knowledge, skills, and technology of the preindustrial town and city. Once the economic egalitarianism of the hunting and gathering existence and of the earliest forms of slash-and-burn agriculture have been left behind, we find that women everywhere have fewer and poorer tools than men and must draw more on their body power for work than do men at comparable tasks. Boserup has effectively demonstrated this for women farmers (1970).

Two other dualisms are superimposed on the gender-based dualism. One is suggested by the term "third world," produced by the most recent, late second-millennium wave of modernization that swept over the temperate zone of the planet and left that third world as the labor-intensive sector of the world economy. The second is the phenomenon to which the word "dualism" usually refers, modernization within third-world countries which leaves a large subsistence sector untouched by industrial development.

It will be argued in this paper that it is the cumulative impact of the triple dualism which creates the poverty trap for so many third-world countries, and that development policies that do not take account of primary, gender-based dualism are doomed to failure. The declining productivity of women in the subsistence sector has to do with disproportionately fewer and fewer resources being available to them. This is part of the general process of resource deprivation which also hits the poorer 40 percent of the male peasantry once the industrial sector begins to develop. It hits both men and women, but it hits women harder. While such sectoral imbalance also accompanied the earlier phase of industrialization in Europe, it was not so extreme because the prior resource depletion by the early medieval colonialist exploiters, the Vikings, was probably modest compared to the resource depletion of the third world by the most-recent European colonialism, particularly in Africa and Asia. Third-world countries began modernization in an already "squeezed" condition.

The condition of triple dualism just described puts such a heavy weight on the least-equipped part of the labor force, in terms of skill and resources—that is, on women—that their daily labor is unable to produce enough food and other home craft products to support an intersectoral flow of goods and services that can improve the standard of life of the total society.

The dualism created in the international economy by colonialism, and the problem of how to trigger the dynamics of a New International Economic Order, will not be dealt with in this paper. It should be understood, however, that third-world countries cannot effectively deal with the problems of internal dualism unless progress is also made at the international level. In fact, the extreme of economic dualism found in developing countries in this century has usually been introduced by a dominant expatriate colonial elite. That same elite stands in the way of the emergence of an indigenous middle class that will provide leadership for the breaking down of the barriers to the free flow of information, skills, and resources between sectors. It also stands in the way of the reconstruction of participatory mechanisms that join the best of traditional values and communication skills with newer organizational and communication technologies, because of the elite's scorn for the traditions on which that reconstruction needs to be based. Even after the expatriate elite has been replaced by an indigenous middle class, it is not necessarily easy for that class to throw off elitist attitudes and identify itself with populist interests.

Adelman and Morris state the problem clearly enough when they suggest that it will be necessary to develop "new political institutions and policies that will ensure development of the people, by the people, and for the people" (1973, p. 202). However, the likelihood of the emergence of such institutions and policies, on the basis of prevailing modes of analysis of the problem, is nil. Expatriate elites, development experts, and indigenous middle-class leadership alike maintain an incomplete if not faulty view of the actual processes of capital formation and productivity and economic decision making on the part of up to 90 percent of a society's population, including the 50 percent which is female. The political consciousness that must be developed before more equitable social policies can take shape depends on a recognition of the resources, productivity, and needs of a hidden sector of society. While the understanding of the day-to-day functioning of the male peasant farmer and the landless laborer is faulty enough, these groups are at least recognized as theoretical targets for economic policy. The female peasant farmer and landless laborer do not exist for the policymaker. Third-world women are seen only as breeders and feeders, not as producers, traders, and performers of a variety of community services in the peasant village as well as in the town. Part of the problem of adequate economic analysis lies in the necessity to assign monetary values to the productive labor and exchange activities of women which do not enter the cash economy; but equally important is to identify and count the monetary transactions of women at the village level, which have stayed hidden to economists because they have not looked for them.

The purpose of this paper is to examine these hidden components of third-world economies and to suggest their policy implications if permanent dualistic structures of poverty are to be avoided. I will examine the more-accessible and routinely enumerated economic activities of women in the framework offered by Adelman and Morris, grouping countries according to the progression delineated by them: from traditional to dualistic to successfully modernizing societies.

Twenty-one countries in various stages of modernization have been chosen from the Adelman-Morris list of seventy-four countries, selected to represent each development stage and a variety of religious and cultural patterns and geographic regions, and also on the basis of the availability of data on women in the labor force. The countries are grouped according to the Adelman formulation (as traditional subsistence, dualistic, and rapidly modernizing) on the basis of the data presented in Adelman and Morris (1967). Data on the participation of women in each society come from a study initially undertaken for the United Nations (Boulding, Nuss, Carson, and Greenstein, 1976). Other country characteristics utilized in the tables that follow are also derived from UN sources. The Adelman and Morris data on income inequality (1973) are also used. Unavoidably, there are blank spaces in the tables where data are missing for a given country.

The data for the twenty-one countries are arranged in a series of tables to enable inspection of cultural and economic characteristics associated with the Adelman-Morris typology, with particular emphasis on occupations and education of women. No statistical analysis is attempted in this exploratory study.

The Data on Dualism

The countries chosen for an analysis of women's participation in societies of varying degrees of dualism are shown in Table 1. The indicators utilized in the typology—percent of the population in traditional subsistence agriculture, extent of sectoral cleavage between modern and traditional economic sectors, extent of bureaucratic efficiency, and extent of development of a significant indigenous middle class, not expatriate-dominated—all come from Adelman and Morris (1967, pp. 9–128). Each of these indicators is judgmental, based on country studies and evaluations made by country experts (pp. 12–13).[1] All judgments refer to the state of a country as of about 1960, and the countries themselves were chosen as representative of societies "which, as of 1950, were underdeveloped with respect to social and economic structure" (p. 9). By 1968, the year to which the UN data on women used in this analysis refers, some of these countries could no longer be characterized as "underdeveloped." This makes possible an examination of the dynamics of change for these countries, particularly for the period 1960 to 1968.

In order to keep the typology as simple as possible, I have collapsed various distinctions made by Adelman and Morris to produce three types of societies, and left out entirely the completely traditional society in which "modernizing" sectoral cleavages have not yet taken place.[2] The societies that will be referred to as "high dualism" societies are those with over 55 percent of the population in traditional subsistence agriculture, with sharp sectoral or geographic cleavage, moderate-to-low bureaucratic efficiency, and a weak indigenous middle class, frequently expatriate-dominated. The "moderate dualism" societies are those with from 25 to 54 percent of the population in traditional subsistence agriculture, with moderate-to-low sectoral or geographic cleavage, moderate-to-high bureaucratic efficiency, and a significant indigenous middle class. The "low dualism" societies are those with less than 25 percent of the population in traditional subsistence agriculture, minimal sectoral or geographic cleavage, high bureaucratic efficiency, and a strong indigenous middle class.

Table 2 gives a picture of the participation of women in the traditional and modern sectors with contextual information about the majority religions for each group of countries. The figures come from 1968 UN data converted into participation units (Boulding, Nuss, Carson, and Greenstein, 1976). Each participation unit indicates the proportion of women in the total population engaged in the activity in

TABLE 1

THE DATA BASE FOR ANALYSIS OF WOMEN'S PARTICIPATION IN DEVELOPMENT:
COUNTRY LISTING, BY EXTENT OF DUALISM[1]

HIGH DUALISM
COUNTRIES:[2]

BLACK AFRICA	WEST ASIA
GABON	IRAN
RHODESIA	
SIERRA LEONE	ASIA
	INDONESIA
NORTH AFRICA	
MOROCCO	
TUNISIA	

MODERATE DUALISM
COUNTRIES:[3]

BLACK AFRICA	ASIA
GHANA	INDIA
NIGERIA	PAKISTAN
NORTH AFRICA	LATIN AMERICA
UAR	ARGENTINA
	COLOMBIA
WEST ASIA	MEXICO
CYPRUS	
SYRIA	
TURKEY	

LOW DUALISM
COUNTRIES:[4]

WEST ASIA	LATIN AMERICA
ISRAEL	CHILE
ASIA	
JAPAN	

[1]Dualism refers to sharp sectoral or geographic cleavages, based on classification in Adelman and Morris (1967: Chapter II), for the time period 1957-1962. The related concepts of bureaucratic efficiency and significance of indigenous middle class are also based on classifications in Adelman and Morris (1967: Chapter II). See definitions in notes 2, 3, and 4.

[2]Countries with over 55% of the population in traditional subsistence agriculture, with sharp sectoral or geographic cleavage, moderate to low bureaucratic efficiency, and a weak indigenous middle class.

[3]Countries with from 25 to 54% of the population in traditional subsistence agriculture with moderate to low sectoral or geographic cleavage and moderate to high bureaucratic efficiency and a significant indigenous middle class.

[4]Countries with less than 25% of the population in traditional subsistence agriculture, with minimal sectoral or geographic cleavage, high bureaucratic efficiency and a strong indigenous middle class.

TABLE 2

WOMEN'S PARTICIPATION IN TRADITIONAL AND MODERN OCCUPATION SECTORS, BY EXTENT OF DUALISM OF THE ECONOMY[1] AND PREDOMINANT RELIGION

COUNTRY	% WOMEN EMPLOYED IN TRADITIONAL SECTOR[2]		% WOMEN EMPLOYED IN "MODERN" SECTOR[3]						MAJORITY RELIGION PERCENT
	AGRICULTURE	OWN-ACCOUNT WORKERS	PROFESSIONAL & TECHNICAL	ADMINISTRATIVE & MANAGERIAL	CLERICAL & RELATED	SALES WORKERS	SERVICE WORKERS	PRODUCTION,TRANSPORTATION, LABORERS	
HIGH DUALISM COUNTRIES									
BLACK AFRICA									
GABON	51	35	--	--	--	--	--	12	50 CATH/ 42 ANIM
RHODESIA[4]	7	16	38	5	56	36	63	4	85 ANIM
SIERRA LEONE	42	13	27	9	16	47	6	--	62 ANIM
NORTH AFRICA									
MOROCCO	8	6	15	3	26	4	27	--	98 MUSL
TUNISIA[5]	2	6	17	4	18	2	19	7	95 MUSL
WEST ASIA									
IRAN	6	7	26	3	7	1	22	25	98 MUSL
ASIA									
INDONESIA	31	23	36	10	11	49	38	31	80 MUSL
MEAN	24	15.14	26.5	5.67	22.33	23.17	29.17	15.8	

TABLE 2 (CONTINUED)

COUNTRY	% WOMEN EMPLOYED IN TRADITIONAL SECTOR		% WOMEN EMPLOYED IN "MODERN" SECTOR						MAJORITY RELIGION PERCENT
	AGRICULTURE	OWN-ACCOUNT WORKERS	PROFESSIONAL & TECHNICAL	ADMINISTRATIVE & MANAGERIAL	CLERICAL & RELATED	SALES WORKERS	SERVICE WORKERS	PRODUCTION, TRANSPORTATION, LABORERS	
MODERATE DUALISM COUNTRIES									
BLACK AFRICA									
GHANA	37	45	20	3	7	80	29	--	42 XIAN / 46 ANIM
NIGERIA	10	--	15	7	10	60	26	21	38 MUSL / 43 ANIM
NORTH AFRICA									
UAR	3	3	24	4	10	6	14	--	92 MUSL
WEST ASIA									
CYPRUS	54	18	33	5	21	13	31	--	80 CATH[6] / 20 MUSL
SYRIA	49	3	27	8	8	0	8	--	87 MUSL
TURKEY	48	4	21	13	13	1	7	10	98 MUSL
ASIA									
INDIA	36	27	16	3	3	11	25	--	84 HINDU
PAKISTAN	14	5	10	1	1	2	15	--	98 MUSL
LATIN AMERICA									
ARGENTINA	5	13	59	7	29	17	62	--	95 CATH
COLOMBIA	4	15	47	15	24	26	75	18	96 CATH
MEXICO	5	15	38	12	30	29	66	17	96 CATH
MEAN	24.09	14.8	28.18	7.09	14.18	32.27	32.55	16.5	

TABLE 2 (CONTINUED)

COUNTRY	% WOMEN EMPLOYED IN TRADITIONAL SECTOR		% WOMEN EMPLOYED IN "MODERN" SECTOR						MAJORITY RELIGION
	AGRICULTURE	OWN-ACCOUNT WORKERS	PROFESSIONAL & TECHNICAL	ADMINISTRATIVE & MANAGERIAL	CLERICAL & RELATED	SALES WORKERS	SERVICE WORKERS	PRODUCTION, TRANSPORTATION, LABORERS	PERCENT
LOW DUALISM COUNTRIES[7]									
WEST ASIA									
ISRAEL	23	19	49	39	39	29	52	--	JUDAISM
ASIA									
JAPAN	53	30	37	5	49	42	58	27	BUDDHIST SHINTO
LATIN AMERICA									
CHILE	3	21	48	9	38	38	73	14	98 CATH
MEAN	26.33	23.33	44.67	17.67	42.0	36.33	61.0	20.5	

[1] Participation figures are in terms of the ratio of women to the total labor force employed in a given occupation. See definitions in Table 1 regarding dualism. -- means information not available.

[2] See E. Boulding, Nuss, Carson, Greenstein for further discussion of these variables which are derived from U.N. data for 1968 or the closest year to that date; both agriculture and own account work may be in the modern sector.

[3] See E. Boulding, Nuss, Carson, Greenstein.

[4] The figures for Rhodesia, as an expatriate-dominated society, are suspect, particularly on participation of women in agriculture. They have probably done little counting of black women.

[5] Tunisia, unlike the other countries in this group, is classified by Adelman and Morris as having a moderately significant indigenous middle class and a high bureaucratic efficiency.

[6] Cyprus Christians are Greek Orthodox, not Catholic.

[7] There is very little subsistence agriculture in these countries, and most of the women employed in agriculture are using some modernized techniques. Many own-account workers in these countries may be in the modern sector.

question. There are as many problems with this supposedly "hard" data on the participation of women as there are with the "soft" data on dualism, though for different reasons. Most of these countries have only recently begun counting women. It is extremely unlikely that any country at any stage of development is accurately counting its women farmers or traders. While I have placed agricultural and own-account workers in the traditional sector, when we get to the low-dualism countries this is no longer an appropriate classification. In these countries, farmer women and self-employed women may well be integrated in the modern sector. In any society, women in the industrial sector are more easily counted, since that sector is urban based. To what extent third-world village women who are engaged in sales, services, and technical work are counted is hard to say. For all these weaknesses, the UN figures represent first approximations of the economic participation of women as seen by a country's bureaucrats.

What is striking, in comparing women's participation rates for differing degrees of dualism, is that the highs and lows of participation in agriculture are the same in all groups of countries. High-dualism countries have as little as 2 percent and as much as 51 percent of women in agriculture. Moderate-dualism countries have as little as 3 percent and as much as 54 percent, and low-dualism countries as little as 3 percent and as high as 53 percent. If we look at cultural regions, there are wide divergences in black Africa, Asia, and West Asia. North Africa and Latin America are more homogeneous.

Looking at the religion column, we see that religious tradition no more determines the participation in agriculture of women than does the culture region; since, while the predominantly Muslim countries of Morocco, Tunisia, and Iran have few women farmers, the predominantly Muslim countries of Indonesia, Syria, and Turkey all have high proportions of women farmers. The only thing all Muslim countries have in common is that they have few women in sales. They may have quite a few women in professional, service, and clerical work—or very few. Catholicism, also considered a restraint on women in the labor force, is consistently associated with few women in farming (at least in Latin America; all the Catholic countries in our list are also

Latin American) but with very high numbers indeed in professional, clerical, and service work. If religion acts as a constraining factor on the participation of women in the labor force, it would appear that the constraints have more to do with the settings in which work is carried out (for example, whether work is done under conditions of seclusion) than with the absolute numbers of women employed.

The variation in the number of women working on their own account is almost as great as the variation in the number of agricultural workers, but the mean of own-account workers is higher for the low-dualism countries than for the high-dualism, less-industrialized societies.

If we read the figures across for the traditional and modern sectors of individual countries in each development category, we find a great unevenness in the extent of participation in various occupational categories in both the high- and moderate-dualism countries. Only in the low-dualism countries is there a tendency for evenly high participation in all categories (except for the administrative field, from which women are uniformly excluded in most countries of the world). Only two categories have high participation of women in all countries at all levels of dualism: professional workers (which means that every country uses women as teachers) and production workers. The latter is an interesting category which includes craftsmen, production-process workers, and laborers not elsewhere classified. Thus it covers both traditional and modern forms of wage labor, from road and construction work to factory work.

Apart from the category of administration, there is no occupation that does not include a substantial number of women in *some* countries at each level of dualism. It would appear that the extent of dualistic structure in a society does not directly affect the frequency of participation of women in the labor force except in the case of low-dualism societies, where participation is more uniformly high than elsewhere.

Table 3 offers a more detailed examination of the patterns of participation of women in the agricultural, own-account, and production sectors reported in Table 2, and does so in a way that breaks down the latter's oversimplified categorization into traditional and modern sectors. The data in Table 3 were compiled by Boserup (1970) from country studies. Figures are available for only thirteen of the twenty-one

TABLE 3

WOMEN IN AGRICULTURE, TRADE AND INDUSTRY: FAMILY WORKERS, OWN-ACCOUNT, AND EMPLOYEES*

| | AGRICULTURE | | TRADE[2] | HOME AND FACTORY INDUSTRY[3] | |
	% FEMALE OF ALL AGRICULTURAL WORKERS	% FEMALE WAGE[1] LABORERS OF ALL AGRICULTURAL WAGE LABORERS	% FEMALE WHO ARE OWN-ACCOUNT WORKERS OF ALL FEMALE TRADERS	% FEMALE IN FAMILY LABOR FORCE	% FEMALE AMONG EMPLOYEES
HIGH DUALISM					
SIERRA LEONE	42	5	75	15	2
MOROCCO	8	5	48	25	15
TUNISIA	2	2	--	--	--
IRAN	6	4	59	36	18
MODERATE DUALISM					
GHANA	37	6	94	39	3
UAR	3	4	81	7	2
SYRIA	49	8	48	14	6
TURKEY	48	23	56	17	10
INDIA	36	44	--	35	12
PAKISTAN	14	6	83	11	2
MEXICO	5	16	--	--	2
COLOMBIA	4	3	26	33	13
LOW DUALISM					
CHILE	3	2	27	35	12

[1]After Boserup (1970:68).

[2]After Boserup (1970:88).

[3]After Boserup (1970:109). Includes home industries, manufacturing industries, and construction activities.

[4]The dates to which the figures for each country refer are as follows: Sierra Leone, 1963; Ghana, 1960; Morocco, 1960; UAR, 1960; Turkey, 1965; Syria, 1960; Iran, 1956; Pakistan, 1961; India, 1961; Colombia, 1964; Chile, 1960; Mexico, not given.

countries we are studying, but those that are available are highly suggestive. The figures on female wage laborers, as a percent of all agricultural wage laborers, are higher in moderate-dualism countries than in high-dualism countries. Further study might indicate that wage-labor employment for women farmers is a transition phenomenon accompanying industrialization in some countries. The percent of women traders who are self-employed probably represents traditional sector employment as opposed to hired salespersons, who are more likely to be in the modern sector. The figures for own-account traders do not differ between high- and moderate-dualism countries—or, rather, the highest figures for self-employed traders are in the moderate-dualism countries. Small-scale trading is a highly adaptive activity that can be carried on under a variety of conditions and degrees of modernization, so we should perhaps not expect to see shifts in the extent of self-employment in trade during the middle stages of development.

TABLE 4

COMPARISON OF UN AND BOSERUP DATA ON WOMEN IN PRODUCTION*

COUNTRY	% FEMALE PRODUCTION, TRANSPORTATION, LABORERS (UN)	% FEMALE IN HOME AND FACTORY INDUSTRY (BOSERUP)	
		% FEMALE IN FAMILY LABOR FORCE	% FEMALE EMPLOYEES
IRAN	25	36	18
TURKEY	10	17	10
COLOMBIA	18	33	13
CHILE	14	35	12

*All figures in this table taken from Tables 2 and 3

The Boserup data on home and factory industry are particularly interesting in that they help us get behind the single aggregate figure on women production workers generally used, and thereby uncover a much larger participation by women in industry than has heretofore been recognized. Table 4 provides a list of the countries from our study for which there are Boserup data, with the UN data and the Boserup data compared. The UN figures for women in production include other categories of labor besides manufacturing and construction, so we would expect it to be larger than the Boserup figure for women employees in industry, but the differences are not great. What is striking is the large number of women in home industries. These home industries are not to be confused with the making of simple craft products to sell in the market. Rather, they should be compared to the industrial home workshops of Europe during the centuries that preceded the industrial revolution. The bulk of the labor in these workshops came from family members, but there were usually one or more paid workers present too, as well as apprentices. (See chapters 10 and 11 of Boulding, *The Underside of History*, 1977, for a discussion of preindustrial workshops in Europe.) The home-industry category is an important factor in the utilization of the productive capacities of women in the development process. It will be noted that two of the countries in Table 4 are Muslim and two Catholic. These countries represent the entire range of dualism, from the high dualism of Iran to the low dualism of Chile; but only Turkey, in the moderate-dualism category, has less than one-third of its women in the home-industrial labor force.

In Table 5 we shift to a focus on the dynamics of dualism by examining GNP and population growth rates for 1961–1968 and 1963–1968, respectively, and the extent of income inequality for countries at each level of dualism. The growth rates in this table come from the Institute of Behavioral Science Global Data Bank, the 1961 figures for GNP per capita come from the Adelman and Morris 1967 study, and columns 4 and 5 on income inequalities are computed from estimates of income inequalities in the Adelman and Morris 1973 study. The shrinkage in the number of countries for which there are income-inequality data is due to the fact that the Adelman-Morris estimates cover only forty-three of the seventy-four countries in their original study. Column 6, on percentage share of income for the poorest 40 percent, comes directly from the Adelman-Morris estimates.

While the extent of dualism has not affected the proportions of women in the labor force, we would expect it to show up in relation to growth rates and income inequalities. Both GNP growth rates and population growth rates have been used for each country, since unless the GNP is growing faster than the population, a country is not improving its economic situation. The countries with an asterisk (*) have

TABLE 5

RELATIVE RATES OF GROWTH OF GNP AND POPULATION, AND EXTENT OF INCOME INEQUALITIES BY EXTENT OF DUALISM[1]

COUNTRY	RELATIVE RATES OF GROWTH OF GNP AND POPULATION		GNP PER CAPITA IN U.S.-$ 1964[4]	INCOME INEQUALITIES		
	GNP GROWTH RATE 1961-1968[2]	POPULATION GROWTH RATE 1963-1970[3]		GNP PER CAPITA FOR LOWEST 40%[5]	GNP PER CAPITA FOR HIGHEST 5%[5]	PERCENTAGE SHARE OF INCOME FOR POOREST 40%[6]
A. HIGH DUALISM						
BLACK AFRICA						
GABON	.7	1.3	200	40#	1880.00	8.0
RHODESIA	.1	3.2	215	14.5	1720.00	12.0
SIERRA LEONE	1.5	1.5	70	17.68#	473.20	10.10
NORTH AFRICA						
MOROCCO	.4	3.0	150	21.75	618.00	14.50
TUNISIA	2.7	--	161	42.75#	722.59	10.62
WEST ASIA						
IRAN	5.0*	3.3	211	--	--	12.50
ASIA						
INDONESIA	.8	2.8	83	--	--	--
B. MODERATE DUALISM						
BLACK AFRICA						
GHANA	-.7	3.0	199	--	--	--
NIGERIA	-.3	2.5	82	28.7	629.43	14.00
NORTH AFRICA						
UAR	1.5	2.5	120	--	--	--
WEST ASIA						
CYPRUS	5.9*	1.0	416	--	--	--
SYRIA	3.5*	3.3	152	--	--	--
TURKEY	3.2*	2.5	193	--	--	--
ASIA						
INDIA	1.0	2.1	80	40.00	320.00	20.00
PAKISTAN	3.1*	2.1	79	34.56	316.00	17.50

TABLE 5 (CONTINUED)

COUNTRY	RELATIVE RATES OF GROWTH OF GNP AND POPULATION		GNP PER CAPITA IN U.S.-$ 1961[4]	INCOME INEQUALITIES		
	GNP GROWTH RATE 1961-1968[2]	POPULATION GROWTH RATE 1963-1970[3]		GNP PER CAPITA FOR LOWEST 40%[5]	GNP PER CAPITA FOR HIGHEST 5%[5]	PERCENTAGE SHARE OF INCOME FOR POOREST 40%[6]
MODERATE DUALISM						
LATIN AMERICA						
ARGENTINA	1.0	1.5	379	163.92	2228.52	17.30
COLOMBIA	1.4	3.2	283	51.64#	2284.38	7.30
MEXICO	3.4	3.5	313	82.16#	1785.35	10.50
C. LOW DUALISM						
WEST ASIA						
ISRAEL	4.7*	2.9	814	325.60	2735.04	16.00
ASIA						
JAPAN	9.9*	1.1	502	192.02	1485.32	15.30
LATIN AMERICA						
CHILE	1.8	2.4	453	169.88	2047.56	15.00

*Countries where GNP growth is outstripping population growth.

#Poorest 40% have 10% or less of total income.

[1]See definitions in Table 1 on dualism.

[2]From Institute of Behavioral Science Global Data Bank.

[3]From Institute of Behavioral Science Global Data Bank.

[4]From Adelman and Morris (1967:88), taken from AID sources.

[5]These figures are computed from estimates in Adelman and Morris (1973:152) on percentage shares by population groups for selected countries, utilizing 1961 GNP per capita data taken from Adelman and Morris (1967:98).

[6]Taken directly from Adelman and Morris (1973:152).

[7]Refers to 1968. From Table 37 in *1974 Report of the World Social Situation* (UN, 1975) based on M.S. Ahlwalia.

GNP growth rates that exceed their population growth rate. The countries marked # are those in which the poorest 40 percent have less than 10 percent of the total income. Large income inequalities are found in both moderate- and high-dualism societies, but not in low-dualism societies. This finding is what we would expect from the Adelman-Morris thesis that dualism creates a poverty trap. However, we find rapid-growth countries, where GNP is outstripping population growth, at all three dualism levels. Unfortunately, income-inequality measures are not available for four of the seven rapid-growth countries, so we can say nothing about whether high-growth countries tend to have lesser or greater income inequalities than countries that are doing less well economically. It happens that in Israel, Japan, and Pakistan, the three countries for which we have data, the poorest 40 percent have a larger share of the income—15-to-17 percent—than most of the other countries in the list. On the other hand, no one could argue that 15-to-17 percent of the total income for the poorest 40 percent is a very impressive figure. We can only say these countries are not the worst offenders in regard to income inequality. Of the seven growth countries, four are predominantly Muslim (Iran, Syria, Turkey, and Pakistan), one is Catholic-Muslim (Cyprus), one is Judaic (Israel), and one Buddhist-Shinto (Japan). It would not seem that Islam is holding back economic development, family planning, or the participation of women in the economy to the extent that it is often accused of doing. Iran and Syria, it must be said, have very high population growth rates. Iran gets away with growth only because of its abundance of natural resources. Syria is just barely outstripping its population with its economic growth, and may not be able to maintain that over time. Only Catholic-Muslim Cyprus and Buddhist Japan have anything like population equilibrium.

Now that we have identified the countries where GNP is outstripping population, we can turn to an examination of the participation of women in these seven countries, grouped by level of dualism (Table 6). It will be seen that women are important in the agricultural labor force in five of the seven countries; Iran and Pakistan are the exceptions. (Women are also important in the wage-labor sector of agriculture in several of these countries; see Table 3. This

TABLE 6

PARTICIPATION OF WOMEN IN THE LABOR FORCE[1] IN SEVEN COUNTRIES WITH GROWTH IN GNP OF 3.1 AND ABOVE, WHERE GNP GROWTH RATE EXCEEDS POPULATION GROWTH RATE[2]

COUNTRY	AGRICULTURE	OWN-ACCOUNT WORKERS	PROFESSIONAL & TECHNICAL	ADMINISTRATIVE & MANAGERIAL	CLERICAL & RELATED	SALES WORKERS	SERVICE WORKERS	PRODUCTION, TRANSPORTATION, LABORERS
HIGH DUALISM COUNTRIES[3]								
IRAN	6	7	26	3	7	1	22	25
MODERATE DUALISM COUNTRIES[3]								
CYPRUS	54	18	33	5	21	13	31	--
SYRIA	49	3	27	8	8	0	8	--
TURKEY	48	4	21	13	13	1	7	10
PAKISTAN	14	5	10	1	1	2	15	--
LOW DUALISM COUNTRIES[3]								
ISRAEL	23	19	49	39	39	29	52	--
JAPAN	53	30	37	5	49	42	58	27

[1] For sources on variables, see footnotes to Table 2.

[2] See Table 4 for the data on which this classification is based.

[3] See definitions in Table 1 on dualism.

TABLE 7

COMPARISON OF COUNTRIES WHERE GNP OUTSTRIPS POPULATION GROWTH AND COUNTRIES WHERE POPULATION GROWTH OUTSTRIPS GNP GROWTH,[1] THE 1960'S, BY RATINGS ON HUMAN RESOURCE IMPROVEMENT PRACTICES, SCHOOL ENROLLMENT RATIOS FOR FIRST AND SECOND LEVEL EDUCATION, WOMEN GRADUATES IN HIGHER EDUCATION, AND AVAILABILITY OF NATURAL RESOURCES

COUNTRY	HUMAN RESOURCES IMPROVEMENT 1961[2]	SCHOOL ENROLL-MENT RATIOS, FIRST AND SECOND LEVEL[3]	% WOMEN GRADUATES IN HIGHER EDUCATION[4]					NATURAL RESOURCES
			EDUCATION	LAW	SOCIAL SCIENCE	ENGINEERING	AGRICULTURE	
A. GNP OUTSTRIPS POPULATION GROWTH								
HIGH DUALISM COUNTRIES[6]								
IRAN	M-L	31	27	13	24	2	7	H
MODERATE DUALISM COUNTRIES[6]								
CYPRUS	H	67	77	--	55	--	--	M
SYRIA	H	36	27	11	21	2	6	M
TURKEY	M	42	44	17	13	8	10	H
PAKISTAN	M	18	36	1	3	0	0	L
LOW DUALISM COUNTRIES[6]								
ISRAEL	H	82	22	31	37	6	5	M-L
JAPAN	H	91	74	--	36	1	5	M-L
B. POPULATION GROWTH OUTSTRIPS GNP, OR HOLDS EVEN								
HIGH DUALISM COUNTRIES[6]								
GABON	M-L	72	--	--	--	--	--	M
RHODESIA	L	--	47	--	7	--	0	H
SIERRA LEONE	L	14	--	--	--	--	--	M
MOROCCO	M-L	20	21	7	7	0	0	H
TUNISIA	M-L	49	20	9	14	0	--	M
INDONESIA	M-L	--	--	--	--	--	--	M

TABLE 7 (CONTINUED)

COUNTRY	HUMAN RESOURCES IMPROVEMENT 1961	SCHOOL ENROLLMENT RATIOS, FIRST AND SECOND LEVEL	% WOMEN GRADUATES IN HIGHER EDUCATION					
			EDUCATION	LAW	SOCIAL SCIENCE	ENGINEERING	AGRICULTURE	NATURAL RESOURCES
MODERATE DUALISM COUNTRIES6								
GHANA	M	43	-	-	-	-	-	M
NIGERIA	L	14	18	11	5	0	1	M
UAR	H	39	32	12	32	8	16	M-L
INDIA	M	28	33	4	2	1	1	M-L
ARGENTINA	H	78	90	30	39	2	8	H
COLOMBIA	M	61	-	11	54	5	4	H
MEXICO	M	64	70	13	9	2	4	H
LOW DUALISM COUNTRIES6								
CHILE	H	83	68	25	53	2	10	H

1See Table 4 for the data on which the classification is based.

2Human Resource Improvement Ratings from Adelman and Morris (1967:123-126); adaptation of Harbison and Myers weighted average of second and third level enrollment ratios.

3Percent girls enrolled in first and second level of all girls of school age, from Boulding, Nuss, Carson, 1976, forthcoming.

4Based on UN data on the ratio of women to all graduates in fields listed (E. Boulding, Nuss, Carson, and Greenstein, 1976).

5From Adelman and Morris (1967:90-93).

6See Table 1 definitions on dualism.

role of women in agriculture, which has been mentioned in connection with earlier tables, requires further discussion, but it should be noted now as a factor of possibly substantial importance to economic development.) Own-account workers do not stand out particularly in the growth countries, but professional and service roles are important in the modern sector. In general, however, except for the two countries in the low-dualism group, the pattern of participation of women in the labor force is spotty by category for any one country.

Table 7 compares the growth countries with the non-growth countries in terms of investment in education in general and investment in the education of women in particular. Column 1 represents human-resources improvement ratings, taken from Adelman and Morris' adaptation of the Harbison and Myers weighted average of second- and third-level enrollment ratios for the total population (1967, pp. 123–126). The figures on enrollment of women (in participation units) in higher education in 1968 in the fields of education, law, social science, engineering, and agriculture, and the first- and second-level school enrollment ratio for women, showing how many women were enrolled of the relevant age groups, come from the UN women's data project at the Institute of Behavioral Science. While it is clear that the growth countries have on the whole invested well in education in general and education for women in particular, there really is not a great deal of difference between the low-growth countries in the moderate- and low-dualism categories and the high-growth countries in these categories in terms of investment in education. If one looks at estimates of natural resources available to countries, it turns out that countries with fewer natural resources (Cyprus, Syria, Pakistan, Israel, Japan) invest more heavily in education, and countries rich in natural resources (Iran, Turkey) invest less heavily in education. If we look at countries high in natural resources, such as Argentina and Chile, which have also invested heavily in education in general and in the education of women in particular, why are they not doing better economically? Egypt has similarly invested in education, but compensatory investment, with a low resource base, has not produced for it the effects the Israeli and Japanese investments have produced in their respective countries.

It has been recognized for some time that it is the type, not the quantity, of education in a society which is related to economic growth. The ratio of vocational education to general secondary education provides a much better predictor of economic development than does the availability of secondary education alone (Bennet, 1967). Adequate vocational education is scarce in most third-world countries, since this type of education has been seen as leading to lower-status employment; policymakers do not provide it, and students do not seek it. Both have been acting on a false image of the skills relevant to creating a productive society. This situation is changing now, and there are increasing numbers of vocational schools giving specific technological skill training for men. However, the same is not true for women. While many women are trained as teachers, they are trained to perpetuate a type of colonial book-learning orientation even in dealing with very young children, an orientation that does not foster problem-solving capabilities in children. Vocational training specifically designed and labeled "for women" is usually thought of in terms of courses in nutrition, child care, and family planning. While this kind of training is useful, it is equally useful for men, and it ought to be part of the general elementary-school curriculum rather than treated as special vocational preparation of women for their economic roles. Women need the same range of vocational training that men do, since on the whole they enter the same range of jobs, whether in agriculture or industry, though at lower status and wage levels.

The data that we have examined in this section on the employment and education of women, in economies characterized by varying degrees of dualism, with varying growth rates, natural resources, and religious traditions, suggest that there is a substantial economic involvement of women in every society which may remain relatively untouched by modernization in terms of increased allocation of skill training, resources, wages, and status to the female labor force. That this picture should emerge with existing data, which we know undercount female labor, is surprising. It is not unlikely that the female work force, particularly the own-account workers, the home-industry workers, and the agricultural workers, is providing a significant amount of the total productivity of the economy, much of it uncounted—thus providing a cushion for modernization that enables planners and policymakers to make poor allocation decisions without causing the economic collapse of a society. More recognition of the actual productivity of female labor, and more allocation of resources to female labor, particularly in agriculture, might well be the decisive factors that determine whether a country's economic growth can outstrip its population growth, and whether the trap of economic dualism can ever be sprung.[3]

None of the data presented in this section can be treated as more than suggestive. Too few countries have been analyzed, and too little data have been available for even the few countries chosen. More research in two areas will be required to present a more conclusive case:

1. At the macrolevel, systematic attention must be paid to the collection of complete and crossnational comparative data on women in agriculture, as unpaid family workers, as women farmers on their own account, and as wage labor. At present no data are collected on independent women farmers, although in some areas up to 50 percent and more of women farmers are *de facto* and sometimes *de jure* heads of households (Boulding, 1975). Similar attention to home industry of all kinds is needed as well.

2. At the microlevel, country studies are needed to investigate the culture-specific patterns of women's labor within individual countries, going beyond existing census data to a more-refined classification of types of work and work sites, and individual case-history studies are needed of women workers in local communities which will include detailed time budgets for women as well as for men, on the model so well developed by the Economic Commission for Africa (United Nations, 1974).

My intentions in choosing the twenty-one third-world countries from the Adelman and Morris studies of economic dualism were to try to bring their data to bear on the problems of gender-based dualism, and to place the two phenomena in a common conceptual framework.[4] As long as "women in the labor force" remains a special category, an economist's afterthought, the basic and ancient economic partnership between woman and man is being distorted in a way that impedes the full economic, social, and political development of any society that engages in that type of categorization of women.

It is clear that women have always been food producers, craft workers, laborers, construction workers, and traders at every period in history. Some social structures have required more elaborate arrangements than others in order to enable women to carry out their economic roles. The activity itself, however, has been a constant, though the formats have varied. As societies have become more complex and more centralized, the women's sector has become progressively less visible, particularly as urbanization has created a class of male clerics and decision makers who are out of touch with the production system of their own economy. The imbalance between perceptions and reality has now gone so far that it is dangerous to the future of the human community. All kinds of international hostilities pile on top of basic failures of perception in relation to primary production processes. The problems of the New International Economic Order are not only problems for all states—first, second, and third worlds equally—of bringing domestic planning into line with a realistic assessment of world needs in a way that will break down have/have-not dualism. They are also the problems of recognizing who the producers are in every society and of bringing the excluded partners into the planning process. The excluded partners are not only women, they are the poverty sector, the subsistence sector, of every society at every level of industrialization.

To emphasize women is not to downgrade the importance of the larger problem of the participation of the poor in societal development. It is, rather, to point to the peculiar multiplier effects of gender-based dualism, once an economy leaves the subsistence pattern and moves to urbanism and industrialization, and to the importance of developing policies that will short-circuit the dynamics of that dualism and release the productivity of women and men alike into the total economy.

Notes

1. These judgments have been sharply questioned by

others, and by Adelman and Morris themselves. I believe they are valuable as first approximations. Recognizing the limitations of the judging procedure, I have nevertheless used their classification in each case, even where my own judgment would differ, for the sake of consistency.

2. While for our purposes this is a most interesting group, statistical data on the participation of women is rarely available for these largely subsistence societies, and therefore they had to be omitted.

3. I have pointed out elsewhere (Boulding, 1975) that women breed the help they need in the absence of other kinds of help, such as tools. The higher the infant death rate, the longer they have to go on breeding to get the necessary help. This is one of the many vicious cycles that result from the phenomenon of triple dualism, and which keep the subsistence sector of an economy from accumulating the surpluses that will enable its members to enter the modern sector.

4. Elsewhere (Boulding, 1976) I have looked at some of the information on the activities of women that comes out of studies undertaken in Morocco and Indonesia (high-dualism countries), Nigeria and India (moderate-dualism countries), and Japan (a low-dualism country). Relevant studies include those undertaken by Maher (1974), Hill (1969), Vreede–De Stuers (1968), Ward (1963), and Boserup (1970), supplemented by the comparative studies of agricultural productivity in the U.S., Japan, and India by Nair (1962, 1969), and Firth and Yamay's (1964) study of capital, saving, and credit in peasant societies. None of these studies was undertaken with the notion of economic dualism in mind, but all of them throw some light on the relationship between the economic roles of women and the economic development of the society in question.

References

Adelman, I., and C. T. Morris (1967). *Society, Politics and Economic Development.* Baltimore: Johns Hopkins Press.

Adelman, I., and C. T. Morris (1967). *Economic Growth and*

Social Equity in Developing Countries. Stanford, Calif.: Stanford University Press.

Bennet, W. S. (1967). "Educational Change and Economic Development." *Sociology of Education* 40 (Spring 1967).

Boserup, E. (1970). *Woman's Role in Economic Development*. New York: St. Martin's Press.

Boulding, E. (1975). "Women, Bread and Babies: Directing Aid To Fifth-World Farmers." Paper prepared for the conference World Food and Population Crisis: A Role for the Private Sector, Dallas, Texas, April 3, 1975.

Boulding, E. (1976) *Women in the Twentieth Century World*. Beverly Hills, Calif.: Sage.

Boulding, E. (1977). *The Underside of History: A View of Women Through Time*. Boulder, Colo.: Westview Press.

Boulding, E., S. A. Nuss, D. Carson, and M. Greenstein (1976). *Handbook of International Data on Women*. Beverly Hills, Calif.: Sage.

Firth, R., and B. S. Yamay, eds. (1964). *Capital, Savings, and Credit in Peasant Societies: Studies from Asia, Oceania, the Caribbean, and Middle America*. Chicago: Aldine.

Hill, P. (1969). "Hidden Trade in Hausaland." *Man* 4.

Maher, V. (1974). *Women and Property in Morocco: Their Changing Relation to the Process of Social Stratification in the Middle Atlas*. London: Cambridge University Press.

Nair, K. (1962). *Blossoms in the Dust: The Human Factor in Indian Development*. New York: Praeger.

Nair, K. (1969). *The Lonely Furrow: Farming in the United States, Japan, and India*. Ann Arbor: University of Michigan Press.

Vreede–De Stuers, C. (1968) *Parda: A Study of Muslim Women's Life in Northern India*. Assen, the Netherlands: Koninklijke Van Gorcum.

Ward, B., ed. (1963). *Women in the New Asia: The Changing Social Roles of Men and Women in South and South-East Asia*. Paris: UNESCO.

United Nations (1974). "The Role of Women in Population Dynamics Related to Food and Agriculture and Rural Development in Africa." ECA/FAO, Women's Program Unit (mimeographed).

United Nations (1974). *1974 Report of the World Social Situation.* New York: United Nations.

Part 3: What To Do About 1

When Planners try to help the poor
They make more misery than they cure,
And every scheme of welfare totters,
Faced by the desperate needs of squatters.

Some cultures can be understood
By Images of Limited Good
But theorist may be imposter
Who does not other models foster.

Is there a culture of the Poor
That keeps them at Starvation's Door?
Or is the only impropriety
Found in the Structure of society?

We should define the Target Groups
And then detect the feedback loops
That lead to the stability
Of Misery, Sickness, and Debility.

If crises leave us in the lurch
We haven't done the right research,
So one of our research devices
Should be to study future crises.

Perhaps we should make some apologies
For battling our ideologies,
But, though we march to different drummers,
Truth, happily, takes on all comers.

Kenneth Boulding

9. Policies for Equitable Growth

Irma Adelman, Cynthia Taft Morris,
and Sherman Robinson

After two decades of concern with the problem of raising
per-capita GNP in low-income developing countries, the
development community of the 1970s has shifted its focus to
the challenge of increasing the equity of the distribution of
income. The shift proved to be dramatically needed, as the
empirical studies of the distribution of the benefits from
economic growth showed that the expected trickle-down was
not taking place. More serious, a number of studies indicated
a systematic worsening, both relative and absolute, in the
position of the poorest stratum of income recipients.

In this paper, we attempt to summarize our insights with
respect to antipoverty policy in developing countries. These
insights were gained in the course of three different major
research projects focused upon the relationship between the
various facets of modernization and relative and absolute
poverty. The first is a cross-section statistical study of the
sources of differences among countries in the relative income
shares of the poorest 60 percent of households.[1] The second is
a historical analysis of processes and initial conditions
leading to extreme poverty in twenty-four countries in the
middle of the nineteenth century.[2] The third is a modeling
effort for the South Korean economy used as a laboratory to
explore the probable efficacy of a large variety of major but

This article was originally published in *World Development* 4, no.
7 (1976): 561–582. Reprinted by permission.

nonrevolutionary strategies, policies, and programs for the alleviation of poverty in the medium run.[3]

Cross-Section Study

Our cross-section study of economic growth and social equity relates interactions among economic and social structures and change to the distribution of income as measured by the income shares of the poorest 60 percent, the middle 20 percent, and the upper 5 percent of the population. The data are for the period 1957–1968 for forty-three underdeveloped countries. They include a wide range of measures of economic structure and institutions and social and political characteristics potentially relevant to poverty.

The statistical analysis attempts to assess the relative importance of thirty-five independent variables in explaining intercountry differences in patterns of income distribution. The analysis selects the independent variable which splits the sample into two subgroups between which the largest difference in scores on the independent variable is obtained. For example, country scores on the share of income of the poorest 60 percent can be split into two groups, the variance between which accounts for 28 percent of the total variance, by the independent variable "socioeconomic dualism"; no other candidate variable accounts for as high a proportion of the total variance. Each of the groups obtained in this way is then treated as a "parent" group and the "best" partition together with the "best" independent variable obtained. The process is stopped when no variable can be found that yields a reduction of variance between group means significant at the 5 percent level. A leading characteristic of the technique is that it permits the selection of different independent variables for different portions of the data.

The results of the study suggest a set of hypotheses regarding the dynamics of economic development and income distribution. The generalizations which follow assume that in its growth path a typical underdeveloped country will embody the average characteristics of the groups of countries which are associated with successive levels of development.

The relationship between levels of economic development and the equity of income distribution is shown to be asymmetrically U-shaped, with more-egalitarian income distributions being characteristic of both extreme economic underdevelopment and high levels of economic development. Between these extremes, however, the relationship is, for the most part, inverse up to a point; higher rates of industrialization, faster increases in agricultural productivity, and higher rates of growth all tend to shift the income distribution in favor of the higher-income groups and against the low-income groups.

The beneficiaries of economic development, as well as the processes by which the poor are penalized by economic development, vary with the level of development of the country. At the lowest level of development, as economic growth begins in a subsistence agrarian economy through the expansion of a narrow modern sector, inequality in the distribution of income typically increases greatly, the income share of the poorest 60 percent declines significantly, as does that of the middle 20 percent, and the income share of the top 5 percent increases strikingly. In these countries the path toward sustained economic growth is eventually blocked unless either the country is sufficiently large or redistributive policies are sufficiently important to generate an internal market for growth.

Once countries move successfully beyond the stage of sharply dualistic growth, the middle-income receivers are the primary beneficiaries of the widening of the base for the economic growth which follows. The position of the poorest 40 percent typically worsens both relatively and absolutely, even where a transition from sharply dualistic growth to more-broadly based economic growth is accomplished. Where relatively high levels of development have been attained and the capacity for more-broadly based economic growth has been established, the poorest segments of the population still typically benefit from economic growth only where widespread efforts are made to improve the human resource base.

Finally, it should be noted that, in order to reach the relatively small positively correlated portion of the equity-level-of-economic-development curve, a country must be among the upper half of those underdeveloped countries at the highest level of development. Indeed, in the absence of domestic policy action aimed specifically at redirecting the benefits of growth, a nation must attain a level of development corresponding to that which exists among the socioeconomically most highly developed of the underdeveloped countries (Argentina, Chile, Taiwan, Israel) before the income distribution tends to become as even as it is in countries that have undergone virtually no economic development (e.g., Dahomey, Chad, Niger).

Perhaps the most interesting policy findings of the study were negative—the paucity of potentially relevant influences that proved to have systematic relationships to variations in shares. As Table 1 shows, the ineffective influences include most of the conventional economic variables as well as most of the social variables which economists stress. Among these are increases in agricultural productivity, changes in degree of industrialization, rates of growth of population, and improvements in tax systems and financial institutions. The unimportance of these variables is reconfirmed by the results of the Adelman-Robinson policy experiments for Korea.

The important economic instruments are quite few. Nor are policies to change them easily designed and carried out. Furthermore, they primarily benefit the middle class. Increasing the rate of economic growth and accelerating modernization have complex consequences that depend upon the stage of economic development; faster growth can achieve a more equal income distribution only at the highest stage characteristic of developing countries. Even then, a favorable impact on distribution is likely only when growth is achieved through a broadly based strategy predicated upon the wide spread and application of educational skills. At all levels, increased access to the acquisition of middle-level skills and professional training contributes to improving the income distribution through its favorable impact on the share of the middle quintile. Policies tending to reduce dualism by widening the base for economic growth are conducive to income equality, benefiting particularly the middle-income groups. The distributional effects of a large government role in industrial production are favorable to lower- as well as middle-income recipients. To implement a major spread of education together with effective use of the

TABLE I

SUMMARY OF RESULTS OF ADELMAN-MORRIS CROSS-SECTION STUDY OF INFLUENCES ON THE DISTRIBUTION OF INCOME

	DIRECTION OF RELATIONSHIP*			FREQUENCY OF SIGNIFICANCE		
	BOTTOM 60%	MIDDLE 20%	TOP 5%	BOTTOM 60%	MIDDLE 20%	TOP 5%
POTENTIALLY EFFECTIVE						
RATE OF IMPROVEMENT IN HUMAN RESOURCES	+	+	−	1	2	1
DIRECT GOVERNMENT ECONOMIC ACTIVITY	+	0	−	1	0	3
SOCIO-ECONOMIC DUALISM	−	−	+	1	1	1
POTENTIAL FOR ECONOMIC DEVELOPMENT	−	+	0	2	2	0
PER CAPITA GNP	−	0	−	1	0	1
STRENGTH OF LABOR MOVEMENT	−	+	−	1	1	1
MODERATELY EFFECTIVE						
ABUNDANCE OF NATURAL RESOURCES	−**	0	+	1	0	1
FACTOR SCORES ON LEVEL OF SOCIO-ECONOMIC DEVELOPMENT	0	+	0	0	2	0
STRUCTURE OF FOREIGN TRADE	+	+	0	1	1	0
IMPORTANCE OF INDIGENOUS MIDDLE CLASS	0	+	−	0	1	1
CHARACTER OF AGRICULTURAL ORGANIZATION	−	+	0	1	1	0
POLITICAL PARTICIPATION	0	+	−	0	1	1
POLITICAL STRENGTH OF TRADITIONAL ELITE	−	0	+	1	0	1
LEVEL OF MODERNIZATION OF INDUSTRY	−	+	0	1	1	0
LITERACY	0	+	0	0	1	0
DEGREE OF CULTURAL AND ETHNIC HOMOGENEITY	−	0	0	1	0	0
LEADERSHIP COMMITMENT TO ECONOMIC DEVELOPMENT	0	−	0	0	1	0
EFFECTIVENESS OF FINANCIAL INSTITUTIONS	0	−	0	0	1	0
URBANIZATION	0	+	0	0	1	0
NOT EFFECTIVE*						

*Where a variable is significant at more than one split in a single analysis, the sign refers to the first split.

TABLE I (CONTINUED)

**This sign is incorrectly stated to be positive in the footnote to Fig. I, p. 163 of Economic Growth and Social Equity in Developing Countries.

***Adequacy of physical overhead capital, rate of population growth, total population, level of modernization of agricultural techniques, improvements in agricultural productivity, change in degree of industrialization, size of the traditional agricultural sector, rate of growth of per capita GNP, level of effectiveness of financial institutions, country size and orientation of development strategy, extent of social mobility, type of colonial experience, length of experience with self-government, and political strength of the military.

increased stock of human capital in a labor- and skill-intensive growth strategy, and at the same time to achieve a significant reduction in dualism and a marked change in the role of the government, requires in most countries a fundamental reorientation of development policies. The required changes are likely to be so far-reaching that they imply a radical transformation of power relationships and economic and social structures.

Historical Analysis

Our analysis of economic growth and impoverishment in the middle of the nineteenth century applies the techniques for the development of "soft" data to gain insight into the historical impacts of economic change on the structure and extent of poverty. A typology of the structure of poverty is constructed for 1850 for twenty-four countries, and the nine types which emerge are ranked by the probable extent of extreme poverty. The nature and ranking of the types is then used to develop hypotheses regarding the historical processes generating poverty. The year 1850 was selected in order to focus on the impact on the poor of the early stages of commercialization and industrialization. The sample consists of countries of widely different levels of development. The countries selected are those where some significant aggregate economic change occurred between 1850 and 1914 for which adequate materials appeared to be accessible.

The concept of poverty applied is that of extreme material poverty. The extremely poor are defined to include three overlapping categories: (a) those who were starving or destitute, (b) those whose food consumption was marked by recurrent inadequacy of their staple food and infrequent consumption of meat, fish, and dairy products, and (c) those subject to very poor health conditions, as indicated by extreme overcrowding, unusually high mortality rates, or disease. The "poverty line" dividing the extremely poor from the rest of the population, while above the level of near-starvation and destitution, lies below a rigorously determined level of adequacy of diet and living conditions.

The sorts of historical data which permit the identification of the major groups in poverty are extremely various:

TABLE 2

A TYPOLOGY OF POVERTY IN 1850

TYPE OF COUNTRY	BRIEF DESCRIPTION OF TYPE	COUNTRIES IN GROUP (a)	STRUCTURAL INFLUENCES AND PROCESSES CONTRIBUTING TO POVERTY IN INDIVIDUAL COUNTRIES (b)
A	RAPIDLY INDUSTRIALIZING AND MOST ADVANCED INDUSTRIALLY; MAJOR POPULATION DISPLACEMENTS	BELGIUM	DIS 1, DIS 2, DIS 4, AG 1 (WEAK), AG 3 (WEAK), AG 4, AG 7, AG 8 (WEAK), URB 2, URB 3 (WEAK)
		ENGLAND	DIS 1, DIS 2, DIS 4 (WEAK), AG 8 (WEAK), URB 2, URB 3 (WEAK)
B	MORE SLOWLY INDUSTRIALIZING COUNTRIES; MODERATE DISPLACEMENTS OF POPULATION	GERMANY	AG 1 (WEAK), AG 2 (WEAK), AG 4 (WEAK), DIS 2 (WEAK), URB 2 (WEAK), URB 3 (WEAK)
		FRANCE	DIS 2 (WEAK), URB 2 (WEAK), URB 3 (WEAK)
		SWITZERLAND	DIS 2 (WEAK), URB 2 (WEAK), URB 3 (WEAK), AG 4 (WEAK), AG 5 (WEAK), DIS 1 (WEAK)
C	NEWLY SETTLED COUNTRIES; SCARCITY OF AGRICULTURAL LABOR; POVERTY CONCENTRATED AMONG URBAN IMMIGRANTS	(U.S.A.)	URB 2, URB 4
		AUSTRALIA	URB 2, URB 4
		(NEW ZEALAND)(E)	URB 2, URB 4, AG 2
		CANADA	AG 2 (WEAK), URB 4
D	EXTREME CONCENTRATION OF LAND OWNERSHIP; MAJOR REGION OF DENSE POPULATION; LOW PRODUCT PER WORKER	ITALY	AG 1 (WEAK), AG 2, AG 4, AG 6, AG 8, DIS 1
		SPAIN	AG 1 (WEAK), AG 2, AG 4, AG 6, AG 8, URB 1, DIS 1
E	SMALL-SCALE INDEPENDENT CULTIVATION; RAPID POPULATION GROWTH IN PRESENCE OF EXPANSION OF EMPLOYMENT OPPORTUNITIES: RESOURCE POPULATION RATIO NOT UNFAVORABLE	NORWAY SWEDEN DENMARK (F)	DIS 1, DIS 4, URB 1, AG 8
F	SLOWLY COMMERCIALIZING; CONSIDERABLE DISINTEGRATION OF FEUDAL-TYPE ECONOMY; DENSE STABLE POPULATION; MODERATE DISPLACEMENTS OF POPULATION	JAPAN	DIS 1, AG 3 (WEAK), AG 2, AG 6 (WEAK), AG 8 (WEAK)
G	DENSE POPULATION: PARCELIZED HOLDINGS BY INDEPENDENT PEASANTS; LOW PRODUCT PER WORKER	INDIA	AG 1, AG 2, AG 3, AG 4, DIS 3
		CHINA	AG 1, AG 2, AG 3, AG 4, VIOL 1

TABLE 2 (CONTINUED)

H	HIGH RATE OF APPROPRIATION OF PRODUCT: SERF, BONDED, OR SLAVE LABOR; LOW PRODUCT PER WORKER	RUSSIA	AG 2, AG 3, AG 4, AG 5, AG 6
		(BRAZIL)	AG 2, AG 3 (WEAK), AG 5, AG 6
		EGYPT	AG 2, AG 3, AG 4, AG 5, AG 6
		TURKEY (ASIAN)	AG 2, AG 3, AG 4, AG 5, AG 6, VIOL 1, DIS 3 (WEAK)
I	FAVORABLE RESOURCE POPULATION RATIO; STABLE POPULATION; PRE-INDUSTRIAL INSTITUTIONS OF SOCIAL INSURANCE	BURMA	AG 1 (WEAK), AG 2 (WEAK)
UNCLASSIFIED		ARGENTINA	AG 2, AG 6
		NETHERLANDS	AG 2 (WEAK), DIS 1 (WEAK), URB 1, URB 2, URB 3 (WEAK)

NOTES:

(a) Countries in parentheses are in some significant respect anomalous for their type; see text for explanation.

(b) The symbols representing structural influences and processes contributing to poverty in individual countries are as follows:

DIS 1: displacement of small agriculturalists because of agricultural commercialization, DIS 2: displacement of craft workers because of domestic industrialization, DIS 3: displacement of craft workers because of foreign imports, DIS 4: unemployment or underemployment because of surge in population growth greater than growth in employment opportunities, URB 1: overcrowding of urban informal sector, URB 2: cyclical unemployment, URB 3: factory wages below subsistence, URB 4: urban foreign immigrants. AG 1: pressure of population on agricultural resources, AG 2: low productivity per worker in agriculture, AG 3: natural disasters, AG 4: parcellization of cultivating units, AG 5: slavery/serf labor/ de facto bonded labor, AG 6: exploitative landholding institutions, AG 7: agricultural indebtedness associated with commercialization of agriculture, AG 8: wages of agricultural laborers below subsistence, VIOL 1: domestic violence

Note that the structural influences and processes are not mutually exclusive. 'Weak' in parentheses indicates that the influence in question contributes to the poverty of relatively few or affects only a single region. The omission of an influence does not indicate that it was not present, only that it does not appear to have operated strongly enough to cause extreme poverty. Influences probably affecting less than 1% of the population are not cited.

TABLE 2 (CONTINUED)

RANK OF TYPE ON EXTENT OF POVERTY (c)	MAJOR SOURCES OF COUNTRY INFORMATION (d)	COUNTRY
5	DECHESNE (1932); CHLEPNER (1956); BAUDHUIN (1928-29); DUCPETIAUX (1850).	BELGIUM
	CHAMBERS AND MINGAY (1966); CLAPHAM (1939); ENGELS (1844); LYONS (1976); USHER (1920); CAIRD (1851); MAYHEW (1860-61); REDFORD (1964).	ENGLAND
3½	HAMEROW (1969); WUNDERLICH (1961); KUCZYNSKI (1945).	GERMANY
	BOGART (1942); CLAPHAM (1921); LEVASSEUR (1904).	FRANCE
	RAPPARD (1914); SCHWIEZERISCHE GES. FUR STATISTIEK (1964); WITTMAN (1963).	SWITZERLAND
	BIDWELL AND FALCONER (1925); GRAY (1925); JONES (1960); WARE (1964); LEGERGOTT (1964); FOGEL (1975); WOODMAN (1966).	(U.S.A.)
2	COGHLAN (1918); GRIFFIN (1970); SHAW (1946).	AUSTRALIA
	CONDLIFFE (1930); SIMKIN (1950); SUTCH (1969); THOMSON (1859).	(NEW ZEALAND)
7	EASTERBROOK AND AITKEN (1956); FIRESTONE (1960); TUCKER (1936).	CANADA
	CLOUGH (1964); ECKAUS (1961); SETON-WATSON (1946); SCHMIDT (1939).	ITALY
	BRENAN (1943); CARR (1966); VIVES (1969); MERIN (1938); HIGGINS (1886); LIVI-BACCI (1968).	SPAIN
	DRAKE(1969); HOVDE (1943); JANSON (1931); LIEVERMAN (1970);	NORWAY
6	NIELSON (1928); YOUNGSON (1959); MONTGOMERY (1939);	SWEDEN
	SOLTOW (1965).	DENMARK
3½	HONJO (1965); SMITH (1959); TSUCHIYA (1937); HANLEY AND YAMAMURA (1971); YAMAMURA (1973).	JAPAN
9	DAVIS (1951); BLYN (1966); BHATIA (1967); GADGIL (1942); SINGH (1965); DIGBY (1901).	INDIA
	FAIRBANK, ECKSTEIN, AND YANG (1960); HOU (1963); TAWNEY (1932); PERKINS (1969); CONDLIFFE (1932); MALLORY (1926).	CHINA

TABLE 2 (CONTINUED)

8	LYASHCHENKO (1949); TUGAN-BARONOVSKY (1907); TUMA (1965); MAVOR (1925); HAXTHAUSEN (1847-48); TOURGUENEFF (1847).	RUSSIA
	GRAHAM (1968); PRADO (1967); STEIN (1957); CONRAD (1972);	BRAZIL
	BAER (1959); DICEY (1881); NAHAS (1901); OWEN (1969).	EGYPT
	MUKDIM (1935); HERSHLAG (1964); ISSAWI (1966); MORDIMANN (1878).	TURKEY
1	FURNIVALL (1931); HLIANG (1964); TUN WAI (1961).	BURMA
	DIAZ ALEJANDRO (1970); SCOBIE (1964).	ARGENTINA
	BRUGMANS (1961); JONGE (1968); BAASCH (1927); KEMPER (1850).	NETHERLANDS

NOTES:
(c) For discussion of empirical bases for the ranking see text.
(d) See bibliography in Adelman and Morris, "A Typology of Poverty," for full references.
(e) Inadequacy of empirical evidence leaves serious doubt about the extent of extreme poverty in this country.
(f) Overall extent of extreme poverty less than characteristic of type.

overt signs of destitution and famine; data on poor relief; data (usually qualitative or impressionistic) on unemployment, vagrancy, begging; descriptive evidence on food consumption; information on the prevalence of land holdings insufficient to support a family; crude estimates of the relative importance of selected occupational groups; indirect indications of undernourishment and malnutrition; and information on extreme overcrowding or the health hazards of housing, water, and sanitation.

The final typology of the structure of poverty is summarized in Table 2. Each type is listed together with a brief indication of its main features in the first column and the countries composing it in the second column. The third column summarizes structural conditions or processes associated with extreme poverty for each country. The fourth column shows the probable ranking of the types by overall extent of extreme poverty, with the lowest number assigned to the type with the least-extreme poverty and the highest number to that with the most. The final column gives the principal sources of information. Since our main interest is in the impact of industrialization and commercialization on poverty, we ordered the types initially by level of industrialization, as judged primarily by the relative importance of the factory sector. The five types in which industrialization was negligible were ordered by extent of commercialization.

An overview of the typology suggests the following generalizations about variations in the structure and extent of poverty in the middle of the nineteenth century:

The comparative abundance of agricultural resources and the nature of institutions for landholding and cultivation differentiated between the extremes of widespread poverty. Poverty was most widespread in India and China (Type G), where parcelized holdings were combined with pressure of population on resources with given technology. Poverty was next most widespread in Types H (Russia, Egypt, Turkey, and Brazil) and D (Italy and Spain), where high rates of appropriation of product existed either because of cultivation by some form of servile or bonded labor or because land ownership was highly concentrated with cultivation by small-scale tenants or landless laborers. Poverty was least widespread in the relatively resource-abundant newly settled countries where internal frontiers were still expanding and the distribution of land was comparatively egalitarian (Type C). In the noncommercial economy of Burma (Type I), abundance of land compared with population and preindustrial village and extended family institutions for social security combined to hold extreme poverty to a minimum.

In countries of the middle range (Types A, B, E, and F), extreme poverty was greatest where economic or demographic change had been widespread or very rapid. In the nonindustrial countries of Scandinavia (Type E), surges of population growth in the absence of sufficient growth of employment led to large numbers of landless unemployed laborers. In the industrially advanced countries of Belgium and Great Britain (Type A), widespread and rapid economic change was associated with major failures to absorb surplus population into the expanding sectors of the economy. In contrast, in Germany, France, and Switzerland (Type B), industrialization had proceeded more slowly, with more-frequent location of factories in rural areas. In Japan (Type F), commercialization of agriculture had spread slowly over a period of many decades, and population growth rates were low.

Several major hypotheses emerge from our historical study of the processes that generate poverty: First, the inherited constraints on economic structure that most affect the incidence of poverty in low-level agricultural economies are the abundance of accessible agricultural resources relative to population and the nature and structure of landholding institutions. Second, the relationship between the level of economic development and the extent of poverty is complex and nonlinear, with extreme poverty possible both at very low and higher levels of development. Third, any kind of structural change, such as industrialization or commercialization, tends to increase poverty among the poorest members of the population. Furthermore, in the early stages of development, the increase in poverty tends to be quite large unless the change is sufficiently slow and of such a kind that the population whose activities are displaced or marginalized can be reabsorbed into expanding sectors of the economy. Our study suggests the hypothesis that both rapid commercialization and rapid industrialization systematically depressed the standard of living of the poorest stratum of the population in the early part of the nineteenth century. Finally, the structure and processes of economic activity matter most in determining the incidence of poverty; the structures of production, the market sector, and the labor force; the processes of technical change, commercialization, and population growth. We will discuss each of these hypotheses in turn.

First, our comparative analysis of poverty in 1850 reinforces the proposition that the constraints on economic structure contributing most to widespread poverty in overwhelmingly agricultural economies in the nineteenth century were the comparative scarcity of agricultural resources and the institutions of land ownership and cultivation. Where population was dense relative to available resources (for example, China and India), increases in population growth to the level of economic opportunity contributed to widespread poverty and recurrent food shortages.

Landholding institutions also affected the structure of poverty. Two kinds of landholding institutions were particularly unfavorable: extreme concentration of landownership with small-scale tenant cultivation (as in Spain and Italy) and large-scale cultivation by servile labor (as in Brazil and Russia); both led to high rates of appropriation by landowners and extreme poverty among agriculturalists. Widespread poverty also occurred with small-scale peasant ownership where population pressed hard against resources and customary or legal constraints on the subdivision of holdings were weak. In India, China, and parts of Belgium and southwest Germany, for example, the incidence of poverty was closely associated with population density and parcelization of small independent landholdings.

Second, our study suggests that the relationship between the extent of poverty and the level of economic development is complex. At the lowest level of economic development there was the most widespread extreme poverty. This level was characterized by either unfavorable resource-population endowments or exploitative landholding institutions. At the highest level of development extreme poverty was much less widespread. However, within the group of high-level countries, the incidence of extreme poverty was greater in the most industrialized countries where economic change had been most rapid and pervasive. Within the group of agricultural economies (above the lowest level) which were undergoing significant commercialization, variations in the incidence of extreme poverty were accounted for by constraints posed by land institutions and the rapidity of economic or demographic change rather than by the level of economic development.

Third, the present analysis suggests strongly the proposition that all kinds of structural change hurt the poor. A leading hypothesis emerging from our study is that during the first half of the nineteenth century, the spread of mechanized techniques and the spread of markets in agriculture systematically increased poverty among the poorest segments of society. The salient features of comparative experience during that period suggest the following model of the key interactions contributing to increased poverty. The extent of increased poverty depended on the nature, strength, and pattern (regional and sectoral) of two processes associated with structural change: first, the process of displacement of one set of economic activities by another as a result of monetization or technological change; and second, the process of expansion associated with the introduction of new economic activities. The impact of structural change on poverty depended upon the net balance of the two processes. Interacting with these patterns were national and regional patterns of population growth and migration.

The process of displacement rarely meant that the outmoded activities disappeared immediately. Rather, the people engaged in such activities were forced through competition with the new activities to accept reduced earnings or reduced employment. The earnings of rural handicraft workers in both Belgium and Great Britain declined steadily after the Napoleonic wars as they faced the cheaper products and rising output of the factory sector. In all countries, the commercialization of agriculture had reduced possibilities for small agriculturalists to obtain a livelihood; enclosures had taken away the use of commonlands on which they depended, rising land values and rents had squeezed small tenants, and the shift to production for the market had led to indebtedness and dispossession of smallholders without the resources to survive market fluctuations. The people engaged in the increasingly marginal activities had joined the permanent wage-earning class or the permanently unemployed only when faced with eviction or incomes below an irreducible minimum.

The processes of expansion associated with the introduction of new economic activities provided for increased employment in both new activities and selected older ones. Factories provided employment directly to only a small proportion of the total labor force in the industrializing countries of northern Europe in 1850. Furthermore, the demand for factory labor was mainly for women and children. Employment had also expanded in such related activities as mining, forestry, and certain handicrafts not yet threatened by mechanization. The demand for unskilled weavers had increased greatly for a time as a result of the mechanization of spinning in England and Switzerland, for example, at the beginning of the nineteenth century. Where commercialization of agriculture had favored the growth of large-scale farming, the demand for agricultural laborers increased substantially (for example, in the north of England, northeast Germany, Normandy, Flanders, and the Po Valley). Commercialization had also provided increased profits and employment to those peasant families with sufficient resources and skills to produce successfully for the market.

Sectoral and regional patterns of displacement, absorption, and population growth mattered greatly. The segmented nature of labor markets implied that labor shortages in particular regions or industries did not cancel out surpluses elsewhere. Institutional, social, and cultural forces limiting geographic mobility thus contributed to an unfavorable net balance of the processes of displacement and absorption. Strong preferences for rural ways of living had led many agriculturalists and rural handicraft workers to accept declining earnings rather than leave their small plots of land. Legal impediments to mobility (for example, the English Settlement Laws) had aggravated regional labor surpluses. Cultural barriers to mobility, such as those posed by Flemish reluctance to move to French Belgium, had intensified unemployment among farmers whose activities had been displaced or marginalized by technical change and commercialization. As a result, detailed net balances—industry by industry and region by region—rather than national balances determined both the pattern and the extent of overall impoverishment associated with structural change.

In the more industrialized countries, cyclical unemployment and fluctuations in prices contributed significantly to poverty. Recurrent unemployment depressed the living standard of urban industrial workers, while price fluctuations contributed to indebtedness and loss of land in agricultural areas.

The extent of imbalance in the labor market was strongly affected by the acceleration of population growth that had occurred during the latter half of the eighteenth century in many countries and regions. The sources of the spurt in population lay in processes that took place as far back as the seventeenth century: improvements in diet related to the spread of new crops, lowered death rates due to mild disease prevention and the lessened impact of wars and domestic violence, and some increases in fertility associated with the weakening of traditional social checks on population growth. The impact of population growth on the extent of extreme poverty operated through its effect on the net balances of the processes of displacement and absorption. Migration, both internal and external, had operated to mitigate the unfavorable effects of segmentation of labor markets, but at that time had generally been insufficient to reduce significantly the net national balance through the evening out of regional imbalances. The pace, distribution, and structure of economic change in turn affected population growth. Where economic change had proceeded slowly, adaptation of population change was possible, and adaptive changes had taken place in some countries and regions. Rapid and pervasive change rendered unlikely adaptive responses of fertility rates to the rate of expansion of economic opportunities. As a result, while rapid economic change meant increased possibilities for absorbing an expanding labor force, the net impact of more-rapid growth was mostly negative because the failure of adaptive population responses more than counterbalanced its positive effects.

Thus, the nature and extent of structural change, together with its rapidity and pattern, determined both the incidence and the characteristics of poverty in the mid-nineteenth century. The critical features whose interrelationships accounted for the incidence of economic change in the poor were the rapidity, breadth, and spread of economic change, landholdings and landholding institutions, and past patterns of population growth. We found no automatic trickle-down to the poorest segments of the population of the benefits of industrialization. On the contrary, economic growth appears to have worked systematically to reduce their levels of living even where average standards of living of workers rose (as in Great Britain between 1800 and 1850).

In summary, the lessons of economic change suggested by our comparative study of the first half of the nineteenth century are that: (a) any kind of structural change in under-developed countries is achieved through processes of net displacement tending to lower the living standards of the poorest members of the society; (b) there is no automatic mechanism ensuring that expanding economic activities will be either appropriate or adequate to reabsorb the population displaced or threatened by structural change; (c) the faster the structural change, the more likely the processes of displacement are to swamp the processes of absorption and result in a marked deterioration in the living standards of the poorest members of the economy; and (d) the impact of economic change on poverty depends critically on the nature of social structure and social responses to economic change. These include social constraints on population growth, the response of fertility and migration rates to changing eco-nomic opportunities, legal and customary barriers to the subdivision of land, arrangements for land tenure and holding, and the strength of extended family protection of the unemployed and underemployed.

Korean Model of Income Distribution

This model is designed to provide a laboratory within which one can explore the potential impact of standard economic policy instruments and programs intended to improve the relative and absolute incomes of the poor. The model traces out both the direct and indirect influences upon the distribution of income. Its structure is set by the nature of the major economic forces determining the distribution of income in the relatively short run and of the major policy instruments which could affect it.

The model is in the tradition of economywide planning models. It has as its primary focus the modeling of the distribution of income, but it also includes all the components of more-traditional planning models as well as some monetary elements typical of macromodels. Its distinguishing features are: (a) it solves for prices endogenously in both factor and product markets; (b) its solution is based on achieving a measure of consistency among the results of individual optimizing behavior by a large number of actors (households, firms); (c) it incorporates income distribution, monetary phenomena, and foreign trade; (d) it is dynamic, with imperfect intertemporal consistency; and (e) it allows for varying principles of market clearing and institutional behavior.

The model operates by simulating the operation of factor and product markets with profit-maximizing firms and utility-maximizing households. Although it is broadly in the neoclassical tradition, it has a number of disequilibrium, nonneoclassical features. The overall model consists of a static within-period adjustment model linked to a dynamic intertemporal model. Within each period, the degree of adjustment is constrained by the existence of capital in place of a specific type, by the immobility of the self-employed both in agriculture and in urban production, by rigidities in wage structures, and by government constraints on firm behavior, especially in the foreign-trade sector. Between periods, some degree of flexibility is provided by capital accumulation, population growth, migration, changes in the amount of self-employment, and changes in the size structure of production. Nevertheless, the ability of the economy to achieve full Walrasian equilibrium remains severely constrained.

The model is quite comprehensive in its degree of "closure," i.e., the number of features of the economy which are endogenous and mutually consistent. The model explicitly goes from endogenously determined factor payments and employment to household incomes, with savings and expenditure decisions being modeled at the household level. The overall size distribution of household incomes is determined by explicit aggregation. Accounting consistency is maintained among: (a) household, firm, government, and trade accounts, (b) national income accounts, (c) input-output accounts, (d) national product accounts, and (e) the labor force and the number of households.

The model's focus on policy experiments led to its being designed in as flexible a manner as possible. The model incorporates optimizing responses by firms and households to a wide range of policy instruments such as indirect tax rates, direct tax rates, tariffs, interest rates, and monetary variables. Furthermore, the model is capable of portraying a variety of institutional principles in the operation of credit markets and factor markets, the degree of monopoly, and even the objective functions of firms.

A summary description of the overall model follows. For each period, the computation of the model is decomposed into three stages. The Stage 1 model describes the contracts made between firms and the financial markets to spend funds on investment goods. Stage 2 describes how factor and product markets reach an equilibrium constrained by the investment commitments undertaken in Stage 1 and by various institutional rigidities imposed by foreign trade and by the operation of product and labor markets. Stage 3 serves to generate the expectations on which Stage 1 decisions are based, some of the rules of its operation (e.g., the credit regime), and to "age" the model economy. Stage 2 is the major simultaneous core of the model; it represents the basic static portion of the model used for comparative-statics experiments. Stages 1 and 3 are used only in the dynamic analysis.

Stage 1 models the loanable funds market. Producers form their demands for loanable funds on the basis of expected sales and expected prices of inputs. Credit is then rationed, either by setting an interest rate and allowing the market to clear at that rate or by setting a target rate of expansion of credit and allowing the rate of interest to adjust in order to clear the loanable funds market. The output of Stage 1 is the allocation of loanable funds among firms and sectors and an overall injection of credit into the economy. Stage 1 is diagramed in Figure 1.

The Stage 2 model is a general equilibrium model in that prices or supplies are assumed to adjust so as to clear all markets, subject to various constraints that prevent the economy from fully adjusting by means of pure market mechanisms. Furthermore, money enters into the Stage 2 model in an essential way.

The Stage 2 model is itself subdivided into a number of

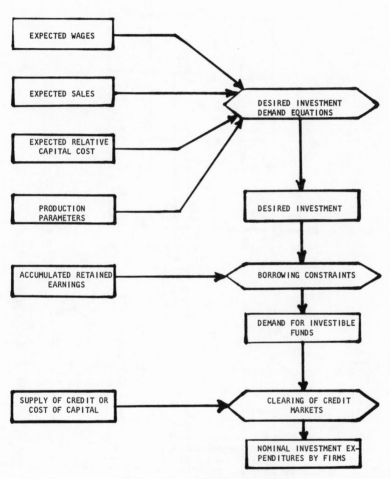

FIGURE 1
STAGE I: DETERMINATION OF INVESTMENT

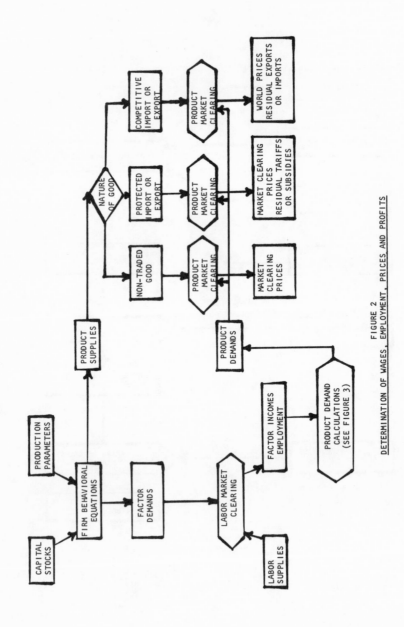

FIGURE 2

DETERMINATION OF WAGES, EMPLOYMENT, PRICES AND PROFITS

parts representing different computational phases: supply, demand, wage, income, and price determination. The output of this stage consists of "actual" production, employment, prices, wages, and income distribution for the period. Figures 2 and 3 portray the basic model structure. In Figure 2, the product and labor markets are pictured. The treatment of traded goods is especially important. Imports and exports which compete in the world market are assumed to sell domestically at the world price plus a fixed tariff (or subsidy). For these goods, imports and exports are determined residually after calculating domestic supply and demand at the fixed prices. For protected goods or nontraded goods, we assume that the domestic markets are insulated from the rest of the world and that prices are determined so as to clear them.

Figure 3 shows the income accounts and especially the steps in translating the functional distribution into the household distribution. There are fifteen different socioeconomic categories of income recipients from whom the model determines income, taxes, allocations to household groups, transfers, savings, and consumption expenditures. For each category, a within-group distribution is calculated by summing the fifteen different group distributions.

The Stage 2 model reaches its solution by means of a *tatonnement* process which simulates market behavior. However, in both Stages 1 and 2, no actual transactions take place until the solution of each stage is reached. Thus, the capital stock of firms is altered only at the end of Stage 1; factors are hired, production takes place, and income is earned and spent only at the end of Stage 2.

The Stage 3 model consists of a set of functions which update the relevant variables and formulate expectations which enter into the Stage 1 model for the next period. Stage 3 can be seen as consisting of a collection of submodels which specify all the dynamic adjustments and intertemporal linkages for the overall model (see Table 3). Our relatively short time horizon has led us to specify a fairly simple set of Stage 3 functions. A number of variables such as population growth are simply assumed to grow at an exogenously specified rate. Rural-urban migration is explicitly modeled as a function of only rural-urban income differentials, with an upper limit on the possible annual rate of migration. In

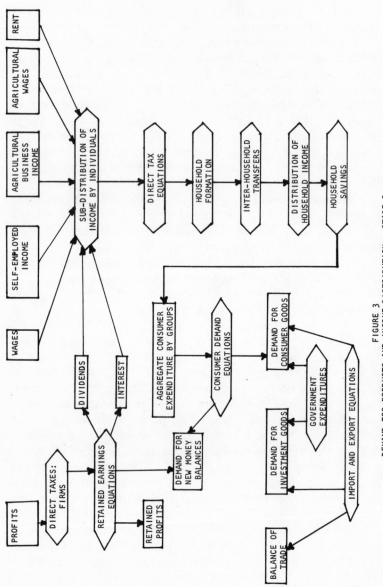

FIGURE 3
DEMAND FOR PRODUCTS AND INCOME DISTRIBUTION – STAGE 2

TABLE 3

MAJOR HYPOTHESES GENERATED BY ONLY ONE STUDY CONCERNING THE IMPACT OF ECONOMIC PROCESSES ON INCOME DISTRIBUTION

HYPOTHESES	STUDY	REASONS FOR IMPORTANCE
AGRICULTURAL TERMS OF TRADE CRITICAL DETERMINANT OF DISTRIBUTION OF INCOME	A-R	INELASTICITY OF DEMAND AND SUPPLY LEADS TO PRICE CHANGES; METHODOLOGY OF OTHER STUDIES DOES NOT PROVIDE TEST.
SIZE DISTRIBUTION QUITE INSENSITIVE TO MAJOR CHANGES IN THE FUNCTIONAL DISTRIBUTION OF INCOME	A-R	HIGH VARIANCE OF EARNINGS WITHIN FUNCTIONAL DISTRIBUTION; SOCIO-ECONOMIC COMPOSITION OF DECILES VARIED AND OVERLAPPING; FUNCTIONAL NOT MEASURED IN OTHER STUDIES.
FUNCTIONAL DISTRIBUTION VERY SENSITIVE TO ECONOMIC POLICY	A-R	ECONOMIC CHANGE IS BOTH ACCOMPLISHED BY AND AFFECTS PEOPLE IN THEIR FUNCTIONAL CAPACITIES AS PRODUCERS; THEREFORE MOST ECONOMIC CHANGE AND ECONOMIC POLICIES IMPINGE DIRECTLY UPON SOCIO-ECONOMIC RATHER THAN INCOME GROUPS.
IMPORT SUBSTITUTION STRATEGY WORSENS DISTRIBUTION OF INCOME	A-R	DETERIORATES AGRICULTURAL TERMS OF TRADE SUBSTANTIALLY; NOT MEASURED IN OTHER STUDIES.
THE IMPACT ON THE POOR OF STRUCTURAL CHANGE IS DETERMINED BY THE DETAILED NET BALANCES OF THE PROCESSES OF DISPLACEMENT, ABSORPTION, AND LABOR FORCE REDISTRIBUTION	HIST	INNOVATION ENTAILS BOTH SUBSTITUTIONS FOR AND COMPLEMENTARITIES WITH EXISTING ECONOMIC ACTIVITIES; THE SUBSTITUTIONS TEND TO BOTH DISPLACE AND ABSORB WORKERS; COMPLEMENTARY ACTIVITIES EXPAND; SEGMENTATION OF MARKETS PREVENTS EVENING OUT OF UNEMPLOYMENT AND LABOR SHORTAGES; EVEN WITHIN A GIVEN MARKET NO AUTOMATIC BALANCING OF EXPANSIONARY AND CONTRACTIONARY INFLUENCES IN EITHER SHORT OR MEDIUM RUN BECAUSE OF SOCIALLY INDUCED RIGIDITIES AND LACK OF ADAPTABILITY OF SKILLS.

general, there are no interactions among the various sub-models, and each is specified as a self-contained set of functions.

In each period, the three stages are solved serially. Variables which are assumed to be fixed in Stage 1 are allowed to vary in Stage 2. Thus the overall model distinguishes between expectations and realizations. In the third stage, the differences between expectations and realizations are incorporated into the forecast functions for the expected variables with which calculations are made in the periods subsequent to the first. In fact, the overall dynamic model represents a kind of "lurching equilibrium" which, it is hoped, represents a more realistic specification of actual growth than would be provided by some intertemporally efficient equilibrium growth model.

We now turn to a discussion of the major implications of the model. The major conclusion from the policy experiments is that the time path of the size distribution of income is exceedingly stable. Under a great variety of experiments, many of which involve quite sizable interventions, there is a marked tendency to return to the basic-path distribution. Even when the policy or program is sustained over time, it is quite rare that, after ten years, there is more than a 5 percent change in the Gini coefficient, or that a percentile's share is altered by more than 20 percent. Most single-policy interventions, with the exception of transfers, even when quite large, do not have lasting effects. Even transfer policies, while to some extent effective, are potentially of quite limited scope in most less-developed countries. Only when a sufficient number of different interventions are applied simultaneously—so that there is, in effect, a change in development strategy—are more-sizable or lasting effects possible. These results support the position that structural change is required to affect inequality and that equity objectives must shape the choice of basic development strategy if they are to be met.

The stability of the size distribution is associated in our experiments with relative instability in factor shares and in the functional distribution of income. This instability indicates that the relative position of various socioeconomic groups is very sensitive to the choice of economic policy. By appropriate choice of instruments, it is easy to favor or discriminate against particular groups. The relative degrees of poverty and wealth in the economy as a whole are little affected, but the composition of the poor and wealthy groups changes dramatically.

Partial analyses are rarely indicative of the ultimate effects of policy interventions, once their impact is allowed to permeate throughout the system. Particular instruments or policies often have different effects than expected. Not only orders of magnitude but also directions of effects are often different. Also, the effects of policy or program combinations are rarely equal to the sum of the effects of their individual components, indicating that interaction effects among policies are significant.

Our results underscore the importance of the agricultural terms of trade and the extent of rural-urban migration for antipoverty policy. In contrast, they indicate that such often-advocated changes as the promotion of small-scale industry and changes in the labor intensity of technology in manufacturing, unless part of a wider package, either are ineffective or are effective for reasons which are different from the grounds on which they are usually advocated. Population policy has relatively little effect on the size distribution of household incomes over the medium time period considered. Indeed, population policies which result in relatively less labor in urban areas tend to deteriorate the distribution of income.

Of the possible instruments for policy intervention to improve the size distribution of income, the agricultural terms of trade are particularly crucial. An increase in the terms of trade raises the incomes of small farmers (and, to a lesser extent, landless labor) and injures urban groups, including the urban poor. Overall, however, even though the incomes of rich farmers are raised more than proportionately and the urban poor are hurt, the net reduction in poverty is significant. Policy actions are required to maintain the agricultural terms of trade, as the terms of trade have a natural tendency to worsen with growth.

Rural-urban migration can affect poverty significantly. In general, the incomes of the urban poor are much higher than the incomes of the rural poor, so that one would expect migration to alleviate overall poverty. However, there clearly can be too much migration, creating a Marxian "reserve army" of the would-be employed and thereby keeping unskilled urban wages at subsistence. If, in addition, agricultural output falls due to outmigration, food prices will rise, raising the cost of living and further impoverishing urban workers.

As expected, choice of trade policies has a significant impact on poverty and equity. However, it is not the direct effects of trade policy on the urban sector which matter—that impact is rapidly dissipated throughout the economy— rather, it is the impact of trade policy on the agricultural terms of trade and upon rural-urban migration that provides the major influences of trade upon poverty and equity. For example, had Korea followed an import-substitution strategy rather than a labor-intense export-expansion policy, our experiments indicate that the resultant deterioration of the agricultural terms of trade would have produced a significantly poorer size distribution of income and significantly greater poverty than were actually experienced. By contrast, a stronger labor-intensive export-promotion package would have had some beneficial effects, the most important of which would have been felt ultimately through trickle-down to the poor farmers.

As for population policy, we found that a reduction in rural population reduces poverty by decreasing the agricultural labor force. It leads to an increase in average land holdings through reductions in the number of farm households and also results in a more intensive use of labor. In contrast, reducing the urban population leads to increases in overall poverty by restricting the supply of urban goods, thus causing their prices to rise, and by lowering the demand for food products, thus causing their prices to fall. The consequence is deterioration in the agricultural terms of trade. The negative effect of urban population reduction can be mitigated by induced increases in migration to replace the lost urban labor and act as a substitute for direct reduction in rural population.

Perhaps the most frequently proposed antipoverty measure is that of direct transfers to the poor. Two different types of transfer program were tried: (a) direct income transfers and (b) price subsidies for consumption of necessities (food, housing, and medical care) for both rural and urban poverty groups. Both types of transfer policies help the specific target groups and have the least leakage and market-distortion effects of any of our experiments. The effects of the price-subsidy program, however, are somewhat eroded over time, because as incomes rise the share spent on necessities falls. The more important problem with transfer programs, however, is that the effects last only as long as the program is in effect. Therefore, if such programs are to be the major tool of antipoverty policy, society must be committed to persistently large welfare budgets and to the resulting dualistic society.

The choice of an appropriate development strategy can lead to major improvements in the share and absolute incomes of the poor, given appropriate initial conditions. The difference to the poor between a labor-intensive export strategy and an import-substitution strategy can be major and lasting. In the presence of reasonably equitable distribution of land ownership and tenure arrangements and widespread ownership of human capital, a labor-intensive export strategy contributes significantly to a more-egalitarian distribution of income. Even with such a strategy and favorable initial conditions, however, a systematic tendency for deterioration to occur in the share of income accruing to the poor appears to be built into the operation of rapidly growing economic systems. To avoid the impact of such deterioration is quite difficult and requires further pervasive reorientation of policy.

To explore the nature of desirable reorientations of policy imposed over and above the basic development strategy, dynamic policy experiments for both rural and urban target groups were carried out. For each sector, packages were investigated containing social development programs, production and employment programs, and programs involving varying degrees of institutional change. Policy experiments with both rural and urban packages showed that the overall program is considerably more effective than the sum of its components. In general, the ultimate impact of the packages is determined largely by the extent and nature of indirect leakage effects, which, in turn, are strongly influenced by interactions among the component sets of programs.

Of the individual rural-development packages, programs to promote increases in agricultural production are not an unqualified blessing. They are ineffective in reducing poverty and improving the distribution after import-substitution possibilities in food are exhausted. They then tend to worsen the position of the rural poor and improve the lot of urban groups, including the urban poor, unless effective price stabilization policies are implemented. In general, who gains from the rural policy packages depends largely on what happens to the terms of trade. If they turn against agriculture, the result is a transfer or trickle-up to the urban groups. Rural groups gain only if special policies are implemented to prevent the terms of trade from deteriorating too much. Rural public-works programs lead to substantial improvement in the real incomes of the poor, especially landless rural labor, and are moderately effective policies. Land reform, which redistributes land to small farmers, is very effective, both in reducing poverty and in narrowing the distribution within the rural sector. Rural cooperatives— which market the crop, subsidize agricultural inputs, and provide low-cost credit—have some beneficial effects and represent a moderately effective program. Of the individual policy packages, land reform has the most effect on the relative distribution and raises the incomes of the poor by almost as much as rural public works.

The implementation of a rural development strategy (including production, public works, cooperatives, social development, and price-stabilization programs) is very effective in alleviating poverty and improving distribution. Under the rural development strategy which includes land reform, the number of people living in poverty is reduced to about one-quarter of the number in the basic run by the final year. The rural strategy without land reform is less beneficial (there are 20 percent more households living in poverty than in the package with land reform), although it is still very effective.

The individual urban programs are all at most moderately effective in reducing poverty and changing the overall distribution. They do, however, exhibit a certain amount of synergism, such that the combination of several urban programs is more effective than the sum of their separate components. The moderately effective individual urban packages are (a) a public-works program in housing construction and transportation and (b) a program to intensify the promotion of labor-intensive and export industries.

However, these programs are successful in alleviating poverty not because of their effect on urban wages and employment but rather through their influence on rural poverty via changes in the terms of trade. A number of programs were ineffective in reducing overall poverty and improving the relative distribution: consumption subsidies to urban working groups, the promotion of small-scale industries, and the adoption of labor-intensive technology (by changes in the production functions). Some programs were harmful. A program to reduce the rate of growth of the urban population (and hence the urban labor force) increased the amount of poverty and worsened the overall distribution. A program to nationalize large-scale manufacturing also increased the degree of poverty, largely because it resulted in lower productivity in the nationalized firms and less manufacturing output overall, and hence drove up the relative price of manufactures. The resulting decline in the agricultural terms of trade lowered rural incomes and so increased poverty.

Despite the largely disappointing nature of the individual urban program, an urban development strategy combining public works and the promotion of labor-intensive industries is effective in reducing poverty and improving distribution. Its effectiveness, however, is not nearly so great as the overall rural strategies and is due largely to indirect effects which improve the agricultural terms of trade and so allow the benefits to leak across to the rural poor. This trickle-down effect is more pronounced with time and, if allowed to operate, would continue to have favorable effects even after the experimental period.

Our experience with the separate rural and urban packages led us rather quickly to examine combined rural-urban packages. We sought an integrated and balanced approach which would affect all sectors of the economy and ensure that leakages to urban groups of rural programs are more than counterbalanced by leakages to rural groups of urban programs (because most of the poor are rural).

Two large across-the-board policy packages were considered in our policy experiments: a "market socialism" package (Package A) and a "reform capitalism" package (Package B). Package A was intended to represent a package of policies similar to those frequently adopted in noncommunist socialist countries. Package A emphasizes land reform, nationalization of large-scale industry, and import substitution, in addition to programs of social development, urban and rural public works, rural cooperatives, and industrial decentralization.

Package B, on the other hand, was intended to illustrate what a capitalist economy could do if it were sufficiently motivated by the goal of poverty alleviation to undertake significant alterations in the structure of its society. This reform capitalism package includes the same programs of social development, urban and rural public works, rural cooperatives, and industrial decentralization that appear in Package A. However, instead of an import-substitution strategy, there is an emphasis on promotion of labor-intensive exports. And, in preference to land reform, Package B introduces rural marketing boards and improvements in agricultural productivity. There is no analog to Package A's nationalization program.

Both Packages A and B were effective. By the end of the decade, in spite of leakages to the rich in Package B and a decline in the growth rate in Package A, all seven of the lowest income deciles of the society remained better off in absolute terms than they were without any policy package at all. The tradeoffs between the two approaches are the familiar ones. The market socialist package leads to better and improving distribution but deteriorating output performance relative to the unperturbed time path of the economy. The reform capitalism package shows evidence of deterioration of the distributional gains over time and of acceleration of production growth. By the end of the decade, everyone (including the lowest decile) is better off with the reform capitalism package than with the market socialism package in absolute terms. However, the seven lowest income deciles are still better off under the socialist package than in the basic dynamic solution, which has no significant antipoverty measures.

On the whole, our results underscore the difficulties of attempting to use effective policy intervention to improve the distribution of income. They emphasize the magnitude of the policy effort necessary to avoid rapid erosion of benefits. Since individual programs tend to be considerably less effective than packages of programs, and the benefits of most single-pronged interventions rapidly trickle up, a big-push balanced strategy appears to be best. However, a successful big push requires major government intervention and large implicit and explicit economic transfers. Therefore, the implementation of a successful antipoverty program would entail either a change in the ideology of the ruling classes towards explicit egalitarian concerns, or a certain degree of centralization of authority in order to overcome resistance by the rich, or, most likely, a combination of both. The problem would then remain of reducing the power of the centralized authority once its basic job is done.

Policy Implications

The present section is devoted to distilling the combined implications for policy emerging from the three studies. To avoid lengthy discussion, the results are summarized in tabular form. Table 4 lists the major hypotheses concerning the relationships between various economic processes and the distribution of income, especially the share of income of the poor. For each variable or influence, the nature of the interaction with income distribution is described, an indication of the studies on which the description is based is given, and the reasons for the impact on income distribution, as we understand them, are summarized. Table 5 lists in similar manner the major policy conclusions about economic influences which emerge from only one study.

All three studies, while utterly different in methodology and in the settings in which the relationships between poverty and growth were investigated, lead to a remarkably consistent and reinforcing set of policy conclusions. As is apparent from Table 4, the results of each study tend to be confirmed and illuminated by those of the other studies, not only in general terms but in specific detail. Since the tables are self-explanatory, we will concentrate here on an elaboration of only the principal conclusions of our work.

A leading conclusion of our studies is that intervention to improve the distribution of income is extremely difficult. The Adelman-Robinson model emphasizes the stability of the size distribution of income in the face of policy interven-

TABLE 4

HYPOTHESES GENERATED BY MORE THAN ONE STUDY CONCERNING THE IMPACT OF ECONOMIC PROCESSES ON INCOME DISTRIBUTION

VARIABLE OR INFLUENCE	NATURE OF IMPACT AND STUDIES BY WHICH GENERATED	REASONS FOR IMPACT
PER CAPITA GNP AND LEVEL OF SOCIO-ECONOMIC DEVELOPMENT	RELATIVE SHARE OF POOREST 60% OF POPULATION SHOWS U-SHAPED RELATIONSHIP TO PER CAPITA GNP (A-M). RELATIONSHIP BETWEEN ABSOLUTE PER CAPITA INCOME AND INCOME DISTRIBUTION COMPLEX; VERY LARGE DIFFERENCES IN DEVELOPMENT LEVELS POSITIVELY RELATED TO BOTH AVERAGE INCOME AND REDUCTION IN POVERTY; BUT RAPID GROWTH TENDS TO INCREASE POVERTY EVEN WHERE AVERAGE INCOME RISES (HIST AND A-M).	AT VERY LOW LEVELS OF DEVELOPMENT SMALL NUMBER OF GROWTH POINTS LEADS TO CONCENTRATION OF BENEFITS OF ECONOMIC CHANGE IN HANDS OF OLIGARCHY OF MERCHANTS, INDUSTRIALISTS, AND PLANTATION OWNERS; INDIRECT EFFECTS OF ECONOMIC CHANGE TEND TO HURT THE VERY POOR BY DISPLACING AND MARGINALIZING THEIR ACTIVITIES; ONLY BEYOND A THRESHOLD DETERMINED BY EXTENT AND SPREAD OF EXPANSION OF ECONOMIC OPPORTUNITIES IS TRICKLE-DOWN SUFFICIENT TO RAISE AVERAGE INCOMES OF URBAN WAGE EARNERS AND AGRICULTURAL LABORERS; EVEN THEN, REDUCTIONS IN EXTREME POVERTY TAKE PLACE VERY SLOWLY BECAUSE OF THE SEGMENTED NATURE OF THE LABOR MARKET AND LACK OF ADAPTABILITY OF HUMAN SKILLS.
SHORT-TERM RATE OF GROWTH OF PER CAPITA GNP.	NO SIMPLE ASSOCIATION WITH THE DISTRIBUTION OF INCOME; STRUCTURE AND COMPOSITION OF THE INCREASE IN INCOME, NOT AVERAGE DEGREE OF INCOME CHANGE, DETERMINES IMPACT (A-M AND A-R).	NATURE, EXTENT, AND RAPIDITY OF STRUCTURAL CHANGE GOVERN THE DIRECTION AND MAGNITUDE OF THE NET BALANCE OF THE PROCESSES OF DISPLACEMENT, ABSORPTION, AND SOCIAL ADAPTATION.
ECONOMIC INNOVATIONS	AT LOW AND MEDIUM LEVELS OF DEVELOPMENT NET IMPACT OF STRUCTURAL CHANGE OF ANY KIND ON THE POOR SYSTEMATICALLY UNFAVORABLE EVEN WHERE AVERAGE INCOMES RISE.	POOR DO NOT HAVE RESOURCES AND SKILLS TO TAKE ADVANTAGE OF EXPANDING ECONOMIC OPPORTUNITIES; THE OPERATION OF PRODUCT AND FACTOR MARKETS TENDS TO MARGINALIZE THEIR EARNINGS OR DISPLACE THEIR SKILLS; ONCE PERMANENTLY MARGINALIZED OR PRODUCTS DISPLACED, THE POOR LACK HUMAN AND FINANCIAL CAPITAL FOR ADAPTATION.
SOCIO-ECONOMIC DUALISM	SHARPLY DUALISTIC GROWTH FAVORS THE RICH AND HARMS THE RELATIVE AND ABSOLUTE POSITION OF THE POOR MORE THAN LESSER DEGREES OF DUALISM (WHETHER AT VERY LOW OR HIGHER LEVELS OF DEVELOPMENT).	CONCENTRATION OF GROWTH IN LIMITED SECTORS OR REGIONS, IN THE PRESENCE OF SEGMENTED LABOR MARKETS CHARACTERISTIC OF UNDERDEVELOPED COUNTRIES, AGGRAVATES DISPLACEMENT AND MARGINALIZATION OF SKILLS, THUS CONTRIBUTING TO POOLS OF SURPLUS LABOR.

TABLE 4 (CONTINUED)

NATURAL RESOURCES	A FAVORABLE RATIO OF AGRICULTURAL LAND TO POPULATION WITH PREVALENCE OF FAMILY-SIZE HOLDINGS RESTRICTS EXTREME POVERTY; AN ABUNDANCE OF NATURAL RESOURCES IS ASSOCIATED WITH EXTREME CONCENTRATION OF INCOME (A-M AND HIST).	AVAILABILITY OF RESERVE OF UNAPPROPRIATED AGRICULTURAL LAND RESTRICTS NUMBERS OF EXTREMELY POOR; PRESENCE OF ABUNDANCE OF NATURAL RESOURCES FOSTERS EXPLOITATION AND THE APPROPRIATION OF THE BENEFITS BY SMALL ELITES, FOREIGN AND INDIGENOUS.
RATE OF POPULATION GROWTH	PAST PATTERNS OF POPULATION GROWTH IMPORTANT DETERMINANT OF RESOURCE-POPULATION RATIOS AND THUS A KEY INITIAL CONDITION DETERMINING EXTENT OF EXTREME POVERTY (HIST AND A-M). IN MEDIUM RUN, POPULATION GROWTH AFFECTS SIGNIFICANTLY NET BALANCE OF PROCESSES OF DISPLACEMENT AND ABSORPTION (HIST AND A-R). IN SHORT RUN, POPULATION GROWTH OF LITTLE SIGNIFICANCE TO THE INCOME DISTRIBUTION (A-R AND A-M).	EXTREMELY LONG LAG (50 YEARS OR MORE) BEFORE CHANGES IN RATE OF GROWTH OF POPULATION AFFECT EXTENT OF EXTREME POVERTY SIGNIFICANTLY; MEDIUM-RUN EFFECTS DEPEND ON INTERACTION OF POPULATION AND MIGRATION AND ARE SUBJECT TO THRESHOLD EFFECT WITH RESPECT TO RESOURCE ABUNDANCE.
RURAL-URBAN MIGRATION	RURAL-URBAN MIGRATION REDUCES RURAL POVERTY AND INCREASES URBAN POVERTY; UP TO A POINT, IT REDUCES OVERALL POVERTY (HIST AND A-R).	IN LABOR MARKET REDUCES URBAN WAGES OR INCREASES URBAN UNEMPLOYMENT, WHILE DECREASING RURAL UNDEREMPLOYMENT OR INCREASING WAGES OF AGRICULTURAL LABOR; IN COMMODITY MARKETS IT SHIFTS THE TERMS OF TRADE IN FAVOR OF AGRICULTURE, THUS FAVORING THE MORE NUMEROUS AND POORER RURAL LOW-INCOME GROUPS; EXTREMELY RAPID RURAL MIGRATION LEADS UNFAVORABLE IMPACT OF THE URBAN POOR TO DOMINATE FAVORABLE RURAL EFFECTS.
EDUCATION	WIDE SPREAD OF EDUCATION AND LITERACY ASSOCIATED WITH LARGER SHARE OF INCOME TO MIDDLE QUINTILE; NO SYSTEMATIC ASSOCIATION WITH OTHER FEATURES OF INCOME DISTRIBUTION (A-M AND A-R).	SPREADS OWNERSHIP OF HUMAN CAPITAL; NARROWS DISTRIBUTION OF WAGE INCOME; INCREASES RURAL-URBAN MIGRATION, THEREBY SHIFTING POPULATION TO HIGHER INCOME AREAS AND IMPROVING AGRICULTURAL TERMS OF TRADE.
LAND TENURE AND HOLDINGS	IMPACT OF CHANGE ON THE POOR CRITICALLY DEPENDENT ON DISTRIBUTION OF LAND OWNERSHIP; PREVALENCE OF SUBSISTENCE FARMING WHERE LAND ABUNDANT IS FAVORABLE TO DISTRIBUTION OF INCOME; PARCELIZATION OF LAND OR MARKED CONCENTRATION OF OWNERSHIP WITH CULTIVATION BY EITHER LANDLESS LABORERS OR SUBSISTENCE TENANTS CONTRIBUTE DIRECTLY TO POVERTY; WIDESPREAD OWNER-OPERATION OF COMMERCIAL FARMS FAVORABLE TO DISTRIBUTION OF INCOME ALTHOUGH MAY NOT HELP THE VERY POOR (A-M AND HIST).	CONCENTRATED OWNERSHIP WHERE CULTIVATORS FACE LACK OF ALTERNATIVE EMPLOYMENTS PERMITS HIGH RATE OF APPROPRIATION OF SURPLUS PRODUCT; OPENING UP OF NEW OPPORTUNITIES IN PRESENCE OF UNEQUAL ABILITIES TO RESPOND WIDENS INEQUALITY; PROCESSES CONDUCIVE TO DISPOSSESSION OR MARGINALIZATION TEND TO BE IRREVERSIBLE.

TABLE 4 (CONTINUED)

VARIABLE OR INFLUENCE	NATURE OF IMPACT AND STUDIES BY WHICH GENERATED	REASONS FOR IMPACT
MODERNIZATION OF AGRICULTURAL HOLDINGS	INCREASES IN AGRICULTURAL PRODUCTIVITY TEND TO WORSEN THE POSITION OF THE RURAL POOR, WHILE BENEFITING BETTER-OFF FARMERS AND THE URBAN POOR (A-R AND HIST). NO SIGNIFICANT CROSS-SECTIONAL RELATIONSHIP.	ACCESS TO COMPLEMENTARY RESOURCES (HELD ONLY BY BETTER-OFF FARMERS) NECESSARY FOR ADOPTION OF IMPROVEMENTS; INCREASES IN OUTPUT WORSEN TERMS OF TRADE, HARMING RURAL POOR AND BENEFITING URBAN POOR; LACK OF CROSS-SECTIONAL RELATIONSHIP DUE TO INTERDEPENDENCE BETWEEN IMPACT OF AGRICULTURAL TECHNOLOGY AND LAND TENURE.
SIZE OF SUBSISTENCE AGRICULTURAL SECTOR	TOTAL ABSENCE OF COMMERCIALIZATION OF AGRICULTURE FAVORABLE TO DISTRIBUTION OF INCOME (HIST). AMONG COUNTRIES WITH SOME COMMERCIALIZATION, NO SYSTEMATIC RELATIONSHIP BETWEEN COMMERCIALIZATION AND DISTRIBUTION OF INCOME (HIST AND A-M).	IMPACT ON THE DISTRIBUTION OF INCOME OF COMMERCIALIZATION OF AGRICULTURE DEPENDENT ON LAND TENURE AND CONCENTRATION OF OWNERSHIP; ALSO DEPENDENT ON COURSE OF TERMS OF TRADE; SHORT-TERM AND MEDIUM- OR LONG-RUN IMPACTS MAY DIVERGE, DEPENDING ON DEMAND AND SUPPLY ELASTICITIES.
TRADE AND INDUSTRIALIZATION STRATEGY	MORE DIVERSIFIED LABOR-INTENSIVE EXPORTS ASSOCIATED WITH LARGER SHARE OF INCOME TO BOTH THE POOR AND THE MIDDLE CLASSES (A-M AND A-R).	IMPROVES AGRICULTURAL TERMS OF TRADE AND INCREASES ABSORPTION OF RURAL-URBAN MIGRATION.
LEVEL AND CHANGE IN INDUSTRIALIZATION	U-SHAPED RELATIONSHIP EVIDENT IN CROSS-SECTION AND HISTORICAL STUDY; MAJOR DIFFERENCES IN LEVEL OF INDUSTRIALIZATION NEGATIVELY ASSOCIATED WITH EXTENT OF POVERTY, BUT AMONG MORE INDUSTRIALIZED COUNTRIES, POVERTY GREATER IN THOSE AT HIGHER LEVELS WHICH INDUSTRIALIZED MOST RAPIDLY (A-M AND HIST).	RELATIONSHIP COMPLICATED; INTERDEPENDENCE BETWEEN LEVEL AND RATE AND THRESHOLD EFFECT. SEE TEXT FOR DISCUSSION.
MARKET SOCIALISM	REDUCES SHARE OF INCOME OF TOP 5%; INCREASES SHARE OF NEXT 15% (A-M AND A-R). REDUCES OVERALL GROWTH RATE AND OVERALL MEAN INCOMES, BUT RELATIVE AND ABSOLUTE INCOMES OF LOWEST 70% HIGHER IN MEDIUM-RUN (A-R).	REDUCES PROFITS AND INTEREST ACCRUING TO TOP 5%; INCREASES TECHNOCRAT AND BUREAUCRAT INCOMES; GIVEN NATIONALIZED FIRMS WHICH LESS DYNAMIC, ABSOLUTE GAINS TO THE POOR EVIDENT IN MEDIUM-RUN EVENTUALLY ERODED, BUT DISTRIBUTIONAL GAINS INCREASE.
EFFECTIVENESS OF AND IMPROVEMENTS IN FINANCIAL INSTITUTIONS	NO SYSTEMATIC ASSOCIATION WITH INCOME SHARES OF THE POOR EVEN THOUGH IMPORTANT FOR GROWTH (A-M AND A-R).	SPREAD OF FINANCIAL INSTITUTIONS EVEN IN RURAL AREAS TENDS TO BENEFIT PRIMARILY THOSE WHO ARE BETTER OFF; IMPROVED ACCESS TO CREDIT FOR POOR FARMERS ONLY BENEFICIAL WHEN COMBINED WITH IMPROVED ACCESS TO TECHNOLOGY AND KNOWLEDGE; INCREASES IN INVESTMENT, EVEN IN SMALL-SCALE INDUSTRY, TEND TO WORK THROUGH THEIR IMPACT ON ECONOMIC GROWTH (RELATIONSHIP OF LATTER TO INCOME DISTRIBUTION COMPLEX).
EFFECTIVENESS OF AND IMPROVEMENTS IN TAX SYSTEMS	NO SYSTEMATIC ASSOCIATION WITH DISTRIBUTION IN CROSS-SECTION (A-M). LITTLE IMPACT IN MODEL (A-R).	STRUCTURE OF TAX SYSTEM INFLUENCES WHO IS POOR AND RICH RATHER THAN HOW MANY; TAX BASE SUFFICIENTLY LOW SO THAT LITTLE SCOPE FOR IMPACT.

tions and the ephemeral nature and inefficacy of most single-pronged antipoverty programs. The cross-section study indicates how few potentially effective policy instruments there are and the difficulties which their very nature poses for efforts at purposive change. The historical study shows the systemic character of the dynamic processes that worked to the detriment of the very poor in the middle of the nineteenth century. The irreversibility of detrimental impacts implies that a remarkably long time is usually required before initially unfavorable effects are counterbalanced.

TABLE 5

MAJOR HYPOTHESES GENERATED BY ONLY ONE STUDY
CONCERNING THE IMPACT OF ECONOMIC PROCESSES
ON INCOME DISTRIBUTION

Hypotheses	Study	Reasons for importance
Agricultural terms of trade critical determinant of distribution of income	A–R	Inelasticity of demand and supply leads to price changes; methodology of other studies does not provide test.
Size distribution quite insensitive to major changes in the functional distribution of income	A–R	High variance of earnings within functional distribution, socio-economic composition of deciles varied and overlapping; functional not measured in other studies.
Functional distribution very sensitive to economic policy	A–R	Economic change is both accomplished by and affects people in their functional capacities as producers; therefore most economic change and economic policies impinge directly upon socio-economic rather than income groups.
Import substitution strategy worsens distribution of income	A–R	Deteriorates agricultural terms of trade substantially, not measured in other studies.
The impact on the poor of structural change is determined by the detailed net balances of the processes of displacement, absorption, and labour force redistribution.	Hist	Innovation entails both substitutions for and complementarities with existing economic activities; the substitutions tend to both displace and absorb workers; complementary activities expand; segmentation of markets prevents evening out of unemployment and labour shortages; even within a given market no automatic balancing of expansionary and contractionary influences in either short or medium run because of socially-induced rigidities and lack of adaptability of skills.

All our studies emphasize that, in a given configuration of structural conditions, it is strategy and process which determine the impacts of economic change on the poor. The historical study indicates that countries sharing a particular mix of poverty also share a set of historical processes of change. The cross-section study stresses the need for certain critical transformations of economies and societies which cannot be brought about without changes in the process and strategy of growth. The Korea model policy experiments show that, as long as policy interventions are tacked onto a given strategy which remains unchanged, the distribution of income tends to revert to the pattern it would have had in the absence of the interventions.

In addition, complicated interactions are evident in our studies between the impact of policy changes, on the one hand, and the initial conditions describing the socioeconomic structure upon which the policies impinge, on the other. Successful antipoverty policy does not merely entail choosing the right development strategy. Initial conditions must also be appropriate. The critical thresholds for successful policy interventions are related to the distribution of ownership of certain assets—those which enter the production functions of the newly expanding activities. In the cross-section results, the existence of thresholds with respect to initial conditions is suggested by the fact that some variables proved important only when countries had achieved minimal levels of education and spread of economic modernization. The historical study shows that the impact of processes of change on the poor depends upon the particular complex of initial conditions. Within complexes there were some possibilities for substitution among conditions; in addition, there were interactions among processes, on the one hand, and initial conditions, on the other.

A further important conclusion of our work is that unbalanced growth strategies are bad for the poor. In the Korea model, the dissipation of the benefits from programs with a single focus was larger and more rapid than from programs with multiple foci. In the cross-section study, sharply dualistic growth led to a worsening of the income distribution. Historically, the concentration of growth in either a few sectors or a few regions has had backwash effects that accentuate new overall displacements arising from commercialization and industrialization.

A final conclusion emerging from our studies is that a systems or general equilibrium approach is required in order to design a strategy which predictably improves the position of the poor in the medium term. Both the historical and modeling studies emphasize the importance of indirect effects and dynamic interactions. Not infrequently, the indirect effects of an initial impact of change swamp the direct effects and even reinforce the need for a careful, systems-wide analysis of the impact of potential policy actions. Taken together, the cross-section, historical, and modeling studies underline the great difficulty which planners face in finding policy instruments or programs which are effective in achieving more equitable paths of economic growth.

Notes

1. I. Adelman and C. T. Morris, *Economic Growth and Social Equity in Developing Countries* (Stanford, Calif.: Stanford University Press, 1973).
2. I. Adelman and C. T. Morris, "A Typology of Poverty in 1850," in *Essays in Honour of Bert Hoselitz*, ed. by Manning Nash (forthcoming).
3. I. Adelman and S. Robinson, *Income Distribution Policies in Developing Countries* (Stanford University Press, forthcoming).

10. Income Inequality and Capitalist Development: A Marxist Perspective

Martha E. Gimenez, Edward Greenberg,
Ann Markusen, Thomas Mayer, and John Newton

Orthodox economic theory does not provide a satisfactory theoretical framework for understanding the relationship between economic development and income distribution. In this paper, we argue that an approach to capitalist development structured largely in terms of Marxist theory, yet one which adopts certain concepts from orthodox social science, offers a more rewarding framework for comprehending the relationship between economic development and income distribution. After outlining our theoretical framework, we demonstrate how it can be applied to several historical cases.

We begin by criticizing orthodox notions of economic growth and well-being, paying particular attention to deficiencies of income as the sole measure of these phenomena. Next we undertake a brief examination of the historical relationship between growth and inequality in the developed world, demonstrating that capitalism has at every stage in its development been plagued by problems of inequality in income, wealth, and the quality of life. In the discussion which follows, we attempt to show how Marxist theoretical concepts—particularly those of class, surplus value, and power—illuminate and explain this persistent (and, we would submit, inescapable) linkage between capitalist production and inequality. We proceed to explore the relationship between growth and equity in the developing countries, explaining why the social position of the majority has deteriorated in the course of capitalist development. Finally, to eliminate any mistaken impression that econom-

ic growth and inequality are inseparable, we examine several
cases of development in postrevolutionary societies.

Deficiencies in the Income Concept

Developmental economists, after encountering a distress-
ing series of problems in the use of such traditional concepts
as stability, efficiency, and growth in their examination of
third-world economies, have increasingly turned their attention to *equity* as an alternative analytic tool. While we
applaud this new concern, we believe that orthodox economists will encounter serious difficulties in their study of
inequality in developing countries because of their excessive
reliance upon *income* as a basic social indicator.

Orthodox economists generally limit their discussion of
equity to income equality. Yet the material existence of poor
people defies reduction to a single economic indicator. In
particular, money income fails to capture the full material
experience of a person who is both a producer (employed or
not) and a member of a society, the values of which are
shaped by economic relationships. At best, money income
expresses only the return to the worker for market production activity. Income differentials reflect relative buying
power in the marketplace but may distort the living standards of various groups, especially if substantial nonmarket
production, in-kind services, and public-sector production
exist as economic activities differentially available to classes.
Of course, income comparisons are subject to the usual
index number problems when groups have differential
access to the necessities of life. For example, income figures
simply lose their meaning in the face of communally provided housing or when good medical care is unavailable at
any price. But even more important is the nonmonetary
material existence of workers.

For example, labor under capitalism is alienated labor.
Alienation is an objective aspect of capitalist relations of
production which (a) forces workers to sell their labor in
order to survive, (b) forces workers to constantly compete for
jobs, (c) expropriates workers from control over the productive process and its outcomes, (d) forces workers to develop
only marketable talents, and (e) robs workers of the product

of their labor, given that wages are equivalent to the value of workers' subsistence needs and not to the value of their total output (Marx, 1887). Alienation, in its multiple dimensions, is an inverse socioeconomic indicator of material well-being. The ideological form in which workers become conscious of alienation and the kinds of behavioral patterns that emerge in their attempt to cope with it on an individual basis is documented in great detail in the growing body of literature describing the links between work dissatisfaction and alcoholism, drug addiction, absenteeism, sabotage, and mental illness (see, for example, Special Task Force Report to the Secretary of Health, Education and Welfare, *Work in America*, Massachusetts Institute of Technology Press, 1973; also Blauner, 1964; Kornhauser, 1965; Mott et al., 1965; Robinson, 1967; Vroom, 1964). It seems reasonable, therefore, to take into account the consequences of alienated labor when considering the performance of a capitalist economic system.

Economic justice is another important feature of economic experience. Whether we focus on "just" participation in production or on the division of the fruits of production or on the right to the fruits of one's own labor, no presently available indicator measures the capacity of an economic system to deliver justice. If we could compare wage and profit rates, appropriately chosen income statistics might function as a remote proxy for exploitation. Unfortunately, such comparisons are almost impossible, since profit in any major production sector is buried under the industrial wraps that clothe international corporations and trade relations. Adequate indicators of economic justice remain to be developed.

Other indicators of the quality of life deserve mention. Infant mortality, morbidity rates, incidence of disease, nutritional levels, pollution levels, and literacy rates are elements of material welfare which may not be reflected in income and distribution figures. Increasingly, indicators of this kind are being incorporated within theoretical models and social accounts.

The economic profession is increasingly compelled to recognize that income and its distribution are hopelessly incomplete measures of economic performance.

The Theory of Capitalist Development

Capitalism has always been an international system. Socioeconomic processes occurring in one national unit of the capitalist world system have always been closely related to processes occurring in other parts of the system. The process of capitalist development in a world which had not witnessed the emergence of universal commodity production was quite different from the process today, when the capitalist world is relatively unified under the dominion of a few advanced capitalist economies. We must therefore consider separately the development of presently advanced economies and that of presently backward economies.

Income Inequality and Capitalist Production in the Developed Countries

Despite the inherent problems attached to the income concept, the relationship between capitalist systems of production and income distribution remains of more than passing interest, not least because of the drift of recent scholarship in development economics. In their widely acclaimed examination of development and inequality in the nonsocialistic world, Adelman and Morris expressed a sense of incredulity and dismay at the results of their research, research which demonstrated that economic development in the third world is *not* tied to the equalization of income.

The results of our analysis came as a shock to us. Although we had believed economic growth to have unfavorable social, cultural, and ecological consequences, we had shared the prevailing view among economists that economic growth was economically beneficial to most nations (Adelman and Morris, 1973).

Ahluwalia, in the World Bank study *Redistribution with Growth* (1975), points to what he calls the "new pessimism" in the development literature, by which he means the growing suspicion among scholars that economic growth does not necessarily bring equalization (Chenery et al., 1974). What we find surprising in these views is, not the recognition of growing inequality within those countries where economic development has taken place under capitalist arrangements, but that orthodox economists can be astonished by such outcomes. Such astonishment, we believe, shows a disregard for both the history of capitalist development in the West and the continuing structure of inequality in the developed capitalist world. No one has ever persuasively demonstrated that capitalist development and income equalization are in any way logically or empirically associated.

Let us examine the relationship between development and inequity in England and the United States. The periods of most dramatic growth in the economies of England and the United States were from about 1780 to 1860 in the former and from about 1870 to the end of World War I in the latter (Kuznets, 1965, p. 276). In the U.S., during its own rapid growth period, Kuznets estimated an expansion of GNP from $10.7 billion in the 1869–1878 period to $67.6 billion in 1914–1923. During this period in England, we have no persuasive evidence that the material standard of living was improved for most of the population. What evidence we do have is conflicting, with no significant indication of a rise in the real level of wages (Flinn, 1974), some evidence of growing inequality in income distribution (Kuznets, 1965) and more than a little evidence of deteriorating quality of life for the masses on the basis of such nonincome indicators as mortality rates, incidence of disease, environmental pollution, and malnutrition (Hobsbawm, 1968).

Rapid growth in England was accomplished mainly through the twin processes of *enclosure* (the forced separation of small farmers and tenants from the land, their means of production), which had the effect of creating a pool of cheap and fitfully employed labor, and *industrialization*, which had the effect of destroying scores of skilled trades, of drawing women and children into the labor process, and of creating vast urban slums. While we cannot place much confidence in income-distribution data from this period of unprecedented growth in the overall economy, we can be fairly confident (on the basis of testimony from various first-hand observers) about the following developments in England (Hobsbawm, 1962 Heilbroner, 1968; Thompson, 1963):

- the creation of an itinerant, free-floating class of unemployed or fitfully employed wage laborers;
- the destruction of the framework of protections provided by traditional society;
- the advent of dangerous and monotonous factory labor and, most dramatically, the intensification of the exploitation of child labor;
- the deterioration of infant mortality rates and life expectancy in mining and manufacturing centers (Friedlander, 1973); and
- the increase of objective alienation—that is to say, the advancement of the division of labor and the loss of control by direct producers over the content and product of their work.

Serious, disruptive, and threatening transformations were occurring among subordinate groups in English society. In the first half of the nineteenth century laws prohibiting vagrancy and idleness proliferated in England; harsh strictures were introduced so as to prevent "illegal combinations" among working people, both in the new factories and in the old trades; game-law offenses were more vigorously enforced; and Dickensian workhouses for the poor became commonplace.

Analogous processes were at work in the U.S. during its own period of rapid growth—expansion of working-class slums, proletarianization of labor, deterioration in the health of blue-collar workers and their families, and so on. Not surprisingly, the period 1870-1920 in the U.S., while one of dramatic economic growth, witnessed the equally dramatic concentration of wealth into a relatively few hands and, most probably, a considerable widening of the income gap (Kuznets, 1965).

Economic growth under capitalist auspices seems to require both painful sacrifices from subordinate nonpropertied groups and an overall accentuation of inequality. Orthodox economists generally believe, however, that once sustained economic growth has been placed on a firm footing (what Rostow calls "takeoff"), capitalism moves toward equalization. In the United States from the end of World War I into the 1950s, average wage rates rose steadily and the share of national income accruing to labor increased; from 1940 onward the general living standards of the wage-earning population visibly improved. Much the same thing happened in England after 1860. Political interventions in the economy seem to have been the principal factor at work in this slight reversal of income trends (Kuznets, 1965, p.276). According to the conventional interpretation, democratic government will act to soften the harsh consequences of economic development and to reverse the trends toward inequality, mainly through the regulation of business and the institution of a progressive tax system.

Many development economists end their story here with the notion that modern capitalist economies, controlled and regulated by democratic governments, will continue on the slow but inexorable march toward greater equality. Kuznets in 1953 confidently announced the continuation of these trends into the future (Kuznets, 1959). Two years earlier, Arthur Burns proudly boasted that "the transformation in the distribution of our national income . . . may already be counted as one of the great social revolutions of history" (Herman, 1975). What has become increasingly evident, however, is that the income and wealth distribution characterizing Western capitalist nations remains frozen in a position of severe inequality.

With respect to the United States, what is striking about the available data is the existence of marked inequality in income distribution and the persistence of this inequality over time. (Note the figures in Table 1, which include the augmentation of family income through government transfers.)

Between 1947 and 1972—during a period of unparalleled growth in the American economy, in educational opportunities, and in government programs to assist the poor and the elderly—the poorest 20 percent of American families increased their share of national income (before taxes) by only .3 percent. The position of the wealthiest 20 percent of families declined only one percentage point during that same period.

As critical as income remains in determining the life chances of Americans, we would argue that wealth in property is, in the long run, even more important. This is so for a number of reasons. First, the ownership or nonownership of wealth is the most important determining factor in the generation of disposable income; it is the very basis for income. To be without wealth in property means that one must sell one's labor in the marketplace, and, for all but a tiny wage-earning elite (doctors, lawyers, athletes, corporation executives, etc.), high incomes are an impossibility. For instance, an annual salary of $30,000 puts one among the top 5 percent of U.S. income earners (Hacker, 1975). Most Americans (almost two-thirds, in fact), take home less than $15,000 per annum, barely enough to surpass the Bureau of Labor Statistics' "intermediate" standard of living. While some very high incomes are based purely on salary (those of professional athletes, for instance), most are derived from wealth in property. For those families in the over-$200,000-a-year bracket, 72 percent of all income is generated from property ownership. For families earning in excess of $1 million annually, 91 percent is generated from the sale or use of property—real estate, corporate stock, savings accounts, bonds, and so on (Internal Revenue Service, 1974). There exists an almost perfect correspondence between annual earnings and the ownership of property in the United States: those without property usually have very low incomes; those with extensive property almost always enjoy high annual incomes.

TABLE 1

SHARE OF AGGREGATE INCOME BEFORE TAXES RECEIVED BY EACH FIFTH OF
FAMILIES, RANKED BY INCOME, U.S.A., SELECTED YEARS, 1947-72* (PERCENTAGES)

INCOME RANK	1947	1950	1960	1966	1972
TOTAL FAMILIES	100.0	100.0	100.0	100.0	100.0
LOWEST FIFTH	5.1	4.5	4.8	5.6	5.4
SECOND FIFTH	11.8	11.9	12.2	12.4	11.9
THIRD FIFTH	16.7	17.4	17.8	17.8	17.5
FOURTH FIFTH	23.2	23.6	24.0	23.8	23.9
FIFTH FIFTH	43.3	42.7	41.3	40.5	41.4

SOURCE: U.S. Department of Commerce, Bureau of the Census
NOTE: Detail may not add to totals due to rounding.
*The income (before taxes) boundaries of each fifth in 1972 were: lowest fifth - under $5,612; second fifth - $5,612-$9,299; third fifth - $9,300-$12,854; fourth fifth - $12,855-$17,759; highest fifth - $17,760 and over. Income includes wages and salaries, proprietors' income, interest, rent, dividends, and money transfer payments.

Moreover, large property owners are in a position to

control major American social institutions. Only those well endowed with property possess the income, assets, technical assistance, investment capability, and time necessary to control corporations, banks, foundations, universities, and news media. To own income-producing property on a large scale is to be among the potential directors of the American social order. To be a wage or salary earner exclusively is to be largely directed and controlled by others.

Clearly, knowledge of wealth distribution yields more understanding of who wins and who loses in American life than does knowledge of income distribution. However, obtaining information about the distribution of wealth is even more difficult than obtaining data about the distribution of income, primarily because wealth is more easily hidden. Information about the property holdings of Americans, unlike income, is nowhere consistently and periodically collected. Nevertheless, every government and scholarly study of the distribution of wealth shows an astounding maldistribution—a maldistribution so extreme that it makes income inequality look quite tame by comparison (see, for example, Parker, 1972).

When we turn to the more-developed welfare states of Western Europe, the picture of inequality is no more encouraging. Whether we measure the phenomenon by mobility rates, by educational opportunity, or by income/wealth distribution, inequality is as pronounced there as in the United States (Parkin, 1971). Evidence suggests that in most European welfare states, income and wealth inequality actually increased during the 1960s because of the declining progressivity of tax systems (Miller and Rein, 1975).

Two inescapable conclusions can be drawn: first, there seems to be no association between equalization and economic growth in the development of advanced capitalist societies; second, unequal distribution of income, wealth, and quality of life is systematically organized around the institution of property, high income being associated with the ownership of income-producing assets and low income with its absence.

The Marxist theory of social classes posits the existence of two basic and historically significant social classes in capitalist society: one which owns and controls the basic means of material production (factories, machinery, tools, raw

materials, investment capital, and the like) and one which
owns nothing but its own labor power. The former class, by
virtue of owning the productive apparatus, derives the
power to direct production, the power to determine what is
produced and how. This class, since it controls access to the
means of production, can buy the labor powers of others,
direct its uses, and, in the form of profits, appropriate the
surplus produced by human labor. The second class, owning
no property, is forced to sell its own labor power for wages
but has the peculiar capacity of producing more value than it
receives in compensation. Labor power, in capitalist society,
becomes a commodity priced by its attractiveness to capital
and discarded when it is no longer required by capital. The
theory of social class can explain a wide variety of phenomena, including the nature of income inequality between
classes, the income differentials within the working class
(based on its attractiveness as a commodity), and the causes
of unemployment and its contribution to the depression of
wage rates.

The Marxist theory of social classes rests at base on the
exploitation of one class by another. It is a theory of exploitation in the double sense that wage labor surrenders both
control of its own use and possession of the surplus value
which it produces. Paradoxically, this double surrender
makes possible the accumulation of capital and the enrich-
ment of the propertied class. Marxists trace the dynamics of
capitalist society in general and income inequality in particular to this unequal control over the productive apparatus.

The Development of Underdevelopment

So far, we have considered the relationship between
growth and inequality in the presently developed countries
in a manner which implies their isolation from the international economy. While this might be permissible for some
few countries, it is plainly inadequate as a general approach.
Each national economy must be located within the context
of an international political economy, since its location
therein has decisive consequences for the internal structure
of the domestic economy. It is particularly important to
locate backward societies within the context of an interna-

tional system of production, an international division of labor, and an international process of capital accumulation.

Economic development within the nonsocialist world must be seen as part of a process of capital accumulation which, from its very inception, has proceeded on a world scale (Amin, 1974). The main structural feature of this accumulation process is the bifurcation of the capitalist world into a *center*, consisting of developed societies in which labor is highly productive, and a *periphery*, consisting of backward underdeveloped societies in which the productivity of labor is relatively low. Moreover, the center-periphery bifurcation is repeated within peripheral capitalist societies. Here we find one sector of the economy which is relatively modernized and typically oriented toward foreign markets, and another (usually larger) sector using primitive production techniques and oriented toward local markets or possibly outside the market system altogether. Frank (1969, p. 9) calls the process by which capital accumulation creates backward economies the "development of underdevelopment." Backwardness, in other words, is not the absence of economic development but rather a special kind of economic development which transforms a precapitalist economy into an underdeveloped capitalist economy.

Before examining how capitalist accumulation on a world scale creates a structural duality between center and periphery, let us clarify a number of points. Marxist theory does not argue that the societies of peripheral capitalism cannot industrialize or achieve significant economic growth. Peripheral capitalist societies, such as Brazil, Hong Kong, Iran, Singapore, South Korea, and Taiwan, are accomplishing just this. Marxist theory does argue that industrialization in the third world is unlikely to loosen the bonds of dependency which presently subordinate peripheral to central capitalist societies, or to enable a particular peripheral society experiencing industrialization to enter the fold of developed capitalist societies. Factually, industrialization in the third world often occurs under the aegis of an autocratic militarist regime with a narrow social base. Capitalist development in backward countries generally exacerbates the existing degree of inequality (perhaps even reducing the absolute amount which the poorer half of the population consumes), disrupts community and culture, lessens local control and self-determination, and introduces alienated, unhealthy working conditions.

That the gap between central and peripheral capitalist societies is expanding can be documented by a mountain of statistical evidence (Adelman and Morris, 1973; Emmanuel, 1974; McMichael et al., 1974). Kuznets' study of growth rates (1971) shows that during the 1950s and 1960s, per-capita GNP was growing much more rapidly in developed countries than in underdeveloped capitalist societies.

How can we distinguish the development of development from the development of underdevelopment? Sutcliffe (1972) has proposed the following four criteria of independent industrialization: (a) development is based primarily on the domestic market; (b) development is not confined to a few industries, but encompasses a diversified industrial structure; (c) the developing society does not rely upon foreign finance except insofar as it can exert strict control over the use of foreign funds; (d) although the developing society may borrow some technology from other societies, it also generates substantial independent technological progress. Applying these four criteria to peripheral capitalist economies, we find that most cannot satisfy even one, and none satisfies all four. On the other hand, the central capitalist economies—with a few exceptions, such as Australia, Canada, and possibly Japan—do indeed satisfy Sutcliffe's four criteria.

Marxist theory posits that the differentiation between central and periperal capitalist economies arises from three features of the international accumulation process: (a) surplus drain from periphery to center, (b) structural distortion of the peripheral economy, and (c) creation of a dependent elite in the periphery. Let us examine each of these in greater detail.

Underdevelopment stems, not from the inability of peripheral capitalist societies to generate an economic surplus, but from the economic relations between center and periphery which drain the surplus—often quite substantial—from the latter to the former. Repatriation of profits on investment and interest payments on foreign loans are important mechanisms of surplus drain (Frank, 1969). Nor do profit figures reveal the magnitude of this transfer, since internal pricing systematically undervalues the domestic product of peripheral capitalist economies.

International trade furnishes another major mechanism of surplus drain from periphery to center (Emmanuel, 1972). The prevailing class structure and the erosion of the self-sufficient agricultural sector generate a large reserve army of labor in the form of both rural and urban poor. Therefore, labor of equal productivity receives far less compensation in peripheral than in central capitalist economies. The nation-state structure of the international system bars labor mobility but fosters capital mobility, thus maintaining dramatic international wage differentials while equalizing rates of return on capital. Under normal conditions of capitalist production, the price of a commodity equals the cost of labor used in its production plus the cost of capital consumed during the production process plus the profit on capital invested. International trade involves an exchange of commodities priced by summation of equally rewarded capital and unequally rewarded labor. The outcome is a net transfer of value from the peripheral capitalist economy to the central capitalist economy.

Structural distortion arises from the international accumulation process. The input requirements of central capitalist societies foster an international division of labor in which peripheral economies concentrate heavily on raw-material production. Such narrow specialization renders the peripheral economy highly vulnerable to the fluctuations of the world market (Prebisch, 1950). In addition, a more-diversified industrial structure would process internally produced raw materials, thereby creating additional employment, demand, and economic growth (Hirschman, 1958; Galtung, 1971). The multiplier effect in an economy which concentrates on raw-material production is weak because income generated in production flows out immediately in the form of interest payments and profits and, secondarily, as payments for imports of basic necessities not produced locally. The cultural hegemony of central capitalist societies over the propertied classes in peripheral capitalism strengthens this tendency to shift demand abroad. Being cemented in the very structure of the peripheral economy, this imbalance is not easily reversed.

Central capitalist-dominated trade orients the infrastructure of production in a peripheral economy, particularly the transportation system, toward export (Dos Santos, 1970; Ehrensaft, 1971; Amin, 1974). It does not establish internal linkages which might foster domestic production and a domestic market. Often, the transportation system of a peripheral society will link the interior with the port city without ever establishing direct connections between cities of the interior. Similarly, the requirements of central capitalism often result in the introduction of highly sophisticated capital-intensive technology which creates quite limited employment opportunities, generates only a very narrow market, and engenders long-run bonds of technological dependency. The peripheral economies would benefit more from use of simpler labor-intensive technologies.

The multinational corporation, however, allocates the resources it appropriates according to its own organizational imperatives with little, if any, reference to the needs of the host society (Beckford, 1971). The commanding position of foreign capital leads to the abandonment of autonomous development policies emphasizing balanced growth and to passive acceptance of those narrow specializations assigned to peripheral economies under the international capitalist division of labor. The initiative of the multinationals in shaping peripheral economies is buttressed by international lending agencies, which use the leverage of credit to create a favorable environment for free enterprise and foreign investment (Hayter, 1971). Dependence upon foreign credit also reduces the domestic propensity to save, thereby curtailing domestic capital formation.

The accumulation process imposes a particular class structure on peripheral capitalism. The overweening presence of foreign capital hinders the development of a self-confident autonomous national bourgeoisie which faces stiff competition from the powerful and long-established bourgeoisie of central capitalist societies. In addition, the national bourgeoisie encounters outright hostility from the landed classes, which—though possibly engaged in capitalist forms of agriculture—retain an aristocratic anticapitalist consciousness and feel threatened by the rise of a manufacturing bourgeoisie (Baran and Sweezy, 1966).

Within peripheral capitalism, both the merchant bourgeoisie and the landed classes have an interest in the export of raw materials. These two social classes often unite with the imperialist bourgeoisie of central capitalist societies in order to inhibit the growth of an indigenous manufacturing bourgeoisie. Thus, the dominant classes of advanced capitalist societies collaborate to preserve backward social classes and suppress modernizing classes within peripheral capitalist societies. This coalition frustrates efforts to accomplish balanced economic development within peripheral capitalism, and confines the society to the economic specializations mapped out for it under the international capitalist division of labor (Galtung, 1971). The alliance between central and peripheral elites also functions to depress wages within peripheral capitalism and to raise the income of ruling classes in all sectors of the capitalist world system.

Testing these propositions is no simple matter. Chase-Dunn (1975) uses panel regression analysis to investigate the effects of economic dependence on development and income inequality during the post–World War II era. Using two different indicators of economic dependence—and three different indicators of economic development—GNP per capita, electricity consumption per capita, and percent of labor outside of agriculture—Chase-Dunn finds that dependence has a significant depressing effect upon economic development. This negative effect persists even when other variables which might explain the relationship between dependence and development are controlled.

Economic growth has not diminished income inequality within peripheral capitalist societies. This basic fact is acknowledged (sometimes reluctantly) by virtually all scholars within the field of economic development, and has caused some to reconsider Marxist analysis. Adelman and Morris summarize the results of their study on social equity and economic development as follows:

> The basic premise of most national and international efforts to aid low-income nations has been that sustained economic growth leads to higher real incomes for even the poorest segments of the population. The statistical analyses of Chapters 3 and 4 strongly suggest that this optimistic assumption has no basis in fact . . . inequality of income tends to be greatest where the exploitation of an abundance of natural resources coincides with a concentration of assets in the hands of

expatriates; it tends to be least where development strategies stress investment in human resources, greater diversity of manufacturing exports, and expansion of public sector output and investment. In short, our analysis supports the Marxian view that economic structure, not level of income or rate of economic growth, is the basic determinant of patterns of income distribution (1973, p. 186).

How can Marxist theory explain the relationship between economic development and income inequality in peripheral capitalist societies? Inequality, we have already noted, has always been associated with the process of capitalist accumulation and is very much in evidence within contemporary highly modernized central capitalist societies. Nevertheless, we would argue that the roots of inequality in peripheral capitalist societies differ significantly from the causes of inequality within central capitalist societies.

Inequality arises from duality within the peripheral economy. For the reasons cited earlier, the modernized or central sector of the peripheral capitalist society interacts continuously with the advanced economies of the capitalist center and, in more extreme cases, even has the character of a foreign enclave. On the other hand, the peripheral sector has little or no direct interaction with central capitalist societies, but does have quite significant interactions with the metropolitan sector of the periphery. Analogous to the relationship between periphery and center, the periphery *within* third-world countries (i.e., the periphery-periphery) serves as a reserve labor source for the center within these countries (i.e., the periphery-center), and the exchange between the two drains surplus from the former to the latter. The periphery-periphery experiences little if any of the modernizing influences felt within the periphery-center; the tendency of demand to shift abroad weakens the multiplier effect and curtails the expansion of income associated with investment. The bifurcation between center and periphery acts as a barrier which radically restricts the trickle-down effects of economic development.

Capitalist accumulation on a world scale is thus a joint process of development and stagnation. On the international level, the peripheral capitalist society is stagnating relative to the central capitalist societies. On the national level, the periphery of peripheral capitalist societies is stagnating relative to the center. It follows that inequality within the capitalist world system accompanies the process of accumulation both internationally—between central and peripheral societies—and domestically—between social classes of peripheral capital societies. Advanced corporate capitalism, like its earlier capitalist predecessors, continues to generate unequal social relationships in great profusion.

A thorough explanation of the center-periphery duality within peripheral capitalist societies requires a careful analysis of peripheral capitalist class structure and its social dynamics. Obviously, each peripheral society has a unique historical experience and hence requires an independent class analysis. Nevertheless, it may be useful to sketch the broad contours of class conflict within peripheral capitalist societies, indicating how this contributes to the center-periphery bifurcation and the entire issue of inequality.

The advance of modernization in England, France, and the United States went hand in hand with a process by which the urban bourgeoisie achieved clear-cut dominance over the landed classes rooted in noncapital forms of agriculture. On the other hand, modernization in Germany and Japan took place without subordination of the aristocratic landed classes to the bourgeoisie. The unresolved tension between these classes—each angling to establish its hegemony over the other and to stamp its imprint on society as a whole—led to an aggressive militarist expansionism. Imperialism was the basis for compromise between contending hegemonic classes in both Germany and Japan (Moore, 1966).

The class structure of contemporary peripheral capitalist societies is in some ways similar to that which formerly prevailed in Germany and Japan. There exists in peripheral capitalist societies an uneasy truce between the landed upper classes and the entrepreneurial bourgeoisie. Neither can establish unambiguous hegemony over the other. In fact, neither dares take forceful action to subjugate the other, since the power of each rests upon the tacit consent of the other. At the same time, the landed classes and the bourgeoisie each recognize that the modes of consciousness and forms of social organization propagated by the other are thoroughly incompatible with the imperatives of its own existence.

The peripheral bourgeoisie emerges with the growth of commerce and modern industry within the peripheral economy. The power of this bourgeoisie is severely limited by the underdevelopment of this indigenous industry within the peripheral economy and by its dependence upon central capitalism. The landed classes are sustained by their traditional social status, by their control over military institutions, and by support rendered to them from the bourgeoisie of central capitalism. The existence of numerous propertyless laborers in both city and countryside confronts the landed classes and the bourgeoisie with the specter of social revolution. This specter is perhaps the strongest bond between them.

Is there any basis for a compromise between the landed classes and the bourgeoisie which will secure their continued joint domination of peripheral society? A satisfactory *modus vivendi* would maintain the social position of the landed classes while simultaneously permitting continued expansion of that capitalist production which constitutes the social foundation of the bourgeoisie. This requires three developmental conditions:

First, and foremost, the compromise entails acceptance of the tutelage of foreign capital by both landed classes and bourgeoisie. Such acceptance is to some extent a matter of simply bowing to necessity, but it has other functions as well. By jointly accepting the tutelage of foreign capital, the landed classes and bourgeoisie help ensure that their own potential conflict will not get out of hand, and that those disputes which do arise will be mediated by a powerful third party. More important, the presence of foreign capital fortifies both of these classes against the possiblity of social revolution, and virtually guarantees them powerful allies in the eventuality of a revolutionary outburst.

Second, the compromise between landed classes and bourgeoisie in peripheral capitalist societies involves the emergence of the *state* as an essential agent of the development process. The bourgeoisie of peripheral societies is not sufficiently strong or self-confident to propel capitalist development on its own. Independently, it cannot mobilize sufficient surplus, discipline the labor force, ensure the loyalty of petty bourgeois and professional elements, or place even minimal restraints on the incursions of foreign capital. A strong state which takes an active hand in the process of capitalist development can accomplish these objectives as well as provide the landed classes with some control over the rate and direction of modernization, thus ensuring that development will not sabotage their social position. The central role of the state in the development process may explain the association earlier noted between economic growth and political autocracy under conditions of peripheral capitalism.

Third, the compromise between landed classes and bourgeoisie entails the division of society into two spheres—one in which the bourgeoisie is socially dominant and another in which the landowning classes are socially dominant. Since dynamism is an essential principle of bourgeois existence, the sphere of bourgeois dominance will exhibit tendencies toward growth. Since tradition and stability are principles which underlie the social hegemony of landed ruling classes, the sphere in which the landed classes are dominant will show an inclination toward stagnation. This is the social basis for the division between center and periphery within peripheral capitalist society.

This last point requires a caveat. Nothing we have said implies that the landed classes cannot participate in dynamic export-oriented capitalist agriculture, even deriving the bulk of their income from such activities. Even so, the maintenance of a stagnant peripheral sector remains essential to secure their social status and general style of life. Similarly, elements of the bourgeoisie may endeavor to set themselves up as a landed gentry with aristocratic pretentions. Nevertheless, the relatively dynamic central sector remains the foundation of their socioeconomic position within peripheral capitalist society. Figure 1 provides a rough outline of the class structure which emerges from the compromise between landed classes and bourgeoisie.

Given this social structure, it is not hard to see why economic development fails to reduce inequality and may actually impoverish the poorer sectors of peripheral capitalist society. The effect of economic development will be to increase the gap between the central and peripheral sectors of peripheral capitalist society and to strengthen the tendencies by which surplus is drained from the latter to the former. Superficially, it might seem that strengthening the bour-

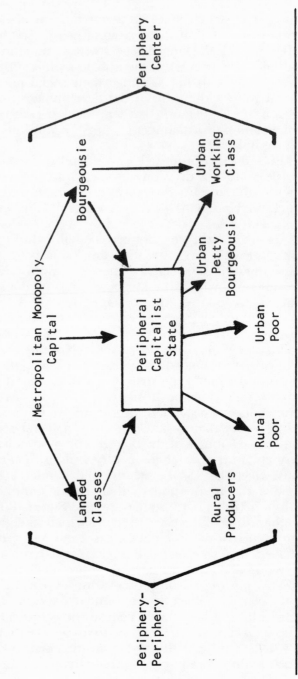

FIGURE 1

NEO-IMPERIALIST DEPENDENCY

NOTE: Arrows indicate lines of direct domination

geoisie at the expense of the landed classes might improve
matters substantially. In fact, however, this would accomplish very little. The bourgeoisie of peripheral capitalist
society is thoroughly dominated by the metropolitan bourgeoisie. Moreover, this class has little stomach for confronta-
tions with revolutionary movements of urban and rural
working people without the sustaining support of the
landed upper classes. We see little hope for the balanced
development of third-world economies, in a manner which
would alleviate gross poverty and inequality, as long as the
class structure engendered by world capitalism prevails
within them.

Evaluation of Socialist Economic Performance

We have noted that the work of some development economists supports our theory of inequality in peripheral capitalist societies (Adelman and Morris, 1973). These scholars
also suggest that the widespread belief in the importance of
increased political participation so as to ensure an equitable
income distribution is not empirically supported, and that
the impotence of political development in that respect might
be explained by the relationship between economic structure
and the structure of political power postulated by Marxist
theory, according to which the former determines the latter.
Furthermore, Adelman and Morris admit that their findings
tend to support Baran's analysis of backwardness as a
product of the exploitation of a country's economic resources by a coalition of native and foreign capitalists (1973, pp.
187–189).

Clearly, the empirical research of some development
economists provides support for the Marxist analysis of
capitalist development and its consequences at the national
and international levels. On the other hand, while recognizing the ability of Marxist political economy to account for
phenomena which remain puzzling to neoclassical economists, Adelman and Morris reject its practical implications.
If, as they acknowledge, what stands in the way of greater
social equity are social relations of production which determine the structure of political power and operate almost
exclusively for the benefit of local elites and their foreign

partners, it follows that nothing short of abolishing those relations is likely to substantially change the situation. Given that the dominant classes can and do manipulate development policies to their own advantage, the evidence produced by several orthodox empirical studies of economic backwardness strongly suggests the futility of policies which do not begin by abolishing those classes. Adelman and Morris avoid this implication by rhetorically advocating an amorphous "development of the people, by the people, for the people" while simultaneously impugning the capacity of revolution to achieve social equity (1973, pp. 201–202).

In our view, such skepticism regarding the accomplishments of revolution cannot be sustained. On the contrary, examination of countries in which the capitalist mode of production has been abolished discloses a greater degree of social equity than is found in capitalist countries at a similar level of economic development. A recent joint study by the World Bank and the Institute of Development Studies at the University of Sussex indicates not only that socialist countries ". . . have the *highest degree* of overall equality in the distribution of income" but also that the 25 percent of total income allocated within these countries to the poorest 40 percent of the population *"may be taken as an upper limit for the target income share to which policy-makers in underdeveloped countries can aspire"* (Ahluwalia, 1975; emphasis added). If the achievement of the socialist countries in the realm of income distribution is to be taken as a model, the structural factors which determine such achievement ought to be given serious consideration.

In terms of our more-broadly conceived criteria, the failure of development policies in third-world countries is demonstrated not only in an overall decline in the income share of the underprivileged masses but also in the exacerbation of all facets of their lives. For example, the so-called Brazilian miracle combines rapid industrialization, high annual growth rates, and increases in per-capita income with a decline in real wages and a rise in infant mortality in major metropolitan areas (Wood and Barros, 1975). If we are to assess the relative potential of social systems for ensuring social welfare, we must conduct a rigorous and critical comparative examination of capitalism and socialist modes of production, distribution, and social organization. Social scientists must not remain oblivious to the economic and political structures which stand in the way of badly needed institutional reforms within third-world countries. Socialist revolution should be soberly evaluated as a rational alternative for people experiencing increased economic exploitation and social oppression in a context of growing wealth. In this section we briefly examine whether revolutions lead to greater social equity, concentrating largely on the experiences of the Russian and Chinese revolutions.

The economic structure of Russia prior to 1917 was overwhelmingly agrarian, with aristocratic landlords and peasants constituting the main social classes. The emancipation of the serfs in 1861, which might have provided the basis for the development of modern agriculture, resulted in the continued subordination of the peasantry to the landlord class through lengthy redemption payments. These payments, in conjunction with the practice of communal agriculture, severely retarded labor transfers from agriculture to industry, since peasants remained tied to the land until the village commune's debt had been paid. Furthermore, the periodic redistribution of land within the communes discouraged efforts to increase productivity. Low agricultural productivity supported only a very meager standard of living. In 1914, Russian national income per capita stood at 25 percent and 15 percent of that existing in England and the United States, respectively. Severe internal income inequality reflected the concentration of land in a few hands: the richest 10 percent of the peasant class owned 35 percent of the land, while the poorest 17 percent owned 2.5 percent of the land (Sherman, 1969, pp. 53–56).

Russia experienced remarkable industrial growth during the twenty years following 1880, and by 1912 had become the fifth-largest industrial power in the world. Foreign capital dominated most industrial sectors; Western shareholders owned 90 percent of Russia's mines, 50 percent of its chemical industry, more than 40 percent of its engineering plants, and 42 percent of its banking stock (Deutscher, 1967, p. 12). Industrialization was concentrated around Moscow and St. Petersburg in large factories generally employing more than 500 workers. The relatively small working class resided in neighborhoods near factories, where living conditions were comparable to those found in nineteenth-century western

Europe. Demographically, Russia's precapitalist population patterns were characterized by high birth and death
rates, which began to decline slowly at the beginning of the
twentieth century but which remained at levels twice the
western-European averages. Educationally, the 1887 census
(the last one taken during the tsarist regime) shows widespread illiteracy; 78 percent of the population over fifteen
was illiterate, while out of a population of 126 million only
1.4 million had been educated beyond the seventh grade.
Only 93,000 had completed higher education (Sherman,
1969, pp. 53–56; Gregory and Stuart, 1974).

Today, fifty-eight years after the revolution, the achievements of Soviet economic development cannot fail to im-
press a fair-minded observer, particularly when conditions
prior to 1917 and the devastation produced by the two world
wars are taken into account. The speed with which Russia
became a modern industrial society, entirely on the basis of
its own resources and the labor of the Russian people,
contrasts sharply with the feeble results achieved by capitalist development policies in third-world countries. In the
brief historical period since the Bolshevik revolution, Russia
has become the second-ranking economic power in the
world.

Today the Soviet Union unquestionably has a more-
equitable income distribution than any capitalist country,
including the United States. The abolition of private ownership of the means of production necessitates the abolition of
property income, the main source of income inequality in
capitalist countries. While the available data are rather
incomplete, careful estimates for 1966 place the income share
of the top 10 percent of Soviet spending units (omitting
collective-farm families) at approximately 4.5 times that of
the lowest 10 percent. The corresponding ratio for the entire
U.S. economy in 1967 was about 28 to 1. Although the
overall Soviet income distribution may become more unequal when farm incomes are included, given the absence of
property incomes, overall inequality would not reach levels
substantially higher than those already cited (Gregory and
Stuart, 1974, p. 399).

While levels of Soviet per-capita consumption and per-
capita GNP are lower than those of the United States, the
annual long- and short-term rates of growth of per-capita

consumption in the Soviet Union (including communal services) exceed comparable rates for the U.S. (Gregory and Stuart, 1974, p. 406). If the pattern is maintained, the Soviet Union is bound to reduce the consumption gap in the future (ibid., pp. 400–406). Despite its consumption lag, the Soviet Union far outstrips the United States in universal provision of the population's basic needs. It is true that Soviet citizens consume fewer automobiles, durable goods, and luxury goods than U.S. citizens, and that their range of choice is limited. It is also true that the housing situation is extremely bad (Sherman, 1969, p. 117). On the other hand, communal free services account for a sizable percentage of the consumption of Soviet citizens (35 percent, according to official figures). Although the actual percentage may be lower, the nature and amount of Soviet communal free goods and services greatly supplements consumption levels of all citizens, with median Soviet consumption surpassing median U.S. consumption in several important categories.

Soviet citizens enjoy substantial free health and education services. Kindergarten and nursery-school care for preschool children are universally available. The impact of child care upon the status of women is tremendous, especially when compared to the United States where women's labor-force participation is seriously retarded by the lack of adequate child-care facilities.

All educational institutions, including universities, are free. Students receive scholarships which, for the more advanced, are sometimes higher than the average industrial wage (Sherman, 1969; Gregory and Stuart, 1974). Recruitment emphasizes intelligence, not the economic positions of students' fathers. While members of the intelligentsia may transmit some advantages to their children via a favorable home background, there is no transmission of property or political privileges from one generation to the next. The high level of aspirations and commitment to higher education found among all strata of the population within socialist countries reflects the opportunities for social advancement open to everyone regardless of social origin (Sherman, 1969; Parkin, 1974). Besides free educational, medical, and dental services, Soviet citizens pay low taxes, low rents, and low transportation costs, and have an array of impressive social-welfare benefits such as social insurance, social security and pensions, and paid holidays (Turgeon, 1962; Nove, 1962).

Under capitalist conditions, health, education, and welfare are precisely the sectors in which the inequality of income distribution has its strongest impact. What the U.S. citizen gains in "consumer sovereignty" does not compensate for the concomitant loss in the quality of life which the "invisible hand" imposes on the majority. The consumption of cars, television sets, and cheap and not-so-cheap "fashionable" clothing, plus a host of artificially differentiated consumer goods, is no substitute for the lack of adequate educational services, the lack of equal opportunity to enter institutions of higher education, the lack of adequate medical and dental care, the lack of adequate services and resources for the elderly and retired, and the lack of adequate housing for much of the U.S. population—which must accept this as the "natural" result of capitalist development. Furthermore, consumption includes payments for both compulsory services, such as insurance, made necessary by the insecurity of capitalism, and the waste involved in product development, such as advertising and market creation.

The Chinese experience is qualitatively different from that of the Soviet Union and must be assessed in its own right. Although Chinese socialism is more recent and therefore less economically developed than that of the Soviet Union, it nevertheless presents unique features relevant for an understanding of the issue of social equity under socialism.

Prerevolutionary China was a predominantly agricultural economy, as was prerevolutionary Russia (Feuerwerker, 1968, p. 25). Problems of land ownership, usury, taxation, and sharecropping plagued the agricultural sector prior to the revolution. Landlords and rich peasant families constituted about 10 percent of the rural population, yet they owned about 70 percent of the land. The poorest 70 percent of the rural population had access to but 10 percent of the land. The middle peasants, about 20 percent of the rural population, owned about 20 percent of the land. While latifundia were relatively uncommon, big landlords dominated the social, political, and economic life in the countryside, perpetuating the backward conditions under which agricultural production took place. The peasantry lived in conditions of utter poverty. Rents were as high as 50 or 60 percent of total crop value; land taxes, corrupt village administrators, and the usury practices of the landlords maintained the rural population in chronic poverty. Famine struck periodically, its remedies barred from reaching affected areas by the prevailing socioeconomic and political system (Mallory, 1926; Nathan, 1965). The detailed information about rural life in prerevolutionary China gathered by Hinton (1966) and others in combination with the actual occurrence of famines, presents an image of Chinese rural life before 1949 as "nasty, short, and poor."

Chinese industrial development began after the mid–nineteenth century and accelerated in the last decade of the nineteenth century. The growth of heavy industry took place mainly in the northeast and was geared to the satisfaction of Japan's economic and military needs. By 1936, foreign capital constituted 73.8 percent of China's total industrial capital (Cheng, 1963, p. 4). China's national industries were small in scale; in 1949, China's industrial base was smaller than Russia's in 1914. China's economy remained fragmented into numerous local and regional markets; it never developed an effective national market capable of providing the demand needed to stimulate industrial production. Furthermore, manufactured goods competed with peasant and urban handicrafts, thus pauperizing both urban areas and the countryside.

Twenty-six years after the revolution, the situation is radically different. Assessing the quantitative performance of the Chinese economy is made difficult by inadequate data. Western social scientists invariably find that Chinese estimates contain upward biases. Corrected estimates, on the other hand, are likely to contain downward biases. Even so— in spite of the setbacks which took place during the Great Leap Forward (1958–1960) and three years of natural calamities (1959–1961), Chinese economic performance is impressive. Between 1952 and 1959, a conservative Western estimate suggests an 8-percent average annual growth rate, which, although lower than the official estimates, ". . . outstripped most countries in the post-war period. The rates were comparable to those of West Germany (7.9 percent) and of Japan (8.8 percent) during the 1950s." However, the long-term growth rate between 1949 and 1969 may range from 4 to 5 percent, appreciably lower than that of 1952–1959 (Cheng, 1971, p. 8).

Using efficiency as the main criterion for evaluating economic performance, Cheng and other Western observers stigmatized Chinese efforts to use nonmaterial incentives and to break down barriers between mental and manual labor as an "anti-modern technology mentality" likely to retard economic growth. From a Marxist perspective, such efforts are essential if economic growth is to occur without the social and intellectual impoverishment of the working population that characterized Western capitalist economic development (Braverman, 1974).

The comparison between China's achievements in food production and distribution and the performance of similarly endowed countries within a developing capitalist framework reveals the enormity of China's progress. Contrary to all expectations, contrary to neo-Malthusian prophecies of doom, China feeds *all* of its people modestly but adequately. A simplistic approach to the relationship between food and people would conclude, on the basis of per-capita grain production, that China is on the verge of starvation. However, the availability of alternative food sources (livestock, fishing), the existence of small-scale domestic food production, the gains made through exporting rice and importing wheat (which is cheaper than rice in the world market), and the social relations of distribution ensure the availability of food for everyone (Orleans, 1972, pp. 150–154). Economist John Gurley testified at hearings before the Joint Economic Committee of the U.S. Congress in 1974:

> . . . the basic overriding economic fact about China is that for twenty years she has fed, clothed, and housed everyone, has kept them healthy, and has educated most. Millions have *not* starved; sidewalks and streets have *not* been covered with multitudes of sleeping, begging, hungry, and illiterate human beings; millions are *not* disease ridden. To find such deplorable conditions, one does not look at China these days but rather to India, Pakistan, and almost anywhere else in the underdeveloped world. . . . The Chinese—all of them—now have what is in effect an insurance policy against pestilence,

famine, and other disasters. In this respect, China has outperformed every underdeveloped country in the world; and even with respect to the richest country in the world, it would not be far-fetched to claim that there has been less malnutrition due to maldistribution of food in China over the past twenty years that there has been in the United States (quoted in Cereseto, 1975, p. 6).

China's performance in health, education, and welfare is also impressive. China's death rate dropped from above 30 per thousand before the revolution to 17 per thousand in 1970. The birth rate, which was about 43 per thousand before 1949, began to decline slowly and may have dropped to 32 per thousand in 1969 (Orleans, 1972). While we lack figures for the country as a whole, information about selected cities indicates a more drastic decline in birth rate since 1969, which now ranges from 27 per thousand to 9.7 per thousand (Chen and Miller, 1975). No other underdeveloped country surpasses this record, which is partly the result of China's unique "planned birth program" made possible by the cooperation and active participation of the broad masses.

Although we could say more about China's accomplishments in other areas, we shall finish this discussion with an examination of China's income distribution. Observers have remarked about the egalitarian appearance of Chinese society. People appear adequately fed and clothed, poverty is not associated with the degradation of body and mind frequently found in other countries, and no extreme wealth is evident. In spite of the equality portrayed by clothing and style of living, there are subtle status and wage differences. On the basis of data collected during a visit in December 1972, Eckstein (1975) indicates that wage differences among industrial workers in factories varied from about 3:1 to 5:1, a range that can be found in the industrial sectors of both developed and underdeveloped countries. He further argues that, as in the United States and in Europe, "... the wage spread within industry seems to be typically around 3:1.... [This example] would suggest that the Chinese industrial wage structure is not significantly more egalitarian than that of other countries" (Eckstein, 1975, p. 348). Such a conclusion, he cautions, may be unwarranted because of lack of comparability of wage data. Wage differentials of 10:1 may exist among

technical and engineering personnel, and differentials of
20:1 characterize top-level personnel and government positions. In the United States, Eckstein admits that ". . . wage
and salary differentials may go as high as 50:1 or even 75:1."
Moreover, comparing wage differentials in China with those
in other underdeveloped areas (Indian and African countries), he concludes that ". . . at the extremes the wage and
salary spread in the United States and in many underdeveloped countries is much wider than in China" (pp. 348-349).
If property incomes are added, the income spread becomes
still larger for capitalist societies, and China compares even
more favorably.

   As in the case of the Soviet Union, meaningful comparison of material well-being ought also to reflect the availability of free communal services in China, as well as price
controls which maintain the prices of necessary goods
within reach of everyone. If money income figures were
adjusted to reflect the availability of free health care for
factory workers and inexpensive care for their dependents, as
well as a price structure which keeps rent, food, and child-
care expenses to a minimum, the meaning of the existing
income gaps in China would change radically.

   While income differentials do exist in China and the
Soviet Union, we conclude that both countries have achieved
a higher degree of social equity than the United States and
other developed and underdeveloped capitalist countries.[1]
The differences lies in the explicit commitment to social
equity which characterizes socialist societies, a commitment
which is maintained even though it may sometimes retard
material expansion. This commitment is institutionalized
in the socialist mode of production, which replaces production for profit with production for use and makes basic
goods and services available to the population as a whole.
The progress which socialist societies have made in the
realm of social equity, less than 60 years after the first
socialist revolution, highlights the relative failure of the
capitalist mode of production, after more than 300 years, to
provide for basic human needs. The available historical
evidence about the consequences of revolutions, contrary to
what Adelman and Morris suggest, offers a solid basis for
optimism about the human capacity to build a better society.[2]

Notes

1. It should be noted that our conclusion is empirically supported by a preliminary analysis of available data on the distribution of income which is part of the World Bank study previously mentioned in this work. The analysis included a "... test for differences between underdeveloped countries on the one hand and the *developed countries* and *socialist countries* on the other. This is done by including two dummy variables, one for the developed countries and the other for the socialist countries. The dummy variable for developed countries is insignificant in all equations, suggesting that the determinants of income shares in these countries are similar to those in underdeveloped countries. By contrast, the dummy variable for socialist countries indicates that the share of the lowest 40 percent and the middle 40 percent is significantly higher than would be accounted for by the influences of other variables. Note that the size of the coefficients is very large, indicating substantially higher equality" (Ahluwalia, 1975, p. 30; emphasis in the text).

2. We define "revolutionary change" as change in the mode of production. This implies changes in the *relations of production*, or relations among the producers mediated through their property relations, to the means of production, as well as changes in the political, legal, and ideological structures and forms of consciousness. Changes in the mode of production presuppose changes in the mode of distribution and exchange.

References

Adelman, I., and C. T. Morris (1973). *Economic Growth and Social Equity in Developing Countries*. Stanford, Calif.: Stanford University Press.

Adler, S. (1957). *The Chinese Economy*. New York: Monthly Review Press.

Ahluwalia, M. S. (1975). "Income Inequality: Some Dimensions of the Problem," in Chenery, H., et al. *Redistribution with Growth*. London: Oxford University Press.

Amin, S. (1974). *Accumulation on a World Scale*. New York: Monthly Review Press.

Baran, P. and P. Sweezy (1966). *Monopoly Capital*. New York: Monthly Review Press.

Beckford, G. (1971). *Persistent Poverty: Underdevelopment in Plantation Regions of the World*. London: Oxford University Press.

Blauner, R. (1964). *Alienation and Freedom*. Chicago: University of Chicago Press.

Braverman, H. (1974). *Labor and Monopoly Capitalism: The Degradation of Work in the Twentieth Century*. (October 1975).

Cheng, C. (1963). *Communist China's Economy 1949–1962: Structural Changes and Crisis*. South Orange, N.J.: Seton Hall University Press.

Cheng, C. (1971). "The Economy of Communist China, 1949–1969." The University of Michigan Center for Chinese Studies, Ann Arbor, Mich., *Michigan Papers in Chinese Studies* no. 9.

Chenery, H., et al. (1974). *Redistribution with Growth*. London: Oxford University Press.

Deutscher, I. (1967). *The Unfinished Revolution: Russia 1917–1967*. New York: Oxford University Press.

Dobb, M. (1973). *Theories of Value and Distribution Since Adam Smith*. Cambridge: Cambridge University Press.

Dos Santos, T. (1970). "The Structure of Dependence." *American Economic Review* 60.

Eckstein, A. (1975). *China's Economic Development: The Interplay of Scarcity and Ideology*. Ann Arbor: University of Michigan Press.

New York: Monthly Review Press.

Cereseto, S. (1975). "How China Solved Its Food Problem." Unpublished manuscript.

Chase-Dunn, C. (1975). "The Effects of International Economic Dependence on Development and Inequality: A Cross National Study." *American Sociological Review* 40.

Chen, P., and A. Miller (1975). "Lessons from the Chinese Experience: China's Planned Birth Program and its Transferability." *Studies in Family Planning* 6, no. 10

Ehrensaft, P. (1971). "Semi-Industrial Capitalism in the Third World." *Africa Today* 10.

Emmanuel, A. (1974). "Myths of Development Versus Myths of Underdevelopment." *New Left Review* 85 (May/-June 1974).

Feuerwerker, A. (1968). "The Chinese Economy, 1912–1949." University of Michigan Center for Chinese Studies, Ann Arbor, Mich., *Michigan Papers in Chinese Studies* no. 1.

Flinn, M. W. (1974). "Trends in Real Wages, 1750–1850." *Economic History Review*, August 1974.

Frank, A. G. (1969). *Latin America: Underdevelopment or Revolution*. New York: Monthly Review Press.

Friedlander D. (1973). "Demographic Patterns and Socio-economic Change in the Coal Mining Population of England and Wales in the 19th Century." *Economic Development and Cultural Change*, October 1973.

Galtung, J. (1971). "A Structural Theory of Imperialism." *Journal of Peace Research* 8.

Gregory, P. R., and R. C. Stuart (1974). *Soviet Economic Structure and Performance*. New York: Harper & Row.

Hacker, A. (1975). "Who Rules America?" *New York Review of Books*, May 1, 1975.

Hayter, T. (1971). *Aid as Imperialism*. Baltimore: Penguin Books.

Heilbroner, R. L. (1968). *The Making of Economic Society*. Englewood Cliffs, N.J.: Prentice-Hall.

Herman, E. (1975). "The Income Counter-Revolution." *Commonweal*, January 3, 1975.

Hinton, W. (1966). *Fanshen*. New York: Vintage Books.

Hirschman, A. (1958). *The Strategy of Economic Development*. New Haven: Yale University Press.

Hobsbawm, E. J. (1966). *The Age of Revolution*. New York: New American Library.

Hobsbawm, E. J. (1966). *Industry and Empire*. New York: Pantheon.

Hunt, E. K., and R. d'Arge (1973). "On Lemmings and Other Acquisitive Animals." *Journal of Economic Issues*, June 1973.

Internal Revenue Service (1974). "Statistics of Income, 1972 Individual Income Tax Returns." Washington, D.C.: U.S. Government Printing Office.

Kornhauser, A. (1965). *Mental Health of the Industrial Worker.* New York: Wiley.

Kuznets, S. (1965). *Economic Growth and Structure.* New York: W. W. Norton.

Kuznets, S. (1971). "Problems of Comparing Recent Growth Rates for Developed and Less Developed Regions." *Economic Development and Cultural Change* 20.

Kuznets, S. (1966). *Modern Economic Growth.* Gienton, Mass.: The Colonial Press.

Kuznets, S. (1959). *Shares of Upper Income Groups in Income and Savings.* New York: National Bureau of Economic Research.

McMichael, P., J. Petras, and R. Rhodes (1975). "Imperialism and the Contradictions of Development." *New Left Review* 85 (May/June 1975).

Mallory, W. H. (1926). *China: Land of Famine.* New York: American Geographical Society.

Marx, K. (1887). *Capital,* 3 vols. Moscow: Foreign Language Publishing House.

Miller, S. M., and M. Rein (1975). "Can Income Redistribution Work?" *Social Policy,* May/June 1975.

Moore, B. (1966). *Social Origins of Dictatorship and Democracy.* Boston: Beacon Press.

Mott, P., et al. (1965). *Shift Work.* Ann Arbor: University of Michigan Press.

Nash, E. (1962). "Purchasing Power of Workers in the USSR," in Holzman, F. D., ed. *Readings on the Soviet Economy.* Chicago: Rand McNally.

Nathan, J. A. (1965). *A History of the China International Famine Relief Commission.* Cambridge, Mass.: Harvard University Press.

Nove, A. (1962). "Social Welfare in the USSR," in Holzman, F. D., ed. *Readings on the Soviet Economy.* Chicago: Rand McNally.

O'Connor, J. (1973). *The Fiscal Crisis of the State.* New York: St. Martin's Press.

Orleans, L. A. (1972). *Every Fifth Child: The Population of China.* Stanford, Calif.: Stanford University Press.

Parker, R. (1972). *The Myth of the Middle Class.* New York: Harper & Row.

Parkin, F. (1971). *Class Inequality and Political Order: Social Stratification in Capitalist and Communist Socie-*

ties. New York: Praeger.

Prebisch, R. (1950). *The Economic Development of Latin America and its Principal Problems.* New York: United Nations Department of Social and Economic Affairs.

Robinson, J. P., et al. (1967). "Measures of Occupational Attitudes and Occupational Characteristics." Survey Research Center, University of Michigan, Ann Arbor, Mich.

Seeman, M. (1972). "Alienation and Engagement," in Campbell, A., ed. *The Human Meaning of Social Change.* New York: Russell Sage Foundation.

Sherman, H. J. (1969). *The Soviet Economy.* Boston: Little, Brown.

Sottow, L. (1968). "Long Run Changes in British Income Inequality." *Economic History Review* 21, no. 1 (April 1968).

Sutcliffe, R. (1972). "Imperialism and Industrialization in the Third World," in Owen, R. and Sutcliffe, R., eds. *Studies in the Theories of Imperialism.* New York: Longman.

Thompson, E. P. (1963). *The Making of the English Working Class.* New York: Vintage Books.

Turgeon, L. (1962). "Levels of Living, Wages and Prices in the Soviet and United States Economies," in Holzman, F. D., ed. *Readings on the Soviet Economy.* Chicago: Rand McNally.

Vroom, V. (1964). *Work and Motivation.* New York: Wiley.

Wood, C. and Y. Barros (1975). "Economic Development and Infant Mortality in Brazil." Unpublished manuscript.

11. Water Supply and Income Distribution in Developing Countries

Anne U. White

Generally speaking, to be "poor" is to lack something. Cash income is one measurement; a recent estimate (McNamara, 1975) puts the number of "absolutely poor" people in the developing world (those subsisting on less than $75 [U.S.] per person per year) at 900 million. An alternative measure that reflects the quality of living arrangements, if not of life itself, is access to water for domestic use. Water is more than a prerequisite for health and well-being; it is a daily necessity for survival. In this sense, water is an element of "real" income.

Approximately 1.2 billion people, about 70 percent of the population of ninety-one developing countries (excluding China), are estimated to lack access to safe water supplies (World Health Organization, 1973). These people must carry their water home from springs, wells, rivers, ponds, or ditches, many of which are contaminated all or part of the time. This group is larger than that of the "absolute poor," as defined in monetary terms, but certainly includes them. With rapidly growing populations in the rural and urban-periphery sectors, the health hazard from unprotected water supplies is increasing. Lack of safe water is an important aspect of being "poor" in many countries.

Distribution

The correlation between the proportion of the population with access to safe water supply and GNP per capita (0.564) suggests that the poorest countries of the developing world have been the least able to provide safe water for their people. Of those countries with GNPs of $100 or less per capita surveyed by the World Health Organization (WHO), none has been able to provide access to safe water to more than 39 percent of its people; the mean for this group is 15 percent. Most countries with GNPs per capita of $500 or more have been able to provide more than half of their people with safe water.

There are exceptions to this general rule: Tanzania, with a GNP per capita of $94, and the People's Republic of China, with a GNP per capita of about $150, appear to have provided a large proportion of their people with basic water and sanitation (White, 1974). In Egypt, a country with a GNP per capita of about $200, a network of standpipes was extended through both rural villages and urban areas in the 1940s. Piped water was further extended after the revolution of 1952, with the result that 90 percent of the people eventually had access to water supplies, although the situation may now be deteriorating with rapid population growth. Colombia, a country with a GNP per capita only one-third that of Argentina, also has managed to serve about 90 percent of its population. These are important exceptions and may point the way to defying the rule, at least for those above the lowest income level.

The distribution of income within a country does not seem to be a critical factor. A comparison of the patterns of income distribution in various countries (as indicated by the Gini index) with the proportion of the population having access to safe water yields a weak inverse relationship (-1.176). In Libya and Peru, where the upper 5 percent of the population receives nearly one-half of national income, 87 percent of the population in Libya and 47 percent in Peru are reported as having access to safe water.

Water supply is sometimes used as a means of income redistribution. More than one-third of the countries surveyed provide rural supplies free, while all but three make some charge to urban customers. While higher-income users frequently subsidize the rest of a water system, very little is known about the price elasticity of water in developing countries. The scattered evidence available, however, indicates that it is relatively inelastic.

Productivity

At the present time it is not practicable to make confident predictions about the total impact of improved water supplies on either health or economy. Productivity, and therefore income, may be affected in three ways: health is improved, women have more time and energy, and new small industries become possible. However, a reduction in disease does not depend on water supply alone, and a recent World Bank panel of medical experts concluded that a large-scale investigation of the relationship between disease and water supply would not be justified (World Bank, 1976).[1] Insofar as parasitic and enteric disease is reduced, better use is made of food resources whether or not individual productivity increases. While it is clear that women may spend up to one-quarter of their daily energy consumption in fetching water (White et al., 1972), and that women in Africa, for example, are responsible for some 80 percent of the agricultural work in addition to this task, it is not clear how women would otherwise spend their time or what their opportunities would be for more productive activities. There is some indication that, although water supply is essential to the formation of such village industries as brick making (Warner, 1973), food processing, or cloth dyeing, it is not in itself sufficient to bring about increased rural development. Despite the fact that there may be few quantifiable contributions to economic growth resulting from improved water supply, it can be argued that providing access to safe water is one way of reducing the gap between the rich and the poor. Yet major questions remain to be answered: What is "adequate"? What is "safe"? How can access to adequate, safe water be obtained?

Basic Needs

The amount of water used by people for domestic needs varies from a little more than a liter per person per day to 25 liters for rural or urban consumers who have no household access to tap connections (see Figure 1). For city or village dwellers with access to standpipes or fountains, the use is about 10–50 liters per person daily. Consumption leaps to 15–90 liters for those with a single tap in the household, and to 30–300 liters for those with multiple taps in the house. This greater use indicates a style of life which includes washing cars and watering lawns and gardens.

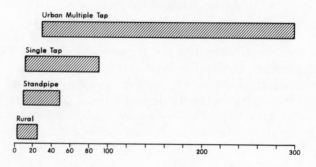

Figure 1. Range of daily domestic water use per capita in liters
(White et al., 1972, and other studies).

In addition to filling basic consumption needs (one to three liters per person daily), water adds to health prospects when it is available for bathing, washing dishes and clothing, and other household uses that protect the human body against disease. Just how much water is required per person daily to ensure health is not yet entirely clear, despite numerous studies; for the effects of nutrition, housing, water supply, hygiene, and environmental stress are so interconnected that it is difficult to isolate one factor.

We do know, however, that the health risk to the nearly three-quarters of the population of the developing world who do not have access to safe water is considerable. What supplies they do have are likely to be contaminated by human and animal feces, and they have difficulty carrying sufficient amounts to ensure cleanliness. Those who have reasonable access to a standpipe are more likely to obtain water of a higher quality, but they still may not be able to carry home enough to obtain maximum health benefits, and a hand in the bucket or in a storage pot may contaminate the supplies. There seems to be no evidence that use in excess of the single-tap amount results in improved health, although it adds much in pleasure.

The Present Situation

The first survey of water service in developing countries was made of cities by the WHO (Dieterich and Henderson, 1963). Researchers found that 33 percent of the urban population of seventy-five developing countries were estimated to have house connections, and another 26 percent were served by standpipes.

In 1970, WHO undertook a more comprehensive survey of ninety-one countries for water supply and sixty-one countries for sewage facilities. This survey (WHO, 1973) divided the population into "rural" and "urban," using whatever definition each country used in its census, and estimated for each the incidence of (a) tap connections within the house, (b) water from a public standpipe which is carried not more than 200 meters to the home, and (c) water from a "safe" (uncontaminated) source to which the household has "reasonable access" (not requiring "a disproportionate part of the day in fetching the family's water needs").[2] The survey did not include the People's Republic of China, but it did cover nearly half the total population of the earth.

The statistics gathered in this survey may overreport the population served, insofar as the assumption is made that facilities once built are always used and in good repair; on the other hand, the data may tend to underreport the population served, since often a number of agencies are involved in water improvements, and one may not know what another is doing. In addition, the data may not reflect modest improvements made by local communities or individuals with little or no agency aid. However, on balance the statistics probably closely approximate the present situation.

In 1970, 50 percent of the urban population of the developing countries were estimated to be served by means of piped water, and another 19 percent by standpipes (see Figure 2). Only 12 percent of the rural population was estimated to have reasonable access to safe water. The situation varied exceedingly from one part of the developing world to another (see Figure 3). The regions which had made

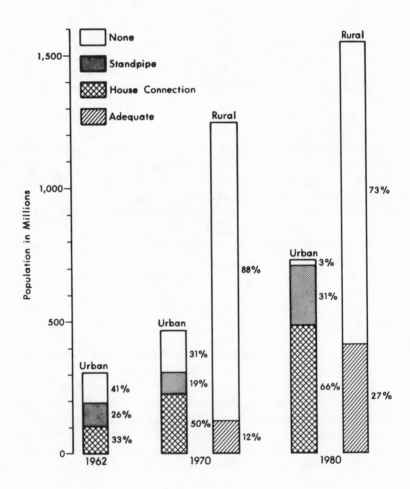

Figure 2. Estimates of water-supply services for developing countries in 1962 and 1970, and goals for 1980 (WHO, 1973).

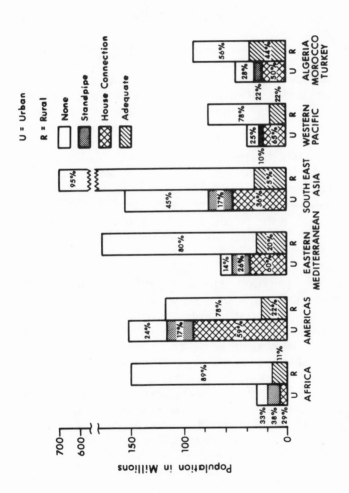

Figure 3. Estimate of water-supply services in 1970 by region (WHO 1973).

the most progress in supplying their people were the Americas (with 76 percent of the urban population and 24 percent of the rural population served), the Western Pacific countries, and three Mediterranean countries. In contrast, Southeast Asia, with the majority of the population, serves only 5 percent of its large rural population and 53 percent of its urban population.

In 1975, an update of this survey, with sixty-one countries answering, indicated that significant progress had been made in rural areas of Africa and in both urban and rural areas of Asia (WHO, 1976). The Americas showed an overall increase of 3 percent. Since the 1970 survey was more comprehensive, the situation as of that date is shown in the figures.

Because of the relatively large amounts of lead time and capital required to effect an increase in the available water supply, many areas in the developing regions are finding themselves unable to meet the rising demand for water. This rise in demand is the result of both population gains and increase in per-capita use. The pressure may be less acute in wetter rural areas, where the water in streams, ponds, springs, and wells may support, at least at a low level of use, an increased population. However, in rural communities and isolated settlements in drier areas, such as Ethiopia, there may be severe restrictions on the amount of water available, even at a high cost.

The health implications of an increased demand for relatively fixed water supplies could be considerable. In peripheral settlements of cities in developing countries, population densities are increasing rapidly, often to as many as 250 people per acre and sometimes reaching as high as 600 people per acre (Tahl, 1965). If few or no excreta disposal facilities are available, water supplies (other than piped water) are inevitably even more contaminated in such settlements than they would be in more-spread-out rural communities. The very economic growth that attracts new settlers to an urban area and provides them with their livelihood may add to the health risk they bear from an unprotected water source, since metals and chemicals from industrial wastes often are disposed of in such fashion that they reach surface and ground water supplies (WHO, 1972a).

That the poorest people are likely to suffer most from this

process is at least indirectly indicated by what has happened to water supplies in the large cities of Latin America since 1962. While great progress has been made in providing water supplies in this region, especially to the medium-sized cities (Pan American Health Organization, 1973), the proportion of people with access to safe water in the cities rose only slightly between 1962 and 1975, moving from 60 percent to 67 percent for those with house connections while decreasing from 27 percent to 14 percent for those with standpipe service. In other regions as well, the proportion with house connections increased while the percentage served by standpipes either dropped or increased only slightly. (Whether the people who gained house connections during this period were the same ones who lost standpipe service has not been investigated.)

In large cities, two kinds of urban settlement are likely to include the poorest people: the older, crowded areas of the central city, where new immigrants may congregate to seek employment, and the peripheral areas of shantytown settlement, to which they may subsequently go in an attempt to improve their living conditions (Turner, 1968). For water service the first of these is likely to have standpipes, but those available are probably overwhelmed by the number of people trying to use them. In Libreville, Gabon, the ratio of standpipes to people in the area needing them is 1:3,000—a grossly inadequate number; most people surveyed used puddles and rainbarrels as supplemental water sources (Gabon, 1972). In the second type of settlement there is usually little or no access to protected supplies. Extended-family systems may mitigate the risk in some places (if one's relative has a tap), but on the whole crowding forces people to use contaminated supplies.

Despite these risks, child mortality in the cities of Latin America seems to be only about half of that among the rural population (Puffer and Sarrano, 1973), possibly because of better access to medical facilities. Whether this will continue to be the case, as populations increase without safe water and excreta disposal systems, remains to be seen.

In the rural sector, which includes many larger villages, countries with vigorous programs—such as those in Latin America—serve a little more than one-fifth of their rural populations (Figure 3); the percentages with safe water are

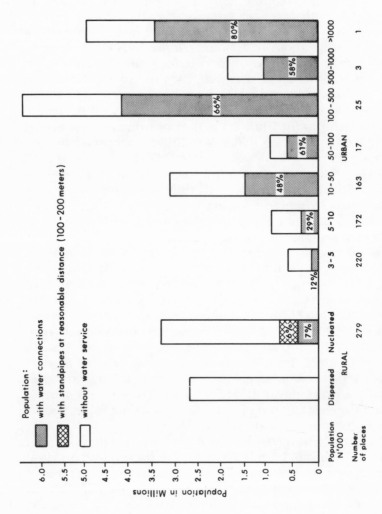

Figure 4. Argentina: Urban and rural settlement groups and water service (Argentina, 1972). In 1970, urban service included 5 percent standpipes (WHO, 1973).

about 11 percent in Africa and about 5 percent in Southeast Asia. According to informed tourists, the People's Republic of China has been able to provide more than two-thirds of its rural people with adequate water and sanitation.

It is difficult to tell who benefits most from improvements in the rural areas. On the whole, the poorer elements of the developing countries live in the traditional agricultural areas. Within these areas, water-supply improvements tend to be made in the more-concentrated settlements, since they are less expensive to serve. Improvements also appear to have been made in the most prosperous settlements, which have access to greater resources of money and community organization.

It may be useful to look at the situation in Argentina, a country with an energetic water-supply program characterized by community involvement and participation, in both organization and funding, and for which data are available. There is no question but that the larger the settlement is, the better are the chances for an individual to obtain access to safe water (see Figure 4). The poorest people, those in the dispersed rural areas, have virtually no safe water unless they have access to private springs or wells. Those in nucleated settlements with populations of under 3,000 have about the same chances as those in the smallest cities, while the chances of those in cities of 500,000 to 1 million people are about twice as great as those in cities of 5,000 to 10,000 people. However, the likelihood of obtaining safe water in the larger cities is now decreasing; the proportion of the total urban population served dropped from 90 percent in 1962 to 64 percent in 1970. Most of the decrease took place in that part of the population served by standpipes, which dropped from 25 percent to 5 percent. These people can be presumed to be among the very poor (WHO, 1973).

Sanitation

While the poor have had a meager share of the world's water supplies, it is probable that they have had an even smaller share of systems for the safe disposal of human excreta and waste water. If there is no safe method for disposing of waste water, especially where water comes from springs, wells, or rivers near crowded peripheral settlements of cities, several health hazards may be created. These hazards may come from the seepage of human or animal excreta into surface or ground water supplies, carrying the causative agents of such diseases as cholera or gastroenteritis, or from ephemeral pools of water which serve as ideal breeding places for the mosquito that carries the vector of the disease filariasis (WHO, 1972a). The installation of stand-pipes may further increase this problem unless there is careful provision for drainage. As Feachem (1976) points out, the assumption that developing countries will provide waterborne sewage for most of their people in a matter of time is totally unrealistic. Unless there is a radical change in investment priorities, and much greater emphasis on non-waterborne schemes of excreta disposal and on health education, the situation is likely to get worse.

Water Quality

Standards for water quality were promulgated by a WHO panel of experts in 1971, drawing largely on the experience of Western countries. These standards propose bacteriological, chemical, physical, and biological requirements. In this context, water is potable if it meets these requirements and not potable if it does not. The developing nations have, for the most part, adapted these standards to their needs or are in the process of doing so (WHO, 1973).

It is possible to look at water quality as a continuum, rather than as a dichotomy. In this view, suggested by White (1974), water quality may be thought of as varying from extremely hazardous to health to only slightly hazardous, and the objective becomes to give as many people as possible access to less-hazardous water.

The level of water service then depends upon the social and economic objectives of the country. That determining the level of service, and which groups of people will benefit from it, is a political decision is illustrated by the following remarks of a minister for water development and power:

. . . in my experience, the implementation of the recommendations of professionals and academics on such topics [water policy, design standards, etc.] will always depend on political decision. For instance, in Tanzania the decision that all water supplied from a public domestic point or kiosk, whether in town or in rural areas, shall be free of charge was a political decision. The purchase or importation of equipment for rural water supplies, including its innovation, must ultimately be the result of a political decision as will also be the provision of necessary finance by governments for the manpower which will be needed for the construction, operation and maintenance of a comprehensive rural water supply programme. . . . even the public health criteria of rural water supply must ultimately be influenced by political decisions based, of course, largely on the advice and recommendations of a country's public health authorities. A case in point in Tanzania is the disturbing fact that water from a large number of our rural boreholes has an undesirable high content of fluoride. . . . Tanzania may be forced by circumstances to accept a higher ceiling of water fluoride content than that currently accepted by the World Health Organization (Chagula, 1971).

A reasonable concept would be one of choosing a level of service concomitant with a risk level acceptable to the people being served. People in the cities would have little choice in the matter, since the central treatment of water would determine everyone's risk; but in the rural areas people could choose a level of improvement which they could afford to operate and maintain.

Prospects for Improvement

The countries involved, and the international agencies interested in aiding them, have not been unaware of the problem. In 1972, goals for water supply and sewerage in the developing countries were set by the World Health Assembly and the Ministers of Health of the Americas. The target date for attaining these goals was set for 1980, during the Second United Nations Development Decade. The goals for water supply were modest:

- for all regions except the Americas, to supply 60 percent of the urban population with house connections, supply 40 percent of the urban population with public standpipes, and supply 25 percent of the rural population with easy access to safe water;
- for the Americas, at minimum, to reduce the portions not supplied in 1970 by 50 percent for city dwellers and by 30 percent for the rural population in each country (WHO, 1973).

If these modest goals could be met, the poorer people would be better off, especially in the cities (Figure 2). The 1975 WHO survey indicates overall increases of 8 percent and 12 percent for Africa and Asia, and the report concludes optimistically that the goals will eventually be met. However, in the Americas the progress from 1970 to 1975 was only 3 percent. Since this region already has a much-larger proportion of the population with access to safe water (57 percent) than other parts of the developing world, the slower progress here may indicate that the remaining sections of the population without such access are the most difficult to reach. Among the reasons proposed to explain why things have not gone better in the domestic water-supply field, the surveyed countries ranked three as most important: (a) insufficiency of internal finance, (b) lack of trained personnel, and (c) insufficiency of external finance. To these might be added: (d) difficulties in operation and maintenance, (e) inadequate legal framework, and (f) inappropriate administrative framework.

Finances

Given present policies, in order to meet the 1980 goal the needed investment is estimated by WHO to amount to $1.4 billion each year until 1980, in contrast to the $938 million invested in 1970 (WHO, 1973).[3] The bulk of the investment has come from internal financing, with about 1 to 5 percent of public-sector development funds going into water supply. External aid for community water supply in the period 1966-

1970 totaled $710 million or about $142 million per year. Thus, either the amount of outside aid would have to be significantly increased or countries would have to increase their allotments to this sector at the expense of other development investments. External aid during that period was not very evenly distributed; 49 percent of it went to the Americas, where there had been much administrative and institutional framework laid in the last decade in order to make use of it, and only 2 percent went to Southeast Asia, the region with the greatest need (Pineo and Subrahmanyham, 1975).

External aid has been closely tied in the past to the philosophies of the international lending agencies, although this situation has changed rapidly during the past few years. The agencies have held that water and sewerage are public utilities, and that charges to the consumer should provide a reasonable rate of return covering construction, operation, and maintenance costs, with a subsidy for a "reasonable household consumption for the poor" (World Bank, 1971). This position is largely accountable for the high proportion of investment in large urban projects which are likely to provide a reasonable rate of return in contrast to rural areas, where costs are high and sufficient returns unlikely. This philosophy has had considerable impact on the internal financial policies of borrowers. The Latin American countries, for example, have made much progress by requiring financial and organizational commitments from the communities involved and by using revolving funds (Donaldson, 1973). Kenya has instituted a program for self-help in some of the rural areas which requires that the community raise 10 percent of the required amount of money before applying for government help (Odingo, 1975). In both these situations, the wealthier communities may be better able to participate, and the government is left with the difficult problem of how to include the poorer communities.

It is not clear how much poor people could or should pay for safe water. In Davao City, Philippines, for example, there is no public water supply, and each family has to make its own arrangements to catch rain water or use surface flows, wells, or other sources. Even in the poorest income group, more than half the people have managed to invest in some sort of tank for catching rain water (Hackenberg, 1973). It is fairly clear that, while the poorest group probably cannot

help finance the construction of projects except by contributing labor, they can afford to pay something for operation
and maintenance. A Latin American rule of thumb is about 5
percent of income.

Lack of Trained Personnel

Difficulties in recruiting trained personnel are evident at
both the planning and construction states and in operation
and maintenance. As for the planning stage, highly trained
engineers are in short supply, and little attempt has been
made to train people for specific tasks rather than for broad
environmental engineering. Simpler systems, such as those
using slow sand filters, coupled with short-term training,
might do much to reduce the problem. The use of such local
materials as burned rice husks for filtration could also reduce
costs (Frankel, 1972).

Much more could be done to train local personnel for
operation and maintenance work. Many of the schemes are
not fully functioning in the rural areas, and in the cities of
Dakar and Libreville only about one-half of the standpipes
are functioning at any one time (WHO/IRC, 1975). This
kind of improvement might benefit poor people as much as
or more than any other. A report in Gabon (1972) concluded
that a very important improvement for the water service in
Libreville would be accomplished by repairing the existing
standpipes and making sure they remained in service. It may
be that new schemes are more likely to benefit the wealthier
segments of the population than are repairs to the old, hence
the latter get scant attention. Self-help projects, such as those
that are proving very effective in Kenya at present (Odingo,
1975), probably have a special need for training components
if they are to continue after outside advisory personnel has
left.

Institutional and Legal Framework

Existing institutional and legal frameworks often lead to
fragmentation of responsibility for water improvements.
Urban works may come under the jurisdiction of local

municipalities, making more-efficient regional development unlikely. In the rural areas, ministries of public works, water development, agriculture, and health are all likely to share in responsibility for water supplies. Where there has been some centralization of authority, as recently occurred in Kenya, a rapid pace of development may follow. Domestic water has only lately begun to be included as an integral part of such development schemes as the Gezira in the Sudan. Even when water supplies are included in development plans, if migratory laborers or others settle where they are not supposed to, some of the population may end up using unsafe supplies of water. Among poorer communities, there seems to have been more rapid progress in countries where there has been much emphasis on involving local people in decisions about improvements in their own water supplies (e.g., Peru, Kenya, Argentina, Mexico).

International Aid

Two recent international efforts may have an impact on the water problem. One is the Ad Hoc Working Group on Potable Water and Sanitation in Developing Countries, made up of various donor groups (including WHO, UNDP, IBRD, UNICEF, UNEP, IDRC, and OECD), which focuses on rural potable water supplies. After about a year of consultation, proposals were submitted to a meeting of this group in November 1975. This meeting was largely devoted to strengthening information links and encouraging regional centers for the interchange of information about water supplies. The original proposals were turned down by the group of prospective donors, and new proposals are now being drawn up. A second effort involves the World Bank, which for the last several years has concentrated upon the problem of poverty in developing countries, especially among the rural poor.

The ongoing programs of UNICEF in the rural areas and of the Pan American Health Organization in both urban and rural settlements have done much to improve the situation, both in specific locations and in training and research operations. In addition, the International Development Research Centre of Canada has sought to foster innovative

research on the technical and social aspects of water supply
and sanitation, especially among workers in the developing
countries.

Robert S. McNamara, president of the World Bank, in an
address to the bank's board of governors in 1975, said: "The
bank can play a significant role in pointing out the extent to
which the government's present policies, practices, and
investment allocations are seriously biased against the poor.
And the bank can expand and redirect its own investments in
urban areas to ensure that they result in increased earning
opportunities and more adequate services for the poor in
both the modern and traditional sectors." The World Bank
has already had considerable effect on urban services
through its lending programs, including the sites and service
program, and this new policy may stimulate more attention
to ways of improving the lot of the urban poor.

Despite the efforts of the countries involved and of international agencies, the general picture that emerges is not
encouraging. There has been considerable progress in developing new supplies for some cities and for the larger and
more prosperous rural settlements, which can afford to share
more fully in the organization and costs of the projects. At
the same time, chronically inadequate supplies are becoming even more inadequate in the large cities of Southeast
Asia; there and elsewhere, population increases threaten to
overwhelm existing supply systems, excluding large
numbers of poor people. The more isolated settlements and
scattered households in rural areas remain outside organized
systems and are likely to continue to remain so, subject to
ever-increasing inconvenience and risk of disease transmission as a result of population growth. If present policies
prevail, the proportion of the population in developing
countries with access to safe water and sanitation will
increase somewhat, but the absolute number of people
without such access will be greater by 1980 than it is today.

There would seem to be no easy answer as to how the
situation can be improved. Yet, because safe water and
sanitation are such a basic part of good health and good
living, their provision could be a rallying point for all
nations that want to improve the life of poor people, either
their own or those in other countries. Some limited steps
toward this end might be taken immediately by national

agencies, with the help of whatever international assistance they can obtain:

1. Ensure that water-supply and sanitation requirements are included in any new rural or urban-periphery development plan. Although domestic water probably cannot claim a significantly increased share of development funds in competition with education, transportation, and other needs, if these needs are considered together the funds are likely to be used more efficiently. A more labor-intensive and participatory growth plan for such development could alleviate the conflict between water goals and growth and distributional objectives.

2. Train people who can assist local community groups in making sound organizational and technical decisions about the level of improvement which they could continue to operate and maintain. Such a training program would create opportunities for people to contribute time as well as money and to receive ongoing technical training for operation and maintenance, as well as providing both training for community development and education of a wider nature than is usually meant by the term "health education."

3. Assist in both developing local manufacture of equipment, which would otherwise require foreign currency, and training innovative engineers who are willing to use local products and devise new methods.

What seem to be needed most are the marshaling of administrative powers, the determination of a clear policy defining access to safe water as a basic element of life, the allocation of a reasonable amount of funds and the drawing together of the resources of poorer people—resources that include organizational ability and labor as well as money.

Notes

1. For a thorough discussion of the health benefits resulting from improved water supplies, see Saunders and Warford (1976).

2. Definitions of "rural" and "urban" vary exceedingly. A useful population division would be: dispersed rural, con-

centrated rural, urban periphery and urban, but there is not
data available to make these distinctions at present.
  3. Basis not stated; assumed to be 1970 U.S. dollars.

References

Argentina (1972). *Plan Nacional de Agua Potable Rural*
    [National Plan for Rural Drinking Water]. National
    Executive Authority, State Secretariat of Public Health.
    Presentation of the Second Phase, 1970–1972.

Chagula, W. K. (1971). "Opening Address." *Proceedings of*
    the Conference on Rural Water Supply in East Africa,
    April 5–8, 1971. Ed. G. Tschennerl. University of Dar es
    Salaam, Bureau of Resource Assessment and Land Use
    Planning, Research Paper no. 20. Pp. 7–10.

Dieterich, B. H., and J. M. Henderson (1963). *Urban Water*
    Supply Conditions and Needs in Seventy-five Develop-
    ing Countries. Geneva: World Health Organization.

Donaldson, D. (1973). *Progress in the Rural Water Programs*
    of Latin America (1961–1971). Washington: Pan Amer-
    ican Health Organization.

Feachem, R. (1976). "Appropriate Sanitation." *New Scien-*
    tist, January 8, 1976, 68–69.

Frankel R. (1974). "Potable Water and the Frankel Filter."
    Inventor 6, no. 5, 313–319.

Gabon (1972). *Projet d'aménagement et d'entretien des*
    bornes fontaines dans les quartiers non urbanisés de
    Libreville [Project for the Management and Mainte-
    nance of Standpipes in the Nonurbanized Sections of
    Libreville]. Gabon Society for Energy and Water.

Hackenberg, R. A. (1973). *A Developing City in a Dual*
    Economy: Economic and Demographic Trends in Da-
    vao City, Philippines, 1972. Davao Action Information
    Center, Davao, Philippines.

Jain, S. (1975). *Size Distribution of Income.* Washington,
    D.C.: World Bank.

McNamara, R. S. (1975). Address to the World Bank board of
    governors, September 1, 1975.

Odingo, R. (1975). *Report to Workshop on Social and Managerial Aspects of Rural Water Supply and Sanitation,* Nairobi, Kenya, December 1–17, 1975 (sponsored by the International Development Research Centre, Canada).

Pan American Health Organization (1973). *Report to the Director.*

Pineo, C. S., and D. V. Subrahmanyham (1975). *Community Water Supply and Excreta Disposal Situation in the Developing Countries: A Commentary.* Geneva: World Health Organization.

Puffer, R. R., and C. V. Serrano (1973). *Patterns of Mortality in Childhood* (Scientific Publication no. 262). Washington, D.C.: Pan American Health Organization.

Saunders, R L., and J. J. Warford (1976). *Village Water Supply: Economics and Policy in the Developing World.* Baltimore: Johns Hopkins Press.

Tahal (Water Planning), Ltd., Tel Aviv, Israel (1965). "Engineering Report for Accra-Tema Metropolitan Area, Vol. 2: Detailed Report."

Turner, J. C. (1968). "Housing Priorities, Settlement Patterns, and Urban Development in Modernizing Countries." *Journal of the American Institute of Planners* 34, 354–363.

Warner, D. (1973). *Evaluation of the Development Impact of Rural Water Supply Projects in East African Villages.* Stanford University, Stanford, Calif., Program in Engineering-Economic Planning, Report no. EEP-50.

White, G. F. (1974). "Domestic Water Supply: Right or Good?" *Human Rights to Health,* Ciba Foundation Symposium 23 (new series). Amsterdam: ASP.

White, G. F., D. J. Bradley, and A. U. White (1972). *Drawers of Water: Domestic Water Use in East Africa.* Chicago: University of Chicago Press.

World Bank (1971). *Trends in Developing Countries.*

World Bank (1976). *Village Water Supply.*

World Health Organization (1971). *International Standards for Drinking Water.* Geneva: Expert Committee on International Standards for Drinking Water.

World Health Organization (1972a). *Health Hazards of the Human Environment.* Geneva.

World Health Organization (1972b). Progress Report to the Director General, Community Water Supply Programme, Geneva.

World Health Organization (1973). "Community Water Supply and Sewage Disposal in Developing Countries." *World Health Statistics Report* 26, no. 11 (783).

World Health Organization (1976). *Community Water Supply and Wastewater Disposal* (mid-decade progress report to the Twenty-ninth World Health Assembly), A29/12.

International Health Organization/International Reference Center for Community Water Supply (1975). *Water Dispensing Devices and Methods for Public Water Supply in Developing Countries*. Netherlands.

12. Intermediate Technology and Income Distribution in Developing Nations

Paul Wehr

> If effective help is to be brought to those who need it most, a technology is required which would range in some intermediate position between the £1-technology and the £1000-technology. Let us call it . . . a £100-technology (Schumacher, 1973, p. 169).

A major policy objective of most governments of developing nations is a significant rise in the income levels of their citizens. The so-called mobilization governments of China, Cuba, Algeria, and Tanzania are notable for their concern with raising aggregate national production and income as well as individual living levels. To achieve these goals, economic planning institutions in third-world states have commonly adopted—with encouragement from their first- and second-world counterparts—the high technology (HT) approach to economic and social development. The HT model relies on heavy injections of capital-intensive advanced technology in both the industrial and agricultural sectors of developing economies. This model likewise requires modern technological and social infrastructures for reasonably centralized industrial operations; mechanized irrigation, cultivation, and harvesting; and rapid and efficient transportation and distribution networks. Such complex machine-based requisites are largely beyond the means of the really poor nations; they tend to aggravate already

Partial support for research for this paper was provided through the National Endowment for the Humanities.

serious urbanization problems and further concentrate existing wealth. In the case of the "green revolution," HT may
even narrow permanently a developing agriculture's options
by eliminating certain genetic strains.

Despite its increasingly obvious inappropriateness for
poor nations, HT until recently was considered *the* methodology and ideology of development. With few exceptions,
third-world planners and statesmen bought the HT message
and its concomitant dependence on Western technology
sources. Only China has for some time been seriously
experimenting with middle-range (and sometimes ill-
conceived) technological innovations.[1] Pushed to a position
of economic and technological self-reliance by food crises
and by their diplomatic and ideological isolation from the
West, the Chinese experimented substantially with intermediate technology (IT) in production and distribution. This is
not to say that IT was completely ignored elsewhere or that
no Western development experts were critical of the application of HT to third-world development problems. René
Dumont (1969) has for two decades vigorously dissented
from the prevailing opinion among Western development
scientists that "what was good for us is good for them."
Dumont cites case after case in sub-Saharan Africa in which
high-technology development schemes either failed misera-
bly because of inappropriate conditions or served to further
tie former colonies, economically, culturally, and politically, to the metropole. Dumont's research suggested indirectly
that HT was a form of neocolonialism and an inhibitor of
self-reliance in newly independent nations.

Gunnar Myrdal likewise became a sharp critic of the
Western tendency to impose the high-technology model on
third-world development problems:

> What is almost inexplicably concealed in economic
> writings is the obvious fact that *scientific and techno-
> logical advance in the developed countries has had, and
> is now having, an impact on the underdeveloped coun-
> tries which, on balance, is detrimental to their develop-
> ment prospects* (Myrdal, 1970, p. 40).

The adverse impact of HT on third-world polities and
economies had deep historical roots and did not commence

with the independent status of these states. A prominent feature of the colonial system was the dual economy it created in colonized areas: (a) the modern sector—created to support, in some cases, a resident community of Europeans and to supply the colonial power with raw materials and foodstuffs, and (b) the traditional, low-technology sector that supported most of the indigenous peoples—albeit insufficiently, as it was undermined by the modern sector. Modern technology was the instrument by which this dual economy was created and maintained in colonized areas, and *thus it became a primary agent of maldistribution of income and life chances.*

My own experience has been with the former French colonial areas of Morocco and Algeria. Algeria, in particular, illustrates the long-term negative impact of colonial high technology on income distribution. Two of Algeria's major problems following the French withdrawal in 1962 were: (a) sustaining the modern economic sector, upon which the majority of Algerians had come to depend but which they were not prepared to operate, and (b) coping with the gross inequities of wealth and privilege among Algerians which had been created by this sector.[2] My research on the development problems of Algeria's rural communes (1968) shows the sharp distinction in productive capacity and living levels between the formerly European communes in the modern agricultural sector and the impoverished communes supported by traditional agriculture depleted by eight years of guerrilla warfare. This residual inequity created immediate and serious political problems for the Algerian government. Despite some amelioration of these problems in the past decade, Algeria remains a two-culture, two-economy nation, and its modern sector remains heavily dependent upon France and, to a lesser degree, on the European Economic Community. In short, it is still largely dependent for high technology and product markets on its former ruler and other Western nations, and it continues to have serious difficulties in eliminating gross income differences. Similar dual-economy problems can be found in any third-world state where a modern commercial infrastructure was installed by a colonial power. While the modern sector may increase the national economic growth rate, as demonstrated in a 1972 International Labor Organization report, it does so at the expense of equitable income distribution within the country (Omo-Fadaka, 1975).

I do not mean to imply that the impact of HT on the third world has been entirely detrimental. The introduction of modern medicine, for example, has decreased mortality and morbidity rates substantially—though its role in the demographic explosion is an ambiguous one, in regard to the economic health of third-world nations. Such other systems as petrotechnology have been productively applied by third-world governments, including Algeria, to accumulate much-needed foreign capital. On the other side of the ledger, however, high technology has helped to generate massive dislocation of populations, the creation of an underproletariat (the underemployed and unemployed), and at least the suggestion of a general increase in the unequal distribution of income within third-world nations, whether through industrialization, the green revolution, or some other process. One can argue that, in general, the third-world experience with the HT model of development has been a sobering and disappointing one which may have produced the opposite results of those desired by displacing traditional forms of production without replacing them.

I should like, in the balance of this paper, to examine two aspects of the technology-income relationship: (a) the nature of the intermediate technology alternative and (b) the potential of that alternative, as suggested in experimentation within three developing nations, for income growth and equalization within poor nations.

Intermediate Technology

During the past decade an alternative to the HT model has emerged, not only directed at third-world development problems but concerned with resource-depletion problems in affluent societies as well. This alternative is termed intermediate, or appropriate, technology.

As early as 1960, Quaker and Mennonite service and relief organizations were exporting modest amounts of intermediate technology to third-world development projects. Treadle sewing machines for Algerian refugee programs, brick-making equipment for Zambian house construction, and simple but effective sanitation and hydrotechnology for Indian villages were among the first such exports.

The idea of fitting the scale of the technology to the task had germinated much earlier in Gandhian economics, and Gandhi's conception of village agriculture and industry generated enough interest among a few Western technologists to produce the Intermediate Technology Development Group (ITDG) in Britain. Its founder, E. F. Schumacher, whose essay on Buddhist economics (1973) is a classic statement of what he calls the "economics of permanence," is concerned that production technology in poor nations (a) be cheap enough to be accessible to the masses, (b) be suitable for small-scale application, and (c) allow for human creativity. The ethical and the practical are combined in Schumacher's economics, which weights the inherent value of creative work as heavily as the consumption of its products.

This approach calls for a conception of income and income distribution different from that used in conventional economics. In Schumacher's estimation, level of consumption is only one element of income—the latter includes, as well, psychic satisfaction derived from creative work and satisfaction from social relationships reinforced by that work. Income maldistribution, for Schumacher, then, involves not only inequity in product consumption but also the conditions of underemployment and unemployment, of social dislocation in a rapidly industrializing and urbanizing society, and so on. This suggests that income production and redistribution policy should do more than produce more material goods and distribute them more justly, it should redistribute social and psychological well-being as well. Schumacher proposes a "technology on a human scale" based on certain fundamental rules:

1. *Make things small* wherever possible.
2. *Reduce the capital-intensity* because labor wants to be involved. We don't want to eliminate the human factor.
3. *Make the process as simple as you can.* (Anyone can complicate things—it takes a genius to keep them simple.)
4. *Design the process to be nonviolent.* The "advanced nations" depend on an extremely violent system. In talking about violence, I don't just mean hitting anoth-

er man over the head. I also include man hitting nature
over the head . . . (1974, p. 274).

The intermediate technology model assumes that production of work places, at least in the third world, is central to a
resolution of the problems of underproduction, income
maldistribution, and underutilization of labor.

The choice of technologies is one of the most important
collective decisions facing a developing country. It is a
choice which affects the whole fabric of the economic
and social structure. It determines *who* works and who
does not; the whole pattern of *income* distribution;
where work is done and therefore the urban/rural
balance; and *what* is produced, that is for whose benefit
resources are used (Intermediate Technology Development Group, n.d., p. 2).

Capital-intensive technology, the intermediate technologists argue, aggravates the income-distribution problem and
decreases individual and national self-reliance, since the HT
model is necessarily dependent on the West, and does not
meet third-world needs. They would agree with Gunnar
Myrdal that poverty is more a sociopolitical problem than an
economic problem.

The IT movement is spreading modestly throughout the
Western world but it is strongest in Great Britain, where the
ITDG has developed scientific and technical programs to
work with developing nations. The ITDG focuses on invent-
ing or discovering simple technology for the 80–90 percent
of the third-world populations living in rural areas—
technology that *uses* labor, the most abundant available
resource (rather than saving it) and makes it more productive. ITDG maintains that IT is *appropriate*, not *second-
rate*, technology. That group assembles data on low-cost
self-help machines and techniques, communicates that
knowledge to developing nations, and tests it through
practical application in field projects in those nations.
While it is a private organization, it contracts with the
British Ministry of Overseas Development and creates IT in
direct collaboration with third-world governments.

Third-World Application of Intermediate Technology

Neither the idea of intermediate technology nor its concretization are products of Western ingenuity. Several third-world governments developed intermediate technology long before Western intellectuals set to work on it.

China. The People's Republic exemplifies perhaps the most explicit and conscious effort in intermediate technological development. Self-reliance, both national and communal, is of course a central ideological tenet of Maoism. Dickinson (1972) cites numerous ways in which intermediate technology is used in Chinese development programs. The "barefoot doctor" represents intermediate medical technology in the Chinese experience and has directly altered the access of the Chinese population to modern medical treatment—physical health being an important element in our revised concept of national income.

The Chinese use of intermediate technology is perhaps most evident in agricultural production. The Chinese commune is designed as a self-sustaining unit, generating all fixed-capital inputs to production (Dickinson, 1972). The less the commune must pay for equipment produced outside the commune, the larger the balance that can be distributed as income to the families of the commune. Communes are thus motivated to maximize internal production of agricultural and industrial equipment, thereby innovating in the pursuit of increased communal income distributed rather equitably within the commune.

> Just as the primary aim is agricultural self-sufficiency, self-reliance is the second important feature of all Communes. In particular, all Communes have workshops where tools and simple machines, such as hand-operated winnowers, huskers, and rice-transplanters, can be fabricated or repaired. These workshops have a variety of simple machine tools as well as carpenter's and blacksmith's shops and may employ from 30 to over 100 workers. As the Communes have become more efficient and productivity has increased, the demand for agricultural labour has lessened and more effort has been put into non-agricultural production units. Using

locally available raw materials, many Communes produce artificial fertilisers and pesticides as well as having
teams engaged in brick making and the construction of
houses and farm buildings. Some Communes now
produce all the furniture necessary for their own needs
and sell part of their production outside the Commune.
The most advanced Communes have complete factories
for quite complex products such as small electric mo-
tors. All these activities add to the Commune revenue
and non-agricultural income may account for 25 percent of gross income (Dickinson, 1972, p. 8).

Among the more common examples of increasing mechanization are simple electrical pumps for irrigation, mechanical rice transplanters, and the walking tractor—a multipur-
pose machine used for cultivation, hauling, compression
power for spraying, and many other purposes. This policy of
mechanization geared to both need and resources also resur-
rects and improves such traditional mechanical devices as
"Persian" wheels and "dragon's spin" water pumps.
 Simple mechanization is now promoted in China by a
separate Ministry for Agricultural Engineering, with thirty
research institutes throughout the nation (Dickinson, 1972,
p. 15). Until the late 1950s, however, there was sharp debate
between proponents of mechanized and labor-intensive
agriculture. In 1958 it was officially acknowledged that both
might be necessary, for,

 while China was still a labor-surplus country in a
 general sense, there existed seasonal agricultural labor
 shortages. This bottleneck limited the further promotion of double or multiple cropping practice. The use of
 machinery . . . might increase farm output not through
 higher yields per unit but through a higher double-
 cropping index (Chao, 1970, p. 97).

From 1958 on, Chinese policy on agricultural mechanization responded rather faithfully to Mao's political control.
During periods of Mao's ascendancy, mechanization was
emphasized. When he was in decline, it was deemphasized.
Much less controversial than complete mechanization was
the policy of improvement of farm implements. In partial

reaction to the earlier disastrous introduction of Soviet two-wheeled plows, the Chinese government from 1958 on gave impetus to "semimechanization," or the modernization of existing farm implements by such methods as installing ball bearings in all turning joints. In 1964, emphasis on such "farm implement reform" and indigenous technology was institutionalized within the national planning process, and it has been a high-priority policy since that time. Chao (1970, p. 104) notes that although this promotion of intermediate technology undoubtedly has had labor-saving and labor-enhancing consequences for Chinese agriculture, they are impossible to measure.

Given the unreliability of agricultural production figures in the People's Republic, our assessment of the impact of its encouragement of intermediate technology in income production and distribution must be largely intuitive. There is some indication that China's semimechanization policy, using local materials in highly intensive agricultural production, has contributed to a general living level increase for the average Chinese. It has helped to produce the 20 percent current savings of annual gross agricultural income by families in communes (Dickinson, 1972, p. 29)—a capital accumulation rare in developing economies. Riskin notes that, in addition to increasing consumption, this policy of encouraging technological experimentation and innovation in communes "along with the movements to visit, study, and catch up with advanced units," produces "a form of demonstration effect that stimulates savings and ingenuity" (Riskin, 1974, p. 85), thus decreasing income maldistribution *between* communes.

Tanzania. Tanzania's experiment with IT is neither so lengthy nor so successful as China's. It began formally in the mid-1960s with President Nyerere's concept of the *ujamaa* village. This was to be a cooperative community that would build on the nation's traditions of agricultural cooperation. These villages—to be created spontaneously, with help from the national government—would become self-sustaining and self-reliant economic and social communities.

In his Arusha Declaration of 1967, Nyerere had laid out his policy of national self-reliance, a policy which viewed capital-intensive development as currently impossible for Tanzania or any other poor nation. Simple and intermediate

technology was seen by Nyerere as an appropriate development tool for the *ujamaa* village.

> To be realistic, therefore, we must stop dreaming of
> developing Tanzania through the establishment of
> large, modern industries. For such things we have
> neither the money nor the skilled manpower required to
> make them efficient and economic. We would even be
> making a mistake if we think in terms of covering
> Tanzania with mechanized farms, using tractors and
> combine harvesters.
>
> We have, instead, to think in terms of development
> through the improvement of the tools we now use, and
> through the growth of co-operative systems of produc-
> tion. Instead of aiming at large farms using tractors and
> other modern equipment and employing agricultural
> labourers, we should be aiming at having ox-ploughs
> all over the country.
>
> Instead of thinking about providing each farmer with
> his own lorry, we should consider the usefulness of
> oxen-drawn carts, which could be made within the
> country and which are appropriate both to our roads
> and to the loads which each farmer is likely to have.
>
> In other words, we have to think in terms of what is
> available, or can be made available, at comparatively
> small cost, and which can be operated by the people
> (Nyerere, 1973, pp. 96–97).

Nyerere has also viewed intermediate technology as a
means to facilitate the acceptance of *ujamaa* socialism.
Production centered around small, shared technological
"plants" would reinforce cooperative activity.

> Thus, for example, in Kilimanjaro a group of farmers
> may get together and jointly organize and run a modern
> poultry unit, or a communal tannery, or a communal
> woodwork shop. Or, again, they may come together to
> share the use of a truck which they jointly own, or to
> organize some new irrigation—perhaps with a water-

wheel which they jointly own—which will benefit all of
them. If people start working together in this way, it
will be possible for these densely populated areas to
become areas of rural industrialization, thus reducing
their dependence on world prices of their cash crops,
and also providing a new impetus to community activity and community life.

Rural industrialization projects must not be thought of
in terms of large modern factories, but more in terms of
"cottage industries" (ibid., p. 139).

Ngotyana (1973) feels that the villagization policy of the
Tanzanian government during the period of the first five-
year plan failed largely because of overcapitalization and a
reliance of the villages on agricultural and marketing technology external to both the villages and the nation. The
ujamaa village was, therefore, designed so as to correct this
problem through, among other things, "a gradual transition
to new simple tools." Evidence suggests, however, that
overly sophisticated and expensive equipment has been only
one of numerous difficulties encountered in the villagization
program, and that those problems persist in the *ujamaa*
villages as well. For example, satisfactory division of labor is
often difficult to achieve, and a system wherein all village
members work on commonly divided tasks sometimes provides a solution. Even then, a family's satisfaction with
others' work on its land is impossible to ensure.
   Ujamaa village income is generated primarily from the
marketing of agricultural produce and from profits from
machinery and shops (Huizer, 1973), and is therefore directly
related to the diligence and productivity of each family. After
construction, contingency, and other costs are deducted, the
balance of village income is distributed to families according
to their workday output. There is, then, a link between labor
and income—a link that restrains somewhat any tendency
toward grossly inequitable income distribution, yet retains
some material incentive. As in the Chinese commune, the
more equipment that is produced internally, the more the
income to be distributed.
   Recent reports suggest that *ujamaa* villagization is not
proceeding smoothly, and that there has been much greater

popular resistance to inclusion in the villages than had been anticipated. Since Tanzania's IT experiment is embodied in its *ujamaa* villagization program, it is difficult to see how the former could be progressing any more rapidly than the latter.

India. The Indian government, perhaps more completely than any other in the third world, bought the HT model for its development plans. Modern industrialization had been rather widely introduced into India by the British, and large numbers of Indian technologists were trained in Britain and in the United States before and after 1947. With the exception of a few dissidents, such as Gandhi, Indian planners and government leaders were wholly taken with HT for both industrial and agricultural development. An Indian industrialist class, long in place at the time of independence, provided its own ethic for development. Unlike most other third-world states, India had the organizational and technical competence to apply high-technology principles of development, but she did not have the necessary capital. India, whose population is still about 85 percent rural and agricultural, is no more an appropriate setting for the application of Western development models than is China or Tanzania.

There has long been a running debate, however, between leaders in the Indian government and leaders in the Gandhian movement. Gandhi, of course, was one of the first proponents of appropriate technology; he modeled it in his ashram communities, which produced human-powered machines to handle every phase of agricultural production and processing. Gandhi was convinced that rural India could eliminate its poverty, while preserving its humanity, only through small-scale industry and agricultural innovation using local resources. For him, self-reliance and appropriateness of technique to need had to coincide in a development ethic.

For a quarter-century, those directing Indian development programs derided the IT model and, in particular, Gandhi's version of it. More recently, however, as the failures of high technology in India have become more glaring and less tolerable as the population swells, planners are desperately considering alternatives, and they are giving somewhat more credence to Gandhian economics.

The Indian government has now created a National Institute of Design, in Ahmedabad, to redesign and invent tools for small-scale agriculture and rural industry. There is some question, however, of how effective this official venture into intermediate technology will be (Naipaul, 1976). In a perverse sort of way, IT has received official sanction as a Western import, not as a process rooted in India's own recent past. Unless this institute produces IT by way of a close relationship of the inventor to rural agroindustrial problems and needs, it will have little effect on the productivity of the Indian peasant.

This new government interest in intermediate technology is, nevertheless, based on some rather successful models of IT experimentation within India itself. The Gandhian movement, through its persistence in pursuing the IT concept since independence, has provided both theory and some test projects in the field. One such program is the Khadi and Village Industries Commission, which promotes and markets homespun textiles and other cottage products throughout India. An extensive operation developed within the Gandhian movement, it fosters the improvement of such simple technology as hand-powered looms in order to meet family and village production needs.

Another Gandhian rural development project that illustrates the potential of intermediate technology is Agrindus, a collection of 100 villages in eastern Uttar Pradesh state. As its name implies, the Agrindus project generates community development through agricultural and industrial growth. It serves 60,000 people, mostly of tribal and outcaste status. Development planning is guided by a very few professionals but comes increasingly from village government.

> The concept of planning and development is not dependent on specialist expertise or administrative directives from above. The *gramsabha*, or village community, has to be the chief agency for planning and implementation. It is envisaged that the new modes of appropriate technology should reach the doors of every villager to increase his ability as a productive unit participating in the process of the total development of the community (*Agrindus*, p. 6).

IT provides a major integrating device for the project, as villages cooperate in the construction of earthen dams for irrigation, brick kilns for housing construction, methane gas plants fed by cow dung, deep water wells, flour mills, oil presses, rice hullers, and agricultural-implement workshops. Increased productivity from IT produces capital for village councils with which revolving loan funds are created. These funds alter the income-distribution and sociopolitical structures of the village in an interesting manner. Short- and long-term indebtedness and indenture to money lenders, both from within and from without these villages, is still quite common. The revolving fund provides loans that release the poorer families from this bondage, thereby permanently altering the wealth and power distribution within the village. Indian planners are watching such experiments as Agrindus very closely and with decreasing skepticism.

Implications of IT for Third-World Development

The impact of intermediate technology on third-world development is hardly measurable at this stage. The best one can do is to thoroughly study cases where it seems to have made a positive difference in the overall productivity of a unit and in income distribution within that unit. As the IT model becomes more widely adopted—Ghana, Zambia, Pakistan, Bangladesh, and New Guinea are currently establishing demonstration and training centers—evaluative research will provide us with an empirical base from which to make comparisons. Until then, one can refer only to isolated cases of success and failure. The exception at this time is, perhaps, China whose heavy use of intermediate technology does seem to have made a discernible difference. The experiments in Tanzania and India are much too young and tentative to permit assessment of their promise for rural development.

In all three IT experiments examined, some common characteristics emerge:

1. IT needs supportive organizational infrastructures in order to produce hardware and use it productively. The Chinese commune, the Indian *gramdan* village, and the Tanzanian *ujamaa* village all provide sociopoliti-

cal settings that, in theory and initial operation at least, lend impetus to the programs.

2. IT must be directly tied to material reward—users must get direct success feedback from its use.

3. IT seems to function as a means of encouraging cohering and collaborating, both in local production process and in the joint rewards of increased productivity.

4. IT does seem to reinforce and operationalize for its users the ideology of self-reliance. Most IT hardware can be produced locally, thereby reducing local dependence on national and external development resources. The future relationship of IT hardware to its organizational infrastructure is unclear. If the hardware does increase productivity and income substantially, will not that infrastructure progressively disintegrate as families, rather than only larger units, become able to afford it? Is the communal or centripetal aspect of IT powerful enough to counter that potential centrifugal force? In the Chinese commune this seems not to be a problem because of enforced common ownership and Maoist ideology. The same is not true in India and Tanzania.

5. In all three cases, IT does seem to alleviate the problems of underemployment and unemployment. Appropriate tools and machines both engage people in work and enhance their ability to do that work more productively.

There is little doubt that a solid critique of both the assumptions and technique of IT development policy is forthcoming. Development theory remains largely committed to the theories of economies of scale and liberal use of capital-intensive technology under diverse conditions. Development economists are joined in this commitment by large numbers of third-world planners. High technology and capital are still regarded as the crucial determinants of economic development. I myself am not wholly convinced by Schumacher's economics, but the success rate of HT in the third world has been dismal enough that we might do well to examine the development model itself more closely— and the skills of third-world users less closely—than we have in the past.

Criticism of the intermediate-technology movement does

not come only from high-technology proponents. Radical technologists fear that, as a "technological fix" in its own right, IT may become just another Western-imposed control used to maintain inequitable distribution of power and income. Dickson maintains that IT can "only be realistically seen as part of a political strategy aimed at liberating the population of the underdeveloped countries from political domination and economic exploitation, whether coming from the industrialized nations, or from their own often Western-oriented elites and bureaucracies" (1975, p. 173).

One might go further and suggest that even high-technology societies might be wise to encourage experimentation with intermediate and appropriate technology in certain domestic problem areas—chronic unemployment and uncertain energy production, by way of illustration. Solar collectors and wind-powered generators are relatively simple machines, and in the long run, if predictions are accurate, they will be more effective and economical as well. As commercial energy costs climb out of sight, the development of simpler and less-centralized energy technology becomes an essential income-leveling device. With an unemployment rate in the 5 percent range projected for years to come in the United States and substantially worse projected for Britain, meaningful and remunerative work will become an increasingly important income-distribution indicator, as it now is in most of the third world.

IT and the Global Distribution of Wealth

Intermediate technology may also have implications for wealth distribution among nations. If, as Barnet and Muller (1974) suggest, multinational corporations and their control of high technology lock the developing nations into dependency relationships, self-sufficiency and decreasing dependency may be facilitated by IT investment in third-world states. One could argue, on the basis of the recent experience of the National Liberation Front in Vietnam, that third-world states relying on simple and intermediate technology can wage defensive war more successfully than countries, such as Iran, who now depend on foreign sources for advanced military technology.

I know of no hard data to support this theory, but a sizable chunk of third-world dependency must be directly attributable to high-technology transfer—via grants, loans, and direct purchase. Some of this technology is beneficial to third-world peoples; much of it is not.

I do not suggest that intermediate technology is a panacea for the problem of either underdevelopment or overdevelopment. I do feel, however, that IT offers an alternate strategy with which to attack underproductivity and maldistribution in developing economies, since it may perform both productive and distributive functions better than high technology. I am also inclined to see much of value in the IT model for our own postindustrial societies. The answer undoubtedly lies in a melding of IT and HT—a combining of both the techniques and the ethics that produced them.

Notes

1. One is reminded here of the ill-fated Chinese experiment with backyard steel furnaces, which never really worked. One is also reminded, however, that Chinese culture has been one of the most technologically inventive in the history of humankind. This inventiveness seems to have reasserted itself, but this time linking ideas to their practical development; not giving them away to other cultures to develop.

2. To illustrate the enormity of the problem—a problem that persists to some degree ten years later—of the 17,400 tractors in the modern agricultural sector in 1966, 1,350 were out of service and 9,300 were in poor condition. Of 2,250 grain harvesters, only 600 were serviceable (Wehr, 1968, p. 24).

References

Agrindus: A Gramdan Development Project (n.d.), 1967–

1973 Report, Banwasi Seva Ashram, Govindpur, Mirzapur, India.

Barnet, R., and R. Muller (1974). *Global Reach: The Power of the Multinational Corporations*. New York: Simon and Schuster.

Chao, K. (1970). *Agricultural Production in Communist China 1949–1965*. Madison: University of Wisconsin Press.

Das, A. (n.d.). "New Frontiers in the Choice of Techniques," in Das, A., ed. *Frontiers of Appropriate Technology*. Varanasi, India: Asian Printing Works.

Dickinson, J. (1972). "Rural China, 1972." Report of the Commission on the Churches' Participation in Development, World Council of Churches, Geneva.

Dickson, D. (1975). *The Politics of Alternative Technology*. New York: Universe.

Dumont, R. (1969). *False Start in Africa*, 2nd revised ed. New York: Praeger.

Goulet, D. (1973). *The Cruel Choice: A New Concept in the Theory of Development*. New York: Atheneum.

Huizer, G. (1973). "The Ujamaa Village Programme in Tanzania: New Forms of Rural Development," in *Studies in International Comparative Development* 8, no. 2 (Summer 1973). New Brunswick, N.J.: Rutgers University.

Intermediate Technology Development Group, London (n.d.). "How the Intermediate Technology Development Group Promotes Appropriate Technology" (mimeographed).

Intermediate Technology Development Group, London (n.d.). *Journal of Appropriate Technology*.

MacPherson, G. (1975). First Steps in Village Mechanisation. Dar es Salaam: Tanzania Publishing House.

Myrdal, G. (1970). *The Challenge of World Poverty*. New York: Random House.

Naipaul, V. S. (1976). "India: Synthesis and Mimicry." *New York Review of Books*, September 16, 1976.

Ngotyana, B. (1973). "The Strategy of Rural Development," in Cliffe and Saul. *Socialism in Tanzania*. Dar es Salaam: East African Publishing House.

Nyerere, J. (1973). *Ujamaa: Essays on Socialism*. London: Oxford University Press.

Omo-Fadaka, J. (1975). "Development: The Third Way." *Alternatives* 1.

Riskin, C. (1974). "Incentive Systems and Work Motivations: The Experience in China." *Working Papers,* Winter 1974.

Schumacher, E. F. (1973). *Small is Beautiful: Economics as if People Mattered.* New York: Harper.

Schumacher, E. F. (1974). "Economics Should Begin with People, Not Goods." *The Futurist,* December 1974.

Sivard, R. (1974). *World Military and Social Expenditures.* New York: Institute for World Order.

Wehr, P. (1968). "Local Leadership and Problems of Rural Development in Algeria." University of Michigan, Ann Arbor, Mich., University Microfilms.